A COLLECTOR'S GUIDE TO:

WORLD WAR 2 GERMAN MEDALS

AND POLITICAL AWARDS

CHRISTOPHER AILSBY

IAN ALLAN
Publishing

First published 1994

ISBN 0 7110 2146 5

Design by Ian Allan Studio

Published by Ian Allan Publishing

an imprint of Ian Allan Ltd, Terminal House, Station Approach, Shepperton, Middx TW17 8AS, and printed by Ian Allan Printing Ltd at their works at Coombelands in Runnymede, England.

Cover photographs by Alan C. Butcher

Distributed in the United States of America by Hippocrene Books Inc, 171 Madison Avenue, New York, N.Y. 10016, USA.

First published 1994

ISBN 0-7818-0225-3

Contents

Note:

The rarity of each individual item is given after the medal's name according to the
following scale:

     * Common

     ** Scarce

     *** Rare

     **** Very Rare

     ***** Extremely Rare

Introduction and Acknowledgements

It is hoped that this book will give you some helpful hints on collecting and information on variations in manufacture of the different pieces, as well as their comparative rarity. I have intentionally not covered values because these are a constantly changing factor. The list of manufacturers given for each medal should not be considered as complete in any way. It should be looked at as a start to a data collecting process and hopefully I will be able to update these sections with the reader's help. The measurements should also be seen in the light of the individual piece used for the research. Having said that all pieces should be, within limits, the same. Wild fluctuations should be considered unusual and a cause for concern and further investigation.

I would like to take this opportunity of thanking those people who have so generously helped with support in all forms. Bob Sevier of the Cracked Pot found some most unusual pieces for my 1992 Max Show exhibition. Adrian Forman, likewise, found some astounding pieces for it and for the inclusion in this book. David Littlejohn is always available for comment and criticism. I highly commend his books as a must for all collectors and I recommend their study in conjunction with this guide. Jack Angolia is also always there to give a helping hand and his books are also a must for the collector. The hospitality my wife and I were accorded at the 1992 Max Show was most pleasing and memorable, especially as it was our first visit to America. The offers of help and encouragement from collectors and the organisers of the show, whom we met while exhibiting, was most welcome. Such shows are so important to the growth of the militaria hobby. The quality and dedication of the exhibitors was remarkable, as was that of the judges of the exhibits. The winner of the Charter Award, Jim Hingley, produced an astounding display of quality. Apart from this attribute, he also showed great personal generosity and cordiality in hosting us for the three days of the show.

Further thanks to: C. Tettinek, T. Stannard, F. Stephens, J. Cross, J. Bowman, M. Young, R. Handford, A. Litherland and B. Simpkin of Spink & Son.

I hope that you find this guide helpful and I look forward to your comments and input for further references. Please write to me c/o Ian Allan Publishing, Coombelands House, Addlestone, Weybridge KT15 1HY.

Christopher J. Ailsby
Peterborough,
England.
May 1993

1. Getting Started

Collecting is a need in many of us, both male and female, and can be as compulsive as smoking, drinking or any of the other vices to which the human race has succumbed. This disease is only partially placated by the acquisition of the items on which we have set our hearts. In fact, the chase is often more rewarding than the physical possession of those long lusted items. On the other hand, the therapeutic value of collecting has been long established as a palliative for stress. Thus convincing myself that collecting is good for me and, I hope, for you, I have endeavoured to try and give some guidelines to collecting medals. The thrill for me is in the skill of the artist who designed the awards and the engravers who produced the dies that fashioned them. Having an interest and collection that covers medals and orders of many countries, including coinage, the Third Reich period never fails to amaze me at the quality and design ingenuity that was employed in the manufacture of their awards.

Whether you are just starting to collect or have decided to restructure your collection, I would like to give some ideas that may prove useful in forming a collection that will give you pleasure in owning and sharing with fellow collectors. Showing your collection, in order to compare its strengths and weaknesses, is surely one of the greatest pleasures that can be derived from our hobby. Our own private museum should be viewed and constructed like the other great national collections. A small collection, carefully chosen for content and quality can shine as a beacon, in comparison to a hotchpotch of artifacts thrown together with little else in common than their historical period. To illustrate this point, I was impressed upon a visit to Scotland where I was privileged to see a group of collectors' artifacts. One collector was reticent in showing his offering. At last he tendered his boxes apologetically and upon opening them I was confronted with approximately 30 pieces of foreign volunteer material, all in exceptional condition, interconnected, captioned and expertly displayed. A real gem of a collection. On the other hand, I visited a collection in Belgium that was housed in three upper rooms and the attic. The owner was well into his late 60s and unfamiliar with the English tongue, except for: 'Original, all original!' His display was awesome and contained over 200 German steel helmets, 1943 pattern, in various conditions from, at best, 'battle worn restored' (which meant he had repainted

them) to 'relic' — the latter being in the majority.

Collecting is about preserving the best examples available and trying to obtain examples in this condition, unless they are so rare that the standard set for the collection has to be compromised by an inferior example. The second most important consideration in forming your collection is in its resale value. I hear the cries of horror: 'I don't want to sell, I am not an investor. Investors push up prices above the real collector's reach. You are not a genuine collector but a dealer in disguise.'

Please read on. I will state my case. Firstly, I am not a dealer. I am what I would like to term a 'professional collector'. A strange statement and one that needs explanation. I am building a collection of as many different medals as possible, from all countries, from which I write books and provide photographs for other authors and agencies, so I can appreciate the problems that you face with what seems to be ever escalating prices of good Third Reich material. I experience it more as I have to obtain more examples. So we have returned to the statement, the high retail price of your collection. If you obtain A1 pieces and preserve them in that condition, as the hobby grows, and that has certainly been the case in our hobby, the supply is reduced by the reservoir effect of collections. If the number in the hobby remains static and each member only adds 10 pieces a year to his collection, the supply must cease in time. Just add a modest growth to your collector base and the supply reduces at a prodigious rate. This pressure leads to, at best, an increase in prices for the varying grades of conditions of individual pieces and, at worst, it spawns a flood of fakes, which range from the ludicrous to the near perfect, to fill the vacuum left. These fakes, in turn, fuel the fire and lead to the production of fantasy pieces. Your collection is your hobby bank, which you should use to achieve your ultimate aim and thus your pieces, on an exchange value, should keep up with the price of inflation to allow you to improve your collection.

One of the most interesting stories that came to my attention was when Richard Kimmel wrote to me with a photograph of a Pilots Badge, the swastika being set with stones. He stated that: 'This piece was bought by a lady as a present for her son while she was on holiday in England. She had obtained it along with a Pour le Mérite at a fund raising sale held at the Imperial War Museum in London, when they had tried to raise money to repair the roof that had been damaged by fire'. This great treasure had returned with her to America where it later turned up at a dealer, who was situated in a Flea Market at New Brunswick. Richard subsequently bought it. His question to me was: 'Is it original?' The general appearance of the badge told all. Firstly, if the Imperial War Museum had required finance, it would have sought other avenues of fund raising rather than the disposal of items from its collection. The museum is also a war memorial to commemorate the dead of WW1. I put it like this: if the White House had fire damage would the President sell something from the Oval Office? However, wishing for the great rarity clouds the impressionable collector's vision. The old saying 'If wishes were horses, beggars would ride' has a parallel in the hobby: many fake pieces with spectacular stories would become original. One must face reality, if there is doubt then usually the piece is bad. Plate 1.

When we visited America, I viewed the great treasure and sure enough, it was as bad as first perceived. But, the collector's view was still hopeful: 'The jury is still out on this!' If I was facing the death penalty, I would still hope for a reprieve but am quite sure I would not get any life insurance. The historical and factual credibility of the story that accompanies a piece is intended to give provenance to that piece and has to stand up. The gullibility of the collector, who wishes to obtain the great rarity at less than a bargain price, means that he is a victim of his own greed. I do not think I have to elaborate upon this further, the connotations will be clear on both sides of the Atlantic.

Having established the principles of the high value of your collection and that the supply will eventually dry up, one has to look at the sources of supply. Initially, these were war souvenirs brought back by ex-service personnel who had been in Europe in the closing stages of WW2 and those stationed there at the conclusion of the war. This may have produced the greatest quantity of artifacts commandeered and then exchanged for cigarettes or other commodities. However, these sources usually relinquished these items soon after their return home, when the initial interest and 'dining out' effect had worn thin, the then recipients holding on until such time as need displaced them. The original owner may have held on to his souvenirs until his first home move, retirement or eventual demise. As service personnel, by nature, were of a similar age grouping, the supply comes, by that fact, in waves. As the war has been finished for some 48 years and the true occupational gleaning period was a further three years, the ages of the personnel added to these dates gives rise to the supposition that the last great wave of veteran acquisitions must now begin to recede.

Where does this leave us collectors? At a very important crossroads, one to which all major antique collectables come. The true 'steel' has come to an end and trading in the antique commodity has to be regularised through a dealer and auction house network. The professionalism of the dealers and auction houses has to match the responsibilities placed upon them by the coming of age of this new antique discipline. Specialisation has to be the order of the day and the vari-

ous sections of Nazi militaria have to be subdivided. In turn, the collector must decide where his interests lie and follow that path. At this point I must clarify this statement. Your collection is what you have decided to try and obtain specimens of and actively study. The fact that you have other artifacts that you like does not mean that you are a collector of them. You own them because you like them. They were a personal gift or one of myriad other reasons. I do not suggest that you rush off to the nearest car boot sale and sell your 'interest' items, enjoy them as you would any other personal belonging. Having clarified your mind as to your intent and hopefully you have decided upon medals and awards, the next stage has to be considered. This may seem patently obvious but nevertheless must be investigated and that is, 'What do I want to collect?' You should look through reference books, consider historical facts and look at personalities. From these you will be able to determine the core element of your collection. Some pointers to this can be that you collect all the awards to one branch of service. Typically, the Luftwaffe would give rise to a large collection or the navy would produce a considerably smaller one. If the navy was chosen, you could eventually expand it further by including the various manufacturers who were engaged in producing the individual awards. Another line of interest is to try and collect all the awards that could be won in a particular theatre of operation or individual battle. Collecting the awards of famous personalities can be expensive but very rewarding. However, if your wallet does not permit this avenue of adventure, some people collect the equivalent awards to replicate the awards won by the chosen personality.

With your core element achieved you can now, by elimination, achieve your wants list. This is the most important part of your collection for it firstly sets the bounds. You have a goal, which allows you to be selective in your purchases thus, hopefully, stopping you from being tempted to make unscheduled purchases. Having said that, if a 'little old lady' gives you a heap of war souvenirs, do not refuse them because they are not on your list. They inevitably will make good exchange items. The list can be forwarded to fellow collectors and dealers allowing them the opportunity to help fill your gaps. It will also act as catalogue for your collection, for cataloguing a collection is one of the most important tasks in the formation. It should have space for the collector to write from where the individual badge was obtained, how much it cost and any further relevant information, such as maker and pin type. This should make collecting a series of medals easier, plus enabling a record of your collection to be portable when visiting arms fairs, gun shows or your favourite dealer. It will also make it easier for your loved ones to buy you that 'super surprise present' by contacting the dealer of your choice whose name, incidentally, is placed conveniently in the front of your records. It beats receiving handkerchiefs and socks for Christmas!

Nothing is more satisfying than completing a set, even if the rare diamond pieces may lie out side your ability financially or by their inherent rarity. Returning to your high values and your hobby bank, do not be afraid to trade lesser items for a great rarity because the more common items, by their very nature, will always be available. Important collections are often broken up and returned to the collecting field of play. So unless the piece has some real sentimental connection be prepared to exchange, even if you end up with only one great rarity in your collection. You formed your collection once, therefore you can repeat it. It is often more fun the second time around and that complete set is most rewarding. Your list sets your limits financially as well as acting as a route map. No traveller would countenance an expedition without a good map. Hopefully I have given you food for thought upon the drawing of your map and I will return to the quality of each individual item that should form your collection. To this end I would like to address the new collector, whether he or she is nine or 90, by passing on the advice I was given many years ago by a delightful young lady of Spink & Sons of St James' London when I was about 11 years old. She advised me to be very selective and collect quality and rarity. She also suggested that I should be very firm in deciding the theme of my collection, so that, having made my decision, I could obtain the specific reference books which all collectors require. Subsequent experience has shown that £20 or more, as is often the case now, spent on a good reference book, can save you far more in the long run. In terms of quality and rarity, your collection will be one of your best investments, particularly if you keep the above observations always in mind. Beware comments like 'combat worn' or 'shows signs of field service use', as these are usually nothing more than a salesman's way of saying 'relic condition'. These comments, from the serious collector's point of view, would indicate a medal which is really not worthy of inclusion in any important collection. Statements by many collectors, such as 'I don't like new looking badges' and 'How do you know they are original, they are too new looking?', are easily rebutted. A mint, original badge will show signs of age patination that is nearly impossible to imitate. This patination in coins greatly enhances their value. The old glow shown on the gold of an Eagle Order or German Cross in Gold belies the fact of their antiquity. On the other hand, the faker often uses wear to reduce or hide imperfections in his work, for a piece of emery paper will round the sharp edges and remove casting marks. The loss of detail in the die striking that accompanies casting is also minimised. Immersion in sulphuric acid will put years of supposed tarnish on the new finish of a badge in a matter of minutes. Natural weathering in soil for a period of time, accompanied by the application of uric acid will produce a natural tarnish. However, all of these are detectable when gauged against an original piece.

To combat the unscrupulous trader, for a person who deals in these forms of fakes is nothing more than a pariah preying on the unknowing and trusting collector, find a reputable dealer who gives a meaningful money back guarantee and will look after you. Send him your wants list and fully understand that he must make an honest profit for, if he does not, he will not be in business to service your collecting needs. Make as many contacts with other collectors and take every opportunity to interchange information and look at rare and interesting pieces. One can look at a hundred pictures but holding a rare piece just once makes you realise its originality. I can coin a phrase: 'It cries out to you, "I'm original".' It has been stated that, for example, the copies of an Iron Cross Second Class are made from one piece stampings, that are produced from a bendy lead alloy and likewise about all other awards. However, there is a brand new breed of reproduction that is currently available, which are near perfect and cover the whole spectrum of the hobby. Contrary to popular belief, not all dealers are experts in the different aspects of their subject. It is true to say that they, like collectors, can also get caught out by fakes occasionally. The fantasy pieces that have been spawned are generally sold as 'rare prototypes' or 'important finds' but collectors can be assured that the chances of stumbling on so much as a single authentic prototype are very rare. It is much wiser to spend your hard earned wages on what is known to be an original medal rather than on what might be a unique, undocumented pattern. Rest assured, it will not be. For the dealers, thoroughly and quite rightly, check what they have to appraise for originality, value and collectors' desirability. This is the sort of professionalism in which they should be indulging to give you, the collector, the best advice possible. Be honest and ask yourself if you were given an unknown badge by a veteran, would you not hope that you had found a valuable rarity and would you not try and contact as many people as possible to ascertain what you had? This is only human nature and dealers, on the whole, are made up of people just like you and are, for the most part, an honest group of people who have a given interest in their subject.

With your reference books read round the subject and try and find the history of the designers of medals as well as the thoughts and diplomatic necessities that brought about their inception. The antecedents of your Third Reich period awares are as important as that period piece, for the latter would not have come into being without the former. A full understanding of the needs of the various organisations, as well as the design styles that the manufacturer and artist employed in the production of the individual awards, is possibly the most useful information that will point you in the right direction for identifying an original piece from that which purports to be so.

To illustrate the various points raised so far, I have undertaken an in-depth look at the two most prestigious of Nazi Germany's awards. These commemorate different aspects of governmental recognition as, on one hand, there was a necessity for the state to honourably acknowledge its friends and, on the other, to reward its heroes. The highest diplomatic award was the Eagle Order and that for valour, the Iron Cross. The study of the Eagle Order shows the number of varieties that can be encountered in one small area of awards and the ways in which it changed due to political pressure and necessity. It clearly illustrates the need to study the changes in the stampings and forms of construction, while an in-depth historical look at the Iron Cross shows a decoration that has spanned the history of medals, been awarded to many different nationalities and witnessed historical design changes that exemplified the political and social changes in Europe. The designer, although relatively unknown in the west, was a very accomplished architect, whose Prussian mentors were fervent in their love of the English style. It is possibly these points that have made it so enthralling to collectors of every nationality, or perhaps it is its simple design, incorporating matt black iron and burnished silver, that inspires them to own one.

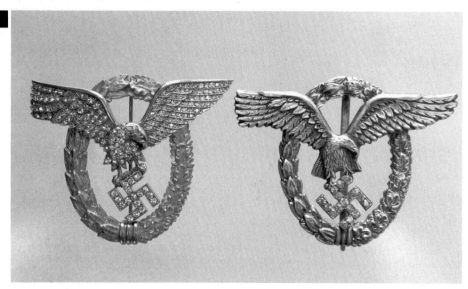

Plate 1 Combined Pilot Observer Badge with Diamonds on the left, with what purports to be such. These pieces turn up frequently and I have closely examined three examples, these have shown the silver content .800 when they are actually cast in base metal.

2. The Meritorious Order of the German Eagle

This chapter concentrates upon the prestigious Meritorious Order of the German Eagle. To understand the implications of this exalted, international award, one has to go back to the situation at the end of WW1. At this time all the awards of the former Second Reich empire were prohibited and only the civilian grade of the Pour le Mérite was allowed to be worn.

In the chaotic period leading up to the Nazi takeover in January 1933 all awards were prohibited except the above mentioned order and certain approved Frei Korps awards. The latter had been subsequently awarded for the struggles that had occurred in what is now Poland, following the collapse of the Czarist government in Russia and the punitive restrictions on territory imposed in 1919 by the Treaty of Versailles. This treaty had dismembered the belligerent powers of Germany and the Austro-Hungarian empire and created numerous small states from the Baltic through to the Adriatic. It was hoped that these countries, with their own nationalistic interests, would never again gravitate to one supreme epicentre which would subsequently threaten the interests of the erstwhile allies, Britain, France and America. To the aforementioned awards, some of the old ducal states were permitted to issue and present orders that had been traditionally theirs to give and not purely Germanic or Prussian ones. These ducal states' orders were permitted to be worn unhindered. Under the Weimar Republic, several of the Länder (German States) issued their own awards for service in industry or the fire brigade, life saving, and mine rescue and continued to do so for the first two or three years of the Third Reich.

With the success of the Nazis in January 1933, Hitler and his confidants grasped the need for a new series of awards and there emerged a desire to reconstruct the various official orders, decorations and medals that applied to every aspect of German military, diplomatic, political and civil life. The role of medals and decorations, combined with the aspects of uniform and pageantry, fitted in well with the newly emergent Nazi ideology that was being crystallised during the heady days of their assent to power through to the spring of 1936. This Nazi ideology and, at times, the almost theatrical splendour of dressing up for occasions of state, presented an occasion to redesign and restrike the official decorations of the new regime, modelled in part upon older awards but restyled and upgraded in keeping with the image of the new Germany. Nazi Germany not only modelled itself on its mythological predecessors, but also encompassed influences it had encountered in the occupation period following WW1, namely those of Great Britain. The necessity for an international order, that reflected the importance of the new state and paralleled those of Great Britain in diplomatic importance, was plainly obvious to such members of the Nazi hierarchy as Ribbentrop, who had a love of theatrical and was also ambassador to Great Britain. He had been much impressed with the funeral of George V and the subsequent coronation of George VI, although he had exhibited the worst possible taste of any ambassador to the Court of Saint James' in its long history, by saluting King George V with 'Heil Hitler'.

The best designers, jewellers and artists, now finding favour and patronage under the national socialist yoke, were commissioned to create the new orders for the new uniforms. Not all of the designers and manufacturers came from Germany itself. For example the most important order of the Luftwaffe was designed by Rudolf Stübiger of Vienna. The Luftwaffe had just emerged from its proving ground in Russia to the glare of the world, which had given the diplomatic prowess to both Hitler and Göring of seeming not unlike a conjurer producing a rabbit from a hat. The Combined Pilots Badge with Diamonds was introduced in 1935 and was to reward the first generals and Göring himself. It was a revival of some of the lost splendour and removed tradition of the old Germany, a hearkening back to old standards and styles under the colours of the new regime, and an encompassing of all that was good in the new German society. The art nouveau trend of the rest of Europe was virtually bypassed in the quest to restore the injured pride of a defeated Germany. The old styles and traditions were revived and ensconced in the new face and image of the Third Reich.

Hitler, an aspiring artist in his youth, took a keen interest in the design and implementation of these new decorations. He understood the sense of importance felt when a man was uniformed and bedecked with medals proclaiming his fine status. Glittering decorations began to adorn the prestigious chests of the new statesmen of the Reich, proclaiming beyond all doubt who worked for the benefit and betterment of the new Reich and who were visibly exalted by its leaders.

Paradoxically, Hitler himself wore few decorations — only his Iron Cross and Wound Badge

Plate 2 Breast Star of the Grand Cross. This is the first type and was produced only for a short period and shows variation in the sunburst.

Plate 3 Close-up view of the eagle to show the hand engraved form.

Plate 4 Close-up view of the hollow formed eagle which was dye stamped.

Plate 5 This shows the flat concave reverse of the early type Grand Cross Breast Star as well as the variation rivet, hinge, pin and hook and silver hallmarks.

Plate 6 Extreme close-up to show the silver hallmark and rivets.

12

Plate 7   The Sash Badge of the Grand Cross showing the form of attachment which did not encompass the later fan in the upper V of the Cross's arms.

Plate 8   The reverse of the badge to show the finish of the eagles.

Plate 9   Close-up of the eagle shown in plates 7 & 8. This eagle is nearly identical to that shown in plate 3.

Plate 10   The positioning of the silver mark on the lower arm of the cross shown in plates 7 & 8.

Plate 11   Hitler and Mussolini taking tea during Mussolini's state visit to Germany, showing him wearing the first pattern Grand Cross prior to his being awarded the Grand Cross with Diamonds.

earned in WW1, and his Golden Party Badge. On high days and holidays he would, when wearing his party uniform, wear his Blood Order. But, unlike the other party members, who always wore their medal or emblem, Hitler seemed only to wear it for these festive occasions. The plain effect of his uniform must have stood in sobering contrast alongside his medal festooned cronies, such as Göring and Ribbentrop.

Hitler's personal quirk in not awarding himself with decorations did not preclude him from constantly reviewing and approving new designs, and seeking occasions to award them. Thus, on one particular occasion, when he received the first example of the German Order which he presented posthumously to Dr Fritz Todt in 1942, after Todt's death in an air accident, he noted that the swastika in the central part of the device was gilded and not silvered, as in the case of the Golden Party Badge. He contacted the manufacturers in Ludenscheid and commented that this must be put right on future examples, and that the other examples of the order, which had been transmitted with the one presented to Todt, he would personally have silvered by a Berlin jeweller. This points out Hitler's attention to detail when medals were involved.

Hitler's international aspirations, linked with diplomatic adventures in Spain, Czechoslovakia and Austria, non-aggression pacts with Stalinist Russia, pacts of steel with Mussolini in Italy and peace with honour for Chamberlain at Munich, were all greased along their way by the honouring of statesmen and the giving of decorations. Palm greasing and playing to the gallery though it was, it worked.

Whatever the murmurings of the evils of Nazism uttered behind embassy doors, over diplomatic lunches or the interminable cocktail parties, Hitler succeeded in getting his own way and appeasing his international political opponents. More to the point, he also established firm political alliances with neighbouring European leaders, in an axis consolidation that was not to separate without the conflagration of war.

In the autumn of 1936 contemplation was given to the introduction of an international order for Germany. This was something that Germany had lacked since 1918, although the gap had been filled by the Order of the German Red Cross up until this time. This practice was unsatisfactory for the emergent Nazi diplomatic corps, who could not readily be identified with the German Red Cross Decoration. Likewise, the International Red Cross were somewhat concerned at the form of awards that were bestowed, which is illustrated by some of the awards to German and foreign dignitaries who could have little to do with the German Red Cross. One such recipient was no less than Hermann Göring himself. On 30.11.36, from the Reichskanzlei, a directive was issued by Ministerialdirektor Dr Doehle stating that 'The Führer and Reichskanzler had personally instructed the Staatssekretars Dr Meissner to formally instruct Prof Klein of München and Profs Rähmisch and Lettre, to look at the problems of the creation of a new international order and submit designs'. This led to the introduction of a revised Red Cross Order which was instituted on 6.4.37 and the introduction of the Meritorious Order of the German Eagle, which was officially instituted on 30.5.37. It was created primarily as an international award designed for presentation to foreign dignitaries and heads of state. By a strange chance, the inauguration of the Eagle Order coincided with the state visit to Germany by Benito Mussolini in September of that year!

The grades of this exalted international award commenced with the Grand Cross of the Order of the German Eagle, which consisted of an eight-pointed breast star. This beautiful order comprised of a fluted sunburst, made of genuine silver and hallmarked on the reverse.

At this point, it is relevant to relate that the markings on the reverse of the order, along with manner of riveting and assembly, changed quite dramatically with the period of manufacture. I will try to bring these differences to the reader's attention as one is guided through the varying classes and grades produced during the time scale of the existence of the order. The first produced pattern is the rarest. Examination of an example of the first pattern has revealed that the initial decoration was partially hand-crafted. There are also distinct differences in the formation of the national eagle emblem, situated between the enamelled arms of the cross mounted on the sunburst.

To describe the Grand Cross set of the 1937 first type, we will commence with the Breast Star, which displays the white enamelled cross with gold edging and gold eagles between the arms of the cross. The whole is mounted on the silver, eight pointed sunburst, which comprises the star of the order. This is illustrated by Plate 2. Plate 3 presents a close up detail of one of the eagle and swastika emblems. The hand finishing of this first type is quite pronounced, particularly in the fletching of the wings and breast of the eagle, as well as in its own distinct outline. There is also a noticeable difference in the shape of the eagle's head. In this case it has a round eye and a large upper portion to the beak, giving it the appearance of a toucan's beak as opposed to the more stylish die struck later versions.

Plate 4, the eagle and swastika pattern of the second type award, is, relatively speaking, the more common of this order. The outline form of the eagle, shape of the head, etc, is noticeably different as is the detail of the fletching. The lessened refinement of the detailed work is exaggerated by the extreme enlargement of the illustration, which is approximately four times life size. In this case, the eagle's head is much more defined, the eye is a smaller dot recessed in a V-shaped eye socket and the beak formation is more as one would find in a lifelike eagle. Whereas in the first type the eye has no eye socket and the top of the beak and the skull forms a straight line, though curved at either end. The other major difference between the two styles is the point at which the wing touches the body of the eagle at its legs. In the first design of eagle there is a gap, as if the last piece of fletching has been cut off mid-way along its length. In the second version there is no such gap, which gives the two distinctive outlines to the wing configuration. In fact, the eagles are produced by being die stamped and usually they are then joined together so that they are formed hollow, and thus attached between the arms of the cross. The reverse of the Breast Star is of a plain, polished type with the silver grade stamped directly on to the reverse, SILBER 800, which is shown in Plate 5. The grade of silver for such a high decoration seems to be unusually low, in that it consists of only 800 parts out of 1,000 parts pure silver; but it seems that this may well have been the usual silver grading for awards of this period, as comparative highest state decorations of the German Red Cross for the period 1934-37 are found in the same silver grading. The two rivets holding the mounted cross into position, visible through the backplate of the star, are of the normal rolled type. This is sometimes also known as a ball rivet, the protecting portion being typical of individual jewellers construction, showing through as a dome ended peening. Plate 6 reveals this feature in extreme close-up (details of the more usual second type construction are shown in Plate 13). Another basic difference between the two patterns of the award is that the first pattern has a narrower securing pin. The second type not only has a securing pin with a swollen centre section but is, in addition, hallmarked on the pin. In addition to the Breast Star the award is accompanied by a special dress sash and sash badge. Worn looped over the right shoulder, the bow of the sash, some 90mm wide, rested on the left hip. From the bow was suspended the sash badge of the order. The sash badge of the order (Plate 7) comprised a silver gilt cross with white enamel centre, with the national emblem placed between the arms of the cross. The reverse of the cross (Plate 8) is virtually identical other than that the eagles' heads face the opposite direction to that on the obverse. The determining feature of the 1937 first pattern is that the eagle emblems are of the same form and hand finished as those found on the star. The suspension ring is mounted through a loop affixed directly into the V section of the upper arm. Comparison with the second type version (Plates 14 and 15) shows that the suspension was modified to affix to a fan shaped projection which protruded from between the V

of the upper arm of the cross. The reason for this modification was because it had been determined that the original basic method of fixing was not overly secure. Using the fan type modification added to the overall strength of the assembly and also possibly lessened the damage from the catch that was attached to the bow of the sash, to which the badge was hooked.

Plate 9 depicts a close up of the first type of the national emblem featured between the arms of the sash badge. The conformity of shape with that depicted on the Breast Star and the formation of detailed fletching is clearly evident. Minute differences between the design work of Plates 3 and 9 are attributed to the variances of hand finishing employed in their construction.

Another point of interest exists in the seemingly apparent fact that two grades of silver were used for the construction of the Breast Star and the Sash Badge. The '800' silver grade mark is clearly evident on the star reverse. The edge of the lower arm of the sash badge, however, is clearly marked with a '900' silver grade, indicating that it was constructed from that material. This marking and its positioning is indicated by One other Grand Cross of this type has been encountered and thoroughly studied and the silver gradings for both pieces for each example of the order are identical, as is the position of those marks on the relative awards that go to complete the Grand Cross set. The construction methods as described above are identical.

On 25.9.37, Hitler awarded Mussolini a special grade of the Order of the German Eagle with Diamonds. This grade had a black outline to the breast star sunburst and the central cross device was studded with diamonds. Plate 11 shows Hitler and Mussolini during an informal break on the occasion of the Duce's state visit. At this point he had not been invested with the special grade with diamonds but is wearing the Grand Cross next to the Grand Cross of the Red Cross decoration 1934, which now currently resides in the collection of Lt-Col J. Angolia. The award presented to Mussolini was a one time special grade and was handcrafted by the firm of J. Godet und Sohn of Berlin. Unfortunately, it has come to light that the actual example was destroyed at the end of the war by being broken down by the Polish troops who overran Mussolini's effects. The special sash for the award was manufactured by the firm of Karl Loy of Munich. It comprised a red sash which was formed and worn over the right shoulder, with the sash badge hanging from the bow at the hip but, in this case, the ribbon, or sash, is totally red and devoid of the white, black, white edgings that are found on the original Grand Cross 1937-43. Two parallel sets of stripes are found on this red field, approximately 1in in from either side, comprising of 1/4in stripes on either side made up of white, black, white lines. Although no part of the original example, to include the sash, has survived the war, a small length was obtained from the firm by Angolia and resides in his collection. The case that housed Mussolini's special grade was an equally magnificent 'one off'. It was an oblong casket with a raised, fluted silver border. The central field was inlaid with amber fashioned in a mosaic of different shades, forming an interconnecting swastika design. On to the centre was placed a finely detailed open winged eagle with a wreath and swastika in its claws. This emblem was fire gilded. The whole work was executed by the master silversmith, Franz Richert of München.

The next grade of decoration was the Order of the German Eagle with Star. This comprised a

Plate 12 The obverse of the 6-pointed Breast Star.

Plate 13 The reverse of the star shown in plate 12, showing the hinge hook and doughnut type rivet.

Plate 14 The Neck Cross of the Eagle Order displaying the fan for the suspender.

Plate 15 Close-up of the fan suspender and showing the ribbed version of the ribbon suspender as well as the .900 silver mark.

16

breast badge, similar to the breast star but slightly smaller — 75mm in size and having only six main points to the sunburst — as shown in Plate 12. The reverse of the decoration was panelled into six distinct sections, as shown in Plate 13. The award was accompanied with a special neck decoration, similar in style to that of the sash badge previously described but now, in the second pattern type construction, it was suspended from the neck ribbon by a specially designed loop and bar, secured to the fluted fan shaped mount on the upper arm. The ribbon itself comprised a bright red coloured, moire ribbon with white, black, white edging. The neck order is shown in Plate 14 and the detail, Plate 15, shows the fan shaped mount with the ring and bar. On this ring is the hallmark '900'. The neck cross measures 50mm across. At this point it is interesting to come to the conclusion that this six-pointed breast star is also found in the first type with no panelling, as is the neck order without the fan. Although I have heard of this type of example I have not, as yet, been able to examine an actual decoration.

Plates 16 and 17 reveal close-ups of the reverse of the star, showing the hallmark '900' on the securing pin, as well as its general swollen form and the ring ended rivets which secure the cross to the base plate of the star.

The third grade of the Order of the German Eagle, first degree, is identical to the neck order of the second grade or degree but was not accompanied by a breast star. Again it has been reported that the first type eagle and suspension are encountered in this type as well.

The fourth grade of the Order of the German Eagle, second degree, is a breast badge measuring 40mm across. It is similar in style to the neck order but single sided and slightly concave. The example depicted in Plate 18 is the 1939 pattern with swords. This type of award is found in the first pattern of Eagle Order. The eagles are as described for the Breast Star (Plate 2) and it has the same thin, slender pin and variant hook and hinge construction being stamped 'SILBER 800'. In the second type of construction, the reverse of this fourth grade is polished and gilded, as it is in the first type but the pin construction is of a bellied design and has the flap at the hinge end, which is semi-circular, acting as a strengthening and retaining arm on the underside of the hinge. This construction is true for all second pattern awards. On to this pin is stamped, to the viewer's surface, the hallmark and silver mark of the maker and grade of silver. In the case of the awards that have swords added to them, these swords are attached through a hole in the centre of the arms of the cross, which are secured by means of one large, domed rivet, which is visible in the centre of the reverse (Plates 19/20). The pin of the fourth grade is marked (Plate 21) this particular illustration showing the silver

content '900' and the manufacturer's code mark 'L/50'. This style is used on pieces produced after 1939 and will be discussed in greater depth further on in the chapter.

The fifth grade is the Order of the German Eagle, third degree. This comprises a 40mm cross suspended from a ribbon of the same colours as the neck order but secured by a free moving ring which is affixed to the upper arm of the cross. Again, this is found in two distinct types. The first type, as previously described with the distinctive eagles and the eyelet that holds the ring from which the ribbon is suspended being affixed directly into the V of the cross. The second type is again suspended from a ribbon of the same colour as the neck order but secured by a free moving ring affixed to a loop on the fan mount (Plate 22). Detailed examination of this ring (Plate 23) shows the silver mark '900' together with a manufacturer's code mark '21'. This style of marking was introduced in approximately 1943. An interesting travesty exists with another mark, the meaning as yet unidentified, being a letter 'T' situated on the very top of the fixed loop of the fan mount (Plate 24). In 1943 it was authorised that the neck order, when awarded with the six pointed star, should have the eyelet stamped with a small capital 'T'. This was to represent 'Teilgenommen', but was incorrectly stamped at the manufacturer's.

The sixth grade is embodied in the form of a standard medal and was known as the German Medal of Merit. A simple disc type silver medal, bearing on the front a representation of the cross with national eagle and swastika between the arms and on the reverse the legend, 'Deutsche Verdienst Medaille'. Two basic patterns to the medal exist, one having the reverse legend formed in Gothic Script, which is thought to be the earlier example with the more usual version having the legend in Roman Script. It was worn suspended from a bright red moire ribbon, with white, black, white edging, which comprise Plates 25/26. Another interesting point of reference is that on the rim or edge of the first described type of medal, is found the silver content which is usually .800 and the Prussian state mint in letters, or a crescent moon logo which is also attributed to the aforementioned mint. The other types are usually found in either fine quality bronze that has been silver-plated or silvered, or in a low-grade zinc based metal, which has again been silvered. This silvering often leads to a dull, pewterish colour which is very unattractive. One point of interest that the collector must take into account, is that in the late war bronze medals, to be described later in the chapter, were produced in a very low grade zinc and then bronzed. As in other war badges that lose their gilding and give the impression of being silver, the bronzing disappears and gives the impression of being a silver award, when indeed they are a

Plate 16 Close-up of the pregnant pin showing the .900 silver mark.

Plate 17 The same view but this time the pin removed to reveal a close-up of the doughnut rivet.

Plate 18 The pin back badge with swords.

Plate 19 The reverse of the badge in 18, showing the pin, hinge and hook as well as the large central rivet that secures the swords to the body of the badge.

Plate 20 An enlargement to show the rivet that holds the swords on to the badge and shown in 19.

Plate 21 Showing the pregnant pin of the badge with the silver mark .900 and the markers' mark, L/50, in recessed box.

very low grade bronze. This quality of badge has little commercial value or collector desirability.

The whole series of the Order of the German Eagle was totally reorganised on 20.4.39, with all its grades being authorised to be awarded with swords as well as a new grade being introduced into the sequence. This was the Grand Cross of the Order of the German Eagle in Gold, which was intended to be awarded to only 16 recipients but, apparently, only eight of the intended recipients actually achieved this recognition. These were: Graf Ciano of Italy (Mussolini's son-in-law); Gen Franco of Spain; Adm Horthy of Hungary; King Boris III of Bulgaria; Ryti (Finnish ambassador to Germany); Marshal Antonescu of Romania; Hiroshi Oshima (Japanese ambassador to Germany); and Field-marshal Mannerheim of Finland. The addition of the swords was to denote an award for military service.

The Order was not intended to be awarded to German nationals but some exceptions were made. The first German national to receive it was Constantin von Neurath, who was Foreign Minister. He entered the Diplomatic Corps in 1901 and, except for a brief period when he served in WW1, he continued in the diplomatic service until 1938 when he was forced to resign as Hitler's Foreign Minister, leaving way for the appointment of Joachim von Ribbentrop. He had, together with Generals Blomberg and Fritsch, tried to dissuade Hitler from moves against Austria and Czechoslovakia. This had angered his master, who took criticism as disloyalty and he knew where the agreement in foreign policy that he wanted could be obtained, from the social climbing ambassador to England, Ribbentrop. Hitler could not ignominiously dispense with Constantin von Neurath after his long and honourable service, so he was later promoted to Reich Protector of Bohemia and Moravia, which could possibly be considered, at best, as a sideways or downwards promotion. He held this backwater position until August 1943, when the post was given to Wilhelm Frick. A 'Special Class' was presented to Constantin von Neurath on 20.4.39 in recognition of his service as Foreign Minister. The same order that established the 'Special Degree' award also served to bring about a revision of the previously established order. At the time of the reorganisation of the award, the category of crossed swords was decreed eligible for those decorations being awarded in recognition in military involvement in the affairs of state. This established the rankings of the order as:

- Golden Grand Cross with Diamonds: a one time award to Mussolini only
- Golden Grand Cross with Swords.
- Golden Grand Cross without Swords.
- Grand Cross with Swords.
- Grand Cross without Swords
- First Class with Swords.
- First Class without Swords.
- Second Class with Swords.
- Second Class without Swords.
- Third Class with Swords.
- Third Class without Swords.
- Fourth Class with Swords.
- Fourth Class without Swords.
- Fifth Class with Swords.
- Fifth Class without Swords.
- Silver Medal of Merit with Swords.
- Silver Medal of Merit without Swords.

The award to Constantin von Neurath set the precedent for the award of the Order to the new Foreign Minister Joachim von Ribbentrop, who had been appointed by Hitler in 1938. This was presumably for diplomatic services for in May 1935, he proved the success of his methods by concluding the Anglo-German Naval Treaty without using Foreign Ministry officials or even officially informing them. This surely must have impressed Hitler. In 1936, once more independently of the Foreign Ministry, he persuaded Japan to join in an Anti-Comintern Pact,. which Mussolini agreed to sign the next year. After his appointment he was at the centre of the Nazi aristocracy and the social standing of his wife, Annalies, lent a glamour no other Party member's spouse could compete with. Ribbentrop's good fortune faltered when he suggested to the Poles the return of Danzig to the Reich and collaboration against Russia. When they failed to agree, Hitler moved into Memel, showing them that diplomacy did not mean debate. In August 1939, however, Ribbentrop negotiated the agreement between Russia and Germany by which they agreed to attack and divide Poland. Thus these two special awards are in fact nothing more than two more additions to the list of Golden Grand Cross without Swords.

The Medal of Merit was enhanced by the extra provision of 'With Swords' (Plate 27) for those recipients who merited its award and to bring it into line with the other degrees of the order. The method of suspension of the swords was not as on the decorations across the arms of the badge of the order but they were attached to the eyelet through which the ribbon ring joined the medal. These swords were finished on both sides, that is to say the design that is found on the obverse is mirrored on the reverse (Plate 30). The ring through which the ribbon passes can be found with a plain number '30' stamped into it.

In 1943 the grades of the order were again redefined with the introduction of two new steps. The new classification of the degrees of the order, inaugurated both the Order of the German Eagle First Class, With and Without Swords and the Bronze Medal of Merit With and Without Swords. The swords attached to the medal ring were also finished on both sides. The bronze medal can be found in either high grade bronze, which is finely die struck, through to very poor

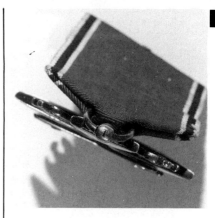

Plate 22   The enamelled cross of the order with swords as worn from a ribbon.

Plate 23   A close-up to the show the silver mark .900 as well as the maker's mark 21.

Plate 24   An interesting additional maker's mark of a double T superimposed on top of each other.

Plate 25   The obverse of the Medal of Merit.

Plate 26 Reverse of the medal showing the later form of inscription.

Plate 27 The obverse of the silver medal with swords. This is the type produced in genuine silver and hallmarked by the Prussian State Mint in Berlin.

Plate 28 Reverse of the same medal showing the first style of legend.

Plate 29 The first and second pattern types of suspension employed in the Neck Order.

Plate 30 A comparison of the two types of reverse of the medals. It is interesting to note that the early silver forms usually have a small ring while the later form have a larger ring on to which is stamped the marker's mark.

Plate 31 A composite shot showing the Sash Badge attached to the Grand Cross Sash and the two Neck Orders, the similarity in the method of suspension of the Grand Cross badge to the ribbon and first pattern Neck Order to its ribbon, as opposed to that finally employed.

affairs which are found in low grade zinc and have been already described. The ring through which the ribbon passes on these bronze versions is normally found with a plain number '30' stamped into it. The ribbon is identical to that found on the silver medal, save in this case, as with the Eagle Order First Class 1943, it has a white stripe breaking the red field of the central band. The purpose was to allow for a more broadly based area of recognition for the award of the lower grade of the series. It was particularly useful for the offering of recognition to foreign workers and military personnel, who were now being increasingly called upon to offer their services to the Reich. This represented the greater awareness of the importance played in the munitions industry by these guest workers and was especially fruitful in rewarding those eastern volunteers who were supporting the Germans in the period 1942-44 in ever increasing numbers. At that time the Germans had introduced a badge or medal, the exact design at the time of writing is still unknown, called the Eastern Workers Achievement Badge. Some of these were volunteers but most were virtually slaves, and the Germans had collectively called them the 'Ostbeiter'. Whether volunteers or not, they were treated more like convicts than war workers and were forced to wear a patch with the word 'Ost' as a mark of their degraded status. As the war situation deteriorated, or as their importance was more greatly appreciated, the detested 'Ost' patch was replaced by more artistically designed national emblems, which fell in line with the more highly honoured volunteer patches of the army and the Waffen SS. As a further honorarium the aforementioned decoration was instituted and was described in the periodical *Deutschland im Kampf* (Germany at War) as being a sword crossed with a hammer, which could be awarded by a factory manager for any act of special merit or achievement on the part of Russian, Ukrainian or Belorussia workers employed in his plant, who had contributed sufficiently to the German war effort. However, in April 1943, which coincides with the reorganisation of the Medal of Merit, foreign workers, 'from countries without diplomatic representation in the Reich', this could only mean in practice those peoples from the aforementioned countries knows as Ostarbeiters, were made eligible for the Medal of Merit of the German Eagle in Bronze With and Without Swords. Normal qualification for the consideration of such an award set out that the requirements were two years of continuous employment with excellent performance in the field of work in which they were employed, or that the proposed recipient should have made some special contribution which had significantly enhanced the German war effort.

The new degrees of the Order of the German Eagle First Class, With and Without Swords, had the difference in design entailing the eagles and the edging of the cross being finished in frosted silver instead of gilt. The sash was also redesigned, with the red field of the moire sash being broken by a white line running down the centre. The Sash Badge of the order was also finished to compliment that of the Breast Star of the order, having the eagles finished in frosted silver as well as the other parts which had previously been gilded.

This gave rise to the final list of the grades and degrees of the Meritorious Order of the German Eagle and comprised:

● Grand Cross of the German Eagle in Gold with Diamonds.
● Grand Cross of the German Eagle in Gold with Swords.
● Grand Cross of the German Eagle in Gold without Swords.
● Grand Cross of the German Eagle with Swords.
● Grand Cross of the German Eagle without Swords.
● First Class of the German Eagle Order with Swords.
● First Class of the German Eagle Order without Swords.
● Second Class of the German Eagle Order with Swords.
● Second Class of the German Eagle Order without Swords.
● Third Class of the German Eagle Order with Swords.
● Third Class of the German Eagle Order without Swords.
● Fourth Class of the German Eagle Order with Swords.
● Fourth Class of the German Eagle Order without Swords.
● Fifth Class of the German Eagle Order with Swords.
● Fifth Class of the German Eagle Order without Swords.
● Silver Medal of Merit with Swords.
● Silver Medal of Merit without Swords.
● Bronze Medal of Merit with Swords.
● Bronze Medal of Merit without Swords.

To bring to a conclusion the varying grades and their interplay at different points of time in their history, I have decided to try and categorise some of the markings to illustrate the type of marks and silver grades encompassed at those times.

The original 1937 type was found with silver marks ranging from .800 or .900 but no maker's mark. This is shown in Plates 6 and 10. Between 1937 and 1939 the pieces were usually produced with a mark on the pin or suspension ring (Plates 15 and 16) and also at this point, the upper arm of the cross was occasionally stamped with the grade or degree of the order. So, for example, the 1939 series Third Class would have a numeral '3' stamped on top of the fan. Also in the 1939 series, the 'L' number was featured in the markings, displayed as letter/number, within a box which surrounded both the letter and the number (Plate 21).

The 1943 series, which was a reorganisation of the 1939 series, would have relegated the former 1939 grade 3 to grade 5, and this numeral '5' would thence appear in the same place on the new series issue. The form of marking also changed to the silver content and the manufacturer's number alone (Plate 23). Also, the markings of the Neck Cross or Third Class of the order, when awarded in conjunction with the six pointed star as a set, had a small capital 'T' for Teilgenommen stamped on the rim. It seems, however, that this practice rarely happened.

If one is lucky enough to possess the original presentation case with an award, the description of the grade or degree of the order was normally displayed by gold blocking inside the upper lid lining of the case (Plate 34).

With the various changes in the gradings of the medals and the subsequent inclusion of swords to the order, it is possible for both grades of the same degree to be worn at the same time. That is to say, the Grand Cross could be awarded to the same recipient With and Without Swords, and could be worn at the same time.

There are a number of strange anomalies in the Grand Cross series and the construction of the Gold Grand Cross of the Order of the German Eagle, which was presented by Hitler to Ribbentrop, affords a good example of such. It is identical to the second type Grand Cross from the obverse, but the reverse has many striking differences. The first of these is in the fact that the reverse of the star sunburst is lined out in a somewhat similar manner to the obverse and the actual gaps between the rays are more deeply sawn down, so that they are in greater silhouette than those on the eight pointed or six pointed sunbursts. The hinge is found higher up the upper part of the reverse of the sunburst and is approximately half as wide as that found on the other two types. Thus the pin that retains the badge to the tunic is equivalently much longer and it is found, although it still has a belly in the middle, to be of a much more slender appearance. Midway on either side of the star are two oval plates, fixed directly on to the back plate. On these are two retaining hooks pointing downwards in the same direction as the hinge pin. These retaining hooks were employed to support the massive weight of the order. The overall piece is gold plated. The major difference between the sash for the Grand Cross in Gold and the standard Grand Cross band is that the black band on the former measures 7mm, while the latter measures only 5mm. Correspondingly, the outer white band on the Grand Cross in Gold is narrower.

Illustrated on p23 of David Littlejohn and Col C. M. Dodkins' book, *Orders, Decorations, Medals and Badges of the Third Reich*, is an eight pointed Grand Cross of the Order of the German Eagle in Silver. The interesting point about this particular piece is that the sunburst is produced by four long rays that are situated at 12, 3, 6 and 9 o'clock respectively and between these rays, emanating from the eagles that are in the quarters of the arms of the enamelled cross, are shorter rays giving the impression of a sunburst surmounting a further sunburst. This does not come to the viewer's attention without careful scrutiny.

There are two further examples that as yet have not been explained.

The illustrations are to be found on p59 of *For Führer and Fatherland, Political & Civil Awards of the Third Reich*, by John R. Angolia. They take a somewhat similar configuration of sunburst to the one previously described but in this case the longer arms are slightly shorter, therefore the difference between the eight arms is not so pronounced. In the case of the first example, the sunburst is silver all over and the eagles between the quadrants of the arms of the cross are gilded, taking the form of the second type of eagle previously described. But in this case, the field behind the swastika clutched in the wreath of the eagle's talons is enamelled red, as opposed to white and the cross itself is enamelled red instead of white, as in the standard pattern. In the second of these two examples the silver sunburst and white cross are exactly identical to the normal piece, but the eagles in the quadrants of the arms of the cross are of a totally different design. They are, to all intents and purposes, identical to the second design, save that they are flat and similar to those found on the Social Welfare Cross, being enamelled black and the fletching and outline of the eagle are raised and polished flat to the upper edge of the enamelled surface and then gilded. The reason for the production of the three aforementioned medals is unknown and any constructive theory would be welcomed by the author.

Plate 32 Obverse Grand Cross of the German Eagle in Gold Without Swords set, belonging to the German Foreign Minister Joachim von Ribbentrop.

Plate 33 Obverse Sash Badge of the Grand Cross of the German Eagle in Gold Without Swords, awarded to Joachim von Ribbentrop.

Plate 34 The titles used to deleniate the Order of the German Eagle. The upper style was used in conjunction with the rare first form, the middle in 1939 and the lower in 1943.

Orden vom Deutschen Adler
Verdienstkreuz 1. Stufe

Verdienstkreuz III. Stufe
des
Ordens vom Deutschen Adler

Deutscher Adlerorden
V. Klasse mit Schwertern

3. The Iron Cross

With such an important decoration as the Iron Cross, I have included a short history of its development from inception to final denazified form. It is not intended to be fully comprehensive, simply to introduce the reader to the subject.

Times were hard and full of dramatic events, when the Iron Cross, the first decoration to be awarded to both officers and other ranks, was instituted. The medal was originally introduced in 1813 to reward the fighting forces of Prussia, whose king had declared war on France and Napoleon on 13.3.1813. On 17.3.1813 King Friedrich Wilhelm III issued at Breslau his passionate 'Appeal to my People' speech, rallying them to respond to the threat from the French during the Napoleonic wars.

On 10.3.1813 the Statute of Institution for the Iron Cross, signed by the King, was published in the *Schlesischer Zeitung*. The details of the medal were announced on 20.3.1813. It was originally intended to be a pure campaign award and was to replace the other state awards such as the Order of the Red Eagle and the Pour le Mérite.

The King, who firstly made designs of his own, then commissioned others to do so as well. The original design submitted by its instigator was that of a cross partée, with a square box centre with chamfered corners. In this box was the royal cipher surmounted by the crown of Prussia. The arms had a sprig of oak leaves superimposed upon them. The quarters of the cross were semifilled and the date of instigation superimposed with one numeral in each quadrant. The medal was to be suspended from a ribbon comprised of stripes of black, white, broad black, white, black, these being the colours of Prussia.

However, another design, submitted by the architect Schinkel, was adopted. The name of Karl Friedrich Schinkel, who was born in 1781, is not been well known in the west. This neglect is largely because his major buildings are in the former East Berlin and German Democratic Republic, which have scarcely gained a reputation as popular touring centres. The lack of appreciation of Schinkel in this country is particularly sad in view of the admiration which he and his principal patrons, the Prussian royal family, had for English achievements in architecture, industry and design. Schinkel made a long study tour to Britain in 1826 observing, among many other things, recent industrial buildings which were to have a marked influence on his subsequent architectural language.

The reasons for his visit were ostensibly to study methods of displaying pictures in public and private collections and to gain ideas for his Altes Museum in Berlin, then nearing completion.

The Altes Museum shows Schinkel's skill as a town planner or environmental designer. His other major buildings in Berlin were the Schauspielhaus, which visually unites the two already classical churches flanking the Platz der Akademie and nearby he built the austerely Greek Doric Neue Wache (New Guard House) the Gothic Werdersche Church and the now destroyed Bavakademie— incorporating the fireproof iron construction with brick cap vaults that had fascinated him in English mills and factories. He enlightened the exterior of the Bavakademie with a series of beautiful figured terracotta reliefs.

That these buildings are mainly cultural, religious and educational is no accident. Schinkel was a product of 18th century enlightened thought and, particularly, German idealism which maintained that, in the ideal state, man could be morally perfect through cultural and aesthetic education. Also, the duty ethic upheld by the philosopher philanthropists of Protestant Prussia, had prepared men like Schinkel to devote themselves to the public good in the service of the state.

In 1810, Schinkel abandoned his brief career as a private architect and entered the service of the King as a civil servant in the Prussian royal building department, where he served until his death in 1841. In 1830 he was appointed director,

a task which, amazingly, involved the direction of all public buildings throughout Prussia. His tour of these provinces added to an already heavy workload which his contemporaries believe was responsible for his early death.

The high moral tone of Schinkel's attempt to make an ideal city of Berlin, then largely known as a barracks town, was shared by his chief benefactor the Prussian crown prince, Friedrich Wilhelm, who succeeded his father as King of Prussia in 1840. A gifted amateur architect, taught by Schinkel himself, the crown prince not only commissioned numerous works from Schinkel but frequently made designs from them. In 1821-22 Schinkel made several classical schemes for a new church in the Werdersche-Markt but the executed Gothic design was made at the request of the crown prince, who thought a building in a mediaeval style would be more suitable for the restricted site and irregular street plan.

Similarly with the Nikolaikirche in Potsdam, the King wanted a cubic basilica, whereas Schinkel and the crown prince had a vision of a centrally planned building with a great dome dominating the skyline of the town, such as St Paul's Cathedral in London and the Panthéon in Paris. After the King's death, the crown prince won. It was also at Potsdam that Schinkel created, for the crown prince and his wife, one of the happiest of all his works, Schloss Charlottenhof, with its adjacent gardener's house and Roman Bath complex. Schloss Charlottenhof, an elegant Greek Doric villa, stylistically influenced by English models, was built between 1826 and 1828 as an idyllic retreat for intellectual and pas-

Plate 35 Obverse Iron Cross Second Class 1914. This piece was taken with the photograph of the Hesse-Darmstadt soldier by Lt J. O. Durham while on a trench raiding party in France from the body of the dead soldier.

35

25

toral refreshment on the western edge of the great royal park of Sanssouci at Potsdam. Brought up on the ideals of Rousseau, the crown prince set his utopian domain in an English landscaped park, which he referred to as 'Siam', also romantically regarded at the time as 'the land of the free', despite there being masonic overtones at Charlottenhof.

Schinkel's design of the Iron Cross was welcomed by the Kaiser who preferred it above his own submission. It was put into immediate production and comprises a cross pattée or formy of blackened iron. This time the centre has a sprig of three oak leaves. The upper arm has the cipher F W, which were the initials of the Kaiser, surmounted by the crown of Prussia, while the lower arm has the date of introduction 1813. The reverse is plain. Originally the plain side was supposed to have been worn to the front. However it is a strange fact that at the express desire of Friedrich Wilhelm the reverse of the Iron Cross, on which were the initials, oak leaves and the date, should be the obverse. So the King issued in June 1813 an order to the effect that 'the underneath side is to be worn upwards'.

Originally the cross was intended to be all black. Only when it was seen that this dark decoration was hardly visible on dark tunics did the thrifty King decide to add the silver edge to the cross. Many experiments were necessary before a way was found of blending the silver edge with the cast-iron part of the cross. By the middle of April 1813 only four crosses had been made, but the method of working had been mastered and by the beginning of May about three hundred were ready. Each cost 2½ talers which was a considerable sum of money for those days. The blackened iron core is surrounded by a silver frame which is in two parts and soldered together. At the apex is an eyelet through which is a ring to hold the ribbon, which is the same as the former design.

In order to recognise merit or bravery by non-combatant personnel, such as medical orderlies, surgeons and doctors as well as military directors, a special ribbon with the colours reversed was produced. The change in the ribbon to a white ribbon with black edge stripes, converted a standard Iron Cross Second Class, into a Non-combatant Iron Cross Second Class.

The Iron Cross First Class consisted originally of two pieces of black and white ribbon sewn over one another in the shape of a cross. It was not until later that it was likewise made of cast-iron. In addition to the Iron Cross, First and Second Class, the King also instituted a Grand Cross which was awarded in four cases during the war and one at the end of the Wars of Independence. The recipients were: Blücher, on 26.8.1813 for the victory at Katzach, Bülow, on 6.9.1813 for the victory at Dennewitz, Tauentzien, on 13.1.1814 for the storming of Wittenberg, Yorck, in 1814 for the Battles from Laon to Paris and the Crown Prince of Sweden, Karl XIV. It is also stated that their were two awards to Friedrick Kleist von Nollendorf and Generalleutnant Ostermann-Tolstoy, made on 29.8.1813 in recognition of the part played by these officers in the victory at Kulm. Doubt exists, however, as to whether the decorations were ever presented and they may have been made on paper only.

The Grand Cross was only to be issued to those commanders who decisively won a battle which caused the enemy to withdraw their forces, decisively besieged and conquered a fortification, or for a total and completely successful defence of a fortification. This was the only deviation from the original concept of a truly democratic order.

A special class, the Grand Cross on a gold radiant star, was created for Prince Blücher which he received for the Battle of Belle-Alliance. It was only awarded one further time and that was 103 years later to Field Marshal von Hindenburg in 1918 for the great battle in France.

The first Iron Cross Second Class, was awarded on 2.4.1813 to Maj von Borcke of the first Pomeranian Infantry Regiment in recognition of his brave conduct at the storming of the strong fortress of Lüneburg. The first Pomeranian Infantry Regiment behaved with such gallantry that five officers, eight NCOs, and two privates were the first to receive the Iron Cross. Maj von Borcke also gained the Iron Cross First Class for the Battle of Katzach. The first woman to be awarded the Iron Cross was Unteroffizier Auguste-Friederike Krüger of the 9.1 Kolberger Regiment on the 3.6.1814, when she was 25. The first Non-combatant Iron Cross Second Class, was awarded to Gen von Esloeg, Military Governor of Berlin. The first Iron Cross First Class, was awarded on 17.4.1813 after the battle of Wanfried to Oberstleutnant von Helwig, officer commanding the ninth Regiment of Hussars.

In addition to those to whom the decoration had been awarded, there was, during and after the Wars of Independence, also a category of individuals 'having acquired the right'. These were persons to whom, for reasons of economy, the Cross was not actually presented. After the decease of a wearer of the Cross the decoration was passed on to another soldier who, according to the regimental list, was next entitled to wear it. It was not until 1837 that this order was cancelled and the King himself presented the Iron Cross to all surviving candidates.

The medal was reintroduced for the subsequent wars of 1870-71 (Franco-Prussian) and 1914-18 (WW1).

In the cases of these two reintroductions the only change in the basic design was that the ciphers were altered, that is to say that on 19.7.1870, Kaiser Wilhelm I reintroduced the Iron Cross in three grades: Second Class, First and Grand Cross. All three had on the obverse, at the centre a W, the top arm the crown and the lower arm the date 1870. The reverse remained the same as the obverse of the decoration of 1813, for the Second Class and Grand Cross. There were almost 42,000 of the Second Class, and about 1,300 First Class Iron Crosses awarded during the Franco-Prussian War. The fact that there were only nine awards of The Grand Cross in the Franco-Prussian War illustrates in what high esteem this decoration was held. The recipients were: Crown Prince Friedrich of Prussia 22.3.1871; Prince of Prussia Friedrich Carl 22.3.1871; Crown Prince Albert of Saxony 22.3.1871; Generalfeldmarschall Graf Helmuth von Moltke 22.3.1871, Kaiser Wilhelm I 16.6.1871 (who wore it at the request of his generals); as well as the four prominent generals — Grand Duke of Mecklenberg-Schwerin 16.6.1871; Count August von Goeben; Baron Edwin von Manteuffel and Count August von Werder.

A number of British recipients of the 1870 Iron Cross are known, generally as non-combatant decorations and include Gen Sir C. P. B. Walker, Surgeon-General J. H. K. Innes, Gen Sir Henry Brakenbury GCB, Surgeon-General W. G. N. Manley VC, CB, and Capt Sir James Lumsden Seaton.

The first award of an 1870 First Class went to Generalfeldmarschall von Steinmek, a veteran of the Freedom Wars who had already won the Second Class Iron Cross of 1813.

The second reinstitution was enacted by Wilhelm II on 5.8.14, which reintroduced the Iron Cross in three grades: Second Class, First Class and Grand Cross. All three had on the obverse, at the centre a W, the top arm the crown and the lower arm:1914. The reverse remained the same as the obverse of the decoration of 1813, for the Second Class and Grand Cross. For the first time, after a further statute was published in 1915, Soldiers of non-German origin belonging to the armies of the Central Powers could receive this high decoration during WW1. A. E. Prowse quotes the case of Chari Maigumeri, who had originally served as a soldier in the Imperial German Army in the Cameroons and had been decorated with the Iron Cross Second Class for gallantry in action against the British during the West African campaign. He was captured by the British and subsequently served with the British West African Frontier Force and distinguished himself again in action with his new masters. By 1928, Maigumeri was an RSM with Third Battalion, the Nigerian Regiment. He won the Military Medal during the 1940-41 campaign in Abyssinia against the Italians and later, on the Far Eastern Front, he was mentioned in dispatches whilst serving in Burma against the Japanese. In 1944, he was awarded the British Empire Medal for long and loyal service to the Crown.

Kaiser Wilhelm II instituted the 1914 Bar to the Iron Cross Second Class 1870 on 4.6.15. It consists of a silver rectangular bar measuring 33mm by 7.5mm, which has a raised burnished outer edge. The field produced is lightly pebbled giving a matt appearance, in the centre of which is superimposed a small Iron Cross measuring 12.5mm. The bar was worn on the ribbon of the 1870 Iron Cross Second Class, just above the 25 Anniversary Oak Leaves.

The recipients of the Iron Cross Second Class 1870, who earned the similar class decoration for special service during WW1, in combat or at home, were rendered this special silver clasp to denote the award. The 1914 Bar to the Iron Cross Second Class 1870 is very scarce, for those still serving would have been very senior officers. Assuming the recipient was 16 in 1871, he would have been 60 years old if he received the Bar in 1915.

The oldest war volunteer was a private, Heinrich Risse, from Aschaffenburg who was 64 years old and had seen service in the wars of 1864, 1866 and 1870-71. He was in action at St Quentin in 1870 and again in 1914 where he received his second award of the Iron Cross Second Class. Another veteran winner was the trumpeter Karl August Voigt from Hamburg who, likewise, had seen service in the wars of 1860, 1864 and 1870-71 where he had been involved in 38 attacks. In WW1, at the time of his bestowal, he held the rank of Wachtmeister in a field artillery regiment.

In all cases the ribbon was the same for each period save that there was a non-combatants version which had the colours reversed, that is to say white, black, broad white, black, white stripes.

The last class, The Star to the Grand Cross of the Iron Cross of 1914, which is known popularly as the 'Hindenburgstern', was awarded only once, to Generalfeldmarschall von Hindenburg, after the Battle of Amiens-Arras, in March 1918.

It is known that Hindenburg had two specimens of the Star. One remained with the Generalfeldmarschall's family until at least 1945 after which, according to Gordon Williamson, it disappeared somewhere into the East. While Vernon Bowen states that 'the present location of the Hindenburgstern is not generally known, though it is believed to be in the possession of the Hindenburg family'. The other example was given by Hindenburg to an officer who was at the time serving with the Armistice Committee. On the death of this officer, his collection was purchased by an East European collector. This story is further amplified in *Fakes & Frauds of the Third Reich* (2nd Ed) by Freiherr von Mollendorf on p14 'In a medal collector's journal, there appeared a story on the medals of Field Marshal Paul von Hindenburg. According to the author, the Field Marshal was so taken by the personality of a very junior German member of the Armistice Commission that he gave him an exact duplicate set of all his orders and decorations! Everything...

even the solid gold Bücherstern. Of course the young German came to the United States and recently did pass away, leaving all these medals to his wife. The wife decided to sell these rare pieces to...guess who? Why the very author of the article! Naturally, he might be persuaded to part with these holy relics... for a price of course'.

Whether or not a second specimen ever existed remains a mystery, as does its present whereabouts as well as the location of the award piece. However, several contemporary museum copies were produced, which feature a variety of construction methods. The descriptions that follow are from two such pieces.

In the first example the insignia consists of a radiant eight-pointed star made of gold plated silver. A standard Iron Cross First Class, 42mm in dimension, is fitted to the obverse and is fixed to the star by small screws, held in position by hexagonal nuts. The star measures 84mm in overall diameter. The reverse of the star is fitted with a broad hinged fixing pin. Two pronged hooks are soldered to the reverse to hook the star to the tunic. The makers stamp, 'GODET BERLIN', may be seen on the upper reverse portion of the star, placed in two lines above and below the upper nut.

The second example is similar on the obverse, but the Iron Cross is held on to the star by a central screw which passes through it and is affixed by means of a large single screw plate. The reverse is plain with no maker stamp, only a small 'O' found on the lowest right arm of the star. It has a broad hinged fixing pin and no hooks. The star in this case is also made of silver which is fire gilded with a matt appearance.

Of 13,400,000 participants in the war, 218,000 were awarded the Iron Cross First Class, while the Iron Cross Second Class was awarded about 5,500,000 times between the date of its institution in 1914 and 1918. The order had come, from a purely Prussian award, to be the highest award of the German empire in all its grades and an internationally acclaimed decoration. With the ending of the monarchy and the abdication of the Kaiser on 9.11.19, everything was temporarily changed. The Iron Cross and Wound Badges continued to be awarded retrospectively, however, right up to 1925. An edict dated 7.3.25 brought an adjustment to the issuing of orders, medals and war badges and the continued awarding of WW1 decorations was halted.

Hitler reinstituted the Iron Cross on 1.9.39. This was to be the last version of the Iron Cross, which was subsequently to be changed to the denazified form by a proclamation on 26.7.57 by the West German Republic Reference BGBL.IS.844. It was stated in contemporary propaganda that 'It is already proudly worn on the breast by many defenders of the Greater Germany' — an allusion to the WW1 version. In addition to the Iron Cross, First and Second Class

and the Grand Cross, Adolf Hitler created the new decoration of the Knight's Cross. This decoration was to be worn round the neck and was awarded not only to officers but also to other ranks. An Order of 8.7.40 stated 'there has also been instituted the Oak Leaves to the Knight's Cross, consisting of three silver leaves on the ribbon clasp'. The propaganda continued, 'By thus distinguishing the bravest of the brave, the Führer has carried on the high tradition of the Iron Cross'. Following this were further orders on the 21.6.41 for the Knight's Cross with Oak Leaves and Swords, on 15.7.41 for the Knight's Cross with Oak Leaves, Swords and Diamonds, and on 29.12.44 for the Knight's Cross with Golden Oak Leaves, Swords and Diamonds. To all intents and purposes, the Iron Cross took the same form as all the previous types, except Hitler recognised the all Germanisation of the award and substituted the oak leaves which formed the central design of the medal with the party or Third Reich emblem of the Swastika. This is referred to as a mobile swastika and can be described as rotated, to stand on the point of one leg, thus giving the impression of an advancing movement. The lower arm had the date 1939 while all the other arms were plain. The reverse was plain also, save for the lower arm which had the year of instigation '1813'. The ribbon in this type also changed to stripes of black, white, broad brick red, white and black. This change has been attributed to the recognition of the blood shed in WW1 and was represented by this broad red stripe. However the real reason for the change was to identify the ribbon colours with those of the national colours of Germany. The ribbon was produced officially in eight sizes the widths of which were 8mm, 10mm, 15mm, 25mm, 30mm, 40mm, 45mm and 56mm— the last two being for the Knight Cross and the Grand Cross respectively.

The great Renewal Order, proclaimed by Hitler on 1.9.1939 for the Iron Cross, stated 'After arriving at the conclusion that the German people must be called to arms in defence of an imminent attack, I will renew for the sons of Germany, as in the past great wars in the defence of the home and the Fatherland, the Order of the Iron Cross'. The Order inevitably precipitated a host of design and manufacturing problems, exacerbated by the suddenness of the proclamation and the urgent demand for Iron Crosses to reward the heroism of the new combatants.

This led to the two main medal contractor firms of Steinhauer & Lück from Lüdenscheid and C. E. Juncker of Berlin being called in to quote for the crosses. They suggested the WW1 rim size be used which, incidentally, has been given by some sources as 42mm, while others say 42.5mm. This would have enabled them to utilise the WW1 Iron Cross rim stocks and benefit from the economies of scale by using the already existing dies for both types. However, the idea was not pursued and a number of designs were submitted, with final approval being given to a Second Class and First Class cross which both measured 44mm and a Knight's Cross measuring 48mm. Steinhauer & Lück's master engraver, Herr Escher, designed the rims as well as the new centre plates for the new crosses. During WW2, the Iron Cross Second Class, Iron Cross First Class and Knight's Crosses were manufactured for the Government by a number of firms, all of whom used the same dies, which were produced by Steinhauer & Lück. This was done so there would be standardisation in the design of the Iron Cross. Work was put in hand and production commenced. Up to 1918, rims had been hand sawn with piercing saws from the sheet strips after pressing, but now all the centre plates were stamped from malleable iron strips and the rims pressed and cut by machine from sheet strips.

Second Class Iron Crosses were made during the early years of WW2 by the fabrication of a cross of a three piece construction, with two flanged beaded rims made of silver-plated nickel silver and a blackened centre plate made from pressed malleable iron sheeting, which were then hand soldered together, the assembled cross being fitted with an eye ring and ribbon suspension ring. By April 1942 the demand by the armed forces for Iron Crosses exceeded stocks and delivery programmes scheduled by the manufacturers. A request by the Präsidialkanzlei for an improved production schedule produced a survey by the Gablonz Arbeitsgemeinschaft (Work Study Group) which was situated in Gablonz in the Sudetenland. They came up with an automatic process for increasing manufacture and delivery of the Second Class Iron Cross. Members of the Gablonzer Arbeitsgemeinschaft worked on preparing the first hand made example from the new production technique and within three months had designed the new tools and instruments for the lap machine appliance, completing the construction of the machinery, together with the test sample. The new machinery, when completed, was ready for a daily output of 1,000 pieces.

The Gablonzer Frame Press gave rise to the Gablonzer system which was a mechanism for winding the wire for the rim. With the new method of production it was no longer necessary to stamp two rims from nickel silver sheeting in order to construct an Iron Cross. Nickel silver wire measuring 4.5mm in diameter was wound by an automatic machine around a jig which formed the shape of the rims. The wire was cut at the ends and compressed at high pressure, thus fusing the metal into a continuous pattern. The edges were then trimmed by a cropper to produce the standard traditional outline. The prepared centre plate, made of black stoved enamelled malleable iron, was then automatically inserted between the rims pressed from the machine stamped wire and a further pressing operation firmly enclosed it within the rims. This method produced a very close fit of the centre plate within the rims and eliminated the loose rattling found in Iron Crosses made from two pressed rims soldered together in the process by the older, more traditional method. The Gablonzer Frame Press also produced a high sheen to the rims, so burnishing them was unnecessary. There was also a 40% saving in material. Not all Iron Crosses made after 1942 were produced by this method. The older, more traditional methods were also used by many firms as they already had material stocks and were tooled up for production. The Chairman of the LDO published an article in 1942 describing the new production method saying that, 'this recognised achievement is appreciated but it would have been appreciated much more if it had been started not in the third year of the war but at the beginning, then it would have been of real use. At this time a lot of orders for materials and completed components are already processed so that the new technique will get the opportunity to be put into action only when all the previous stock is used up. Firms without reserves of stock and material will get permission to start on the new technique through the Präsidialkanzlei. All rights and ownership belong to the Arbeitsgemeinschaft für Metall-Kunstoff in Gablonz, only they can give permission for further production and basically, they have nothing against other firms using this system, in fact they are quite agreeable to its use'.

IRON CROSS: SECOND CLASS*

Known Makers: 3, 4, 5, 6, 13, 16, 22, 23, 24, 25, 27, 33, 35, 40, 42, 44, 49, 55, 65, 75, 93, 95, 100, 108, 113, 120, 122, 123, 125, 128, 133, 142, L/3, L/11

The Iron Cross Second Class measured 44mm in diameter and, as already described, was produced from three parts, a central core, an obverse and reverse rim. The obverse of the core has a mobile swastika at its centre and the date 1939 on its lower arm. The reverse is plain except for the date of institution, 1813, which is placed at the bottom of the lower arm. The core is normally of solid iron either chemically treated to give a matt or semi-matt finish or, for economy, painted black with an enamelled paint. From the upper arm, through an eyelet, is positioned the ribbon ring. Many of the suspension rings are stamped with the manufacturer's code number. Through the ring is placed the ribbon that comprises a 4mm black edge stripe, 4mm white stripe and 14mm central brick-red stripe. When the Iron Cross Second Class was presented, it was hung from the second buttonhole of the tunic in the traditional German manner. Afterwards, the recipient usually sported the ribbon alone, either from the buttonhole or on a ribbon bar above the left breast pocket.

The criteria for the award were:
- outstanding service of combatant personnel and for bravery in the face of the enemy.
- a higher grade cross must be preceded by the award of this grade.

Hitler, however, did not reintroduce the non-combatants version of the award but introduced the War Merit Cross series in its stead, which will be covered later in the book.

The Iron Cross could also be conferred on foreigners as well as being awarded *en masse*, as happened on 1.4.41 when some 1,300 men, who comprised the whole compliment of the *Admiral Scheer*, received the award. Similar awards were rendered to the crews of the auxiliary cruiser *Kormoran* and the U47 which sunk the *Royal Oak*. Awards of the Iron Cross were also made to boys of the Hitler Youth fighting in the defence of Berlin in 1945. The youngest recipient was 12-year old Hitler Youth Alfred Zeck of Goldenau, who rendered first aid to 12 wounded German soldiers pinned down by enemy fire in his home town in March 1945.

The medal was usually awarded in a blue paper packet, with the name printed on it. But it is also found in a black presentation box, which sometimes has a see-through lid, with a white flock lining and recess for the medal and a recessed area for the ribbon. The lid is lined with white satin. The overall appearance is that of a miniature Knight's Cross box. This type of box is considered very rare. During 1939-45 it is estimated that nearly 5,000,000 awards were bestowed and these covered all the nationals fighting with the Germans, including a unit to which Eddy Chapman, the triple spy, was attached, although whether he received the award personally is in some doubt.

IRON CROSS: SECOND CLASS 1939 BAR: FIRST TYPE**

Known Makers: L/4, L/11, L/12, L/14, L/16, L/18, L/56

This bar was introduced on 1st September 1939 to reward recipients of the Iron Cross Second Class of 1914 who had distinguished themselves again in WW2.

It comprises an eagle with outstretched wings, spread legs and clutching in its talons, an oak leaf wreath with a Swastika inside it. The field around the Swastika is pebbled. Beneath this wreath is a box with diagonal sides at each end. Round the edge of the box is a lip and in the centre the date, 1939. The overall colour of the badge is matt silver with the high parts polished. The overall size is 30mm by 39mm and it was worn

on a piece of 1914 ribbon, which was placed through the second buttonhole of the uniform jacket. The reverse is flat save for four lugs which are pushed through the fabric of the ribbon to secure it.

The criteria for the award were identical to the previous medal.

The badge usually came in a brown or blue paper packet but it was occasionally found in a small square box of either black, green or burgundy. These boxes were usually unlined and sometimes they had the LDO logo or just these letters stamped into the inner lid. Another rarer version is an oblong box which is quite plain and black in colour. The badge is fastened by the described method above to a full length of ribbon, which is secured at the top and bottom of the lower portion of the box. That is to say, the lid section and the lower section of the box are in two separate halves. With this is the ribbon bar to which a miniature emblem is attached.

For very high ranking officers an example has been encountered which contains both the Second Class Bar with a First Class Bar. The latter on the left and the former on the right, with a piece of ribbon at the top positioned horizontally across the case. The badges are on a black velvet base. The case is red, pebbled simulated leather with a gold political eagle stamped on to it. The whole case is finely made with a hinge and press-stud opener. The upper, inner lining is of white satin.

IRON CROSS: SECOND CLASS 1939 BAR: SECOND TYPE**

Known Makers: L/4, L/11, L/12, L/14, L/16, L/18, L/56

This medal is, in all respects, identical in style to the former medal except for its size, which is 25mm by 25mm. The reverse has only two prongs for attachment and the gauge for the material from which the badge is made was correspondingly thinner. This type is known as the 'Prinzen' version and was obtained by private purchase. The purpose of this size was for being attached to the ribbon of the Second Class 1914 Iron Cross when it was worn on formal occasions. This is usually of a much finer quality than that found on the awarded type.

Being private purchase the form of containers for the medal were numerous and the quality therefore of these containers depended greatly on the store from which the badge was obtained.

IRON CROSS: FIRST CLASS**

Known Makers: 4, 6, 8, 15, 20, 26, 52, 65, 100, 107, L/10, L/11, L/12, L/13, L/15, L/16, L/18, L/19, L/50, L/52, L/53, L/54, L/55, L/56, L/57, L/58, L/59,

L/73, L 55 L/50 (in an oblong box)
Again this medal was introduced on 1st September 1939 taking the form of its predecessor but with the Swastika at its centre and the date at the bottom of the lower arm. The centre is blackened iron which is either painted or chemically blued. The reverse is flat and silvered with a straight bladed pin. Usually this pin has the maker's mark on it, either on the top or bottom face. In rarer cases the pin is omitted and has been replaced by a screw post with a large screw cap, which might be plain or have a raised line to help fasten or unscrew it. Three variations in construction are encountered and have been separately catalogued.

Two interesting variations are the Japanese made silver variety and the Spanish made pieces. The Japanese manufactured cross was made from Japanese silver and it is believed that only 26 of these silver crosses were produced. The German Naval Attaché in Tokyo, Admiral Paul Werner Wenneker, who had taken up the position on 1.4.35 and remained until the end of the war, supplied the names of two Japanese firms of jewellers, who had been commissioned by him previously, and they undertook the order. This had been brought about by the need to award the Cross to service men serving in the Far East when no on hand stock was available. One such instance occurred on 17 October, when the cruiser Michel, ship 28 in the German Navy list, was torpedoed off Yokohama by the US submarine Tarpon. Obermaat Konrad Metzner rescued 39 men and thereby earned the Iron Cross 1st Class. A presentation ceremony was held shortly after this incident at which Admiral Wenneker issued the citation documents and awarded 26 Iron Crosses 1st Class to Obermaat Konrad Metzner and 25 other men who had also earned the award for their bravery.

Spanish soldiers serving in the Blue Division received Iron Crosses which had been made in Spain. An interesting point is that after the war had ended, these Spanish made crosses were available to veterans from military tailors and could be worn in their Nazi uniform.

A cloth version of the badge was produced and a few variations are encountered. On the whole they seem to be a little crude in their manufacture. These items were private purchase and the reason for them is uncertain. However, a theory has been put forward that they were intended for use in situations which required no magnetic sparks, as in the case of the new jet fighters or no sound, as in the case of submarine personnel for in the latter days of the war, when British sound locaters had greatly improved, they could hear the smallest metallic noise.

The criterion for the award was for the recipient to have distinguished himself at least three times more than he had for the Second Class award.

However, in the case of the navy the cross was considered on a tonnage basis, with the commander of a U-Boat having to sink approximately 50,000 tons of enemy shipping to be nominated for this class. In the Luftwaffe it was awarded on a points basis, one point was given for the shooting down of a single engine fighter, two for a twin-engine aircraft and three for a four engine bomber. Night victories were assessed double. It was considered that five points were required for the bestowal of the Cross. On occasions the Iron Cross Second Class could be awarded in conjunction with the First Class to facilitate the necessary criteria for its award.

The badge was awarded in a black box with a white flock base and silk lid liner and on the outer lid was stencilled the outline of the award. It is estimated that 300,000-750,000 awards were made. It is very unlikely that the exact figure for awards of the medal is known.

IRON CROSS: FIRST CLASS: VARIATIONS 1 & 2**

Known Makers: L/11, L/18, L/53, L/54
A standard First Class Cross as described but with slightly convex arms, which was supplied with both pin or screw attachment. However in a memorandum dated 5.9.40 it was stated that, on instructions received from the LDO, Steinhauer and Lück informed their customers that they were unable to supply 1939 EK 1s in curved form with screw backed fasteners as it was forbidden. The existence of this type, it would seem, is due to some firms manufacturing and supplying such items prior to this. In a directive issued on 5.3.41 by the LDO, the following announcement appeared 'after agreement with the Oberkommando das Wehrmacht I have permitted dealers to sell 1939 1st Class Iron Crosses with screw attachments. Forbidden still as previously 1939 1st Class Iron Crosses in curved form'.

The criteria for the award were the same as the standard Iron Cross First Class.

IRON CROSS: FIRST CLASS: VARIATION 3**

Known Makers: Godet u. Sohn
The firm of Godet & Sohn of Berlin produced a smaller version for General Officers, which measured approximately 41mm by 41mm. This was usually produced in silver .800 standard and occasionally the metal centre was black enamelled.

The criteria for the award were the same as the standard Iron Cross First Class.

Plate 36   Obverse Iron Cross First Class 1914.

Plate 37   Reserve Iron Cross First Class 1914.

Plate 38   Obverse of the Iron Cross Second Class 1939. That on the left is the rarer, slightly larger, framed version. This example was awarded to George Miller on 9 July 1941, who was then with Jäger Regiment 253.

Plate 39   Reverse of the standard Iron Cross Second Class 1939.

Plate 40   Obverse Iron Cross-Second Class 1939 Bar- First Type

Plate 41   Bar to the Iron Cross. On the left the standard size and on the right the scarcer 'Prinzen' version.

Plate 42   Obverse of the Iron Cross First Class 1939.

Plate 43   Reverse of two Iron Crosses First Class illustrating two of the numerous pin, hinger and hook assemblies employed. The maker's stamp, 107, is clearly visible on the broad bellied pin while the other, L/52, is stamped just below the 'C' hook and is indistinguishable in the picture.

Plate 44   Obverse of the Iron Cross First Class 1939 Bar. This example is of the highest quality.

Plate 45   Reverse of the Iron Cross First Class 1939 Bar showing two types of hinge, pin and hook assembly. The pin on the right hand badge has a recessed L/21 and the back of the badge has been privately engraved with 'Ein Reich, Ein Volk, Ein Fuhrer'.

33

IRON CROSS:
FIRST CLASS: VARIATION 4**

Known Makers
For use by members of the German Navy, the iron centre was substituted by a brass or copper core which was chemically blackened. The reason for this was that the salt water rusted the iron centre.

The criteria for the award were the same as the standard Iron Cross First Class.

IRON CROSS:
FIRST CLASS 1939 BAR**

Known Makers: L/11, L/21, L/56, L/57
Again, this badge was introduced on 1.9.39 and is identical to the Second Class Bar. There are two slight variations in the style of the eagle's chest and the fletching thereon but this does not warrant an introduction of a second type. The reverse is flat and has a pin of the broad blade type. Occasionally it is found with a thin needle pin. This type is usually encountered with the trade mark L/11 stamped on to the reverse and is generally of a poor quality of manufacture.

The criterion for the award was to have been awarded the Iron Cross First Class again in WW2.

The presentation box is black and pebbled with an exact facsimile of the badge in silver stencilled on to the outer lid. The base on which the badge rests is black velvet or flocking and the lid liner is white silk.

IRON CROSS:
FIRST CLASS 1939 BAR: VARIATION 1**

Known Makers
This award takes the exact design of the previous award, save that the hinge, hook and pin are replaced by a large screw post that has a fluted, domed plate which is screwed to the post. This form of award was a private purchase option and the screw post enabled the award to be more firmly attached to the uniform.

IRON CROSS:
FIRST CLASS 1939 BAR: VARIATION 2**

Known Makers
This variation consists of a combination of the First Class 1939 Bar and a 1914 Iron Cross First Class. The Bar is attached at the top of the upper arm of the Cross. The reverse of the Cross has the standard pin to the Iron Cross with the reverse of the Bar being completely plain. This variation is also encountered with a screw post instead of the pin. This type was again a private purchase item and it is supposed it was to facilitate easy removal from one tunic to another.

KNIGHT'S CROSS OF THE IRON CROSS***

Known Makers: 4, 20, 64, L/12, L/15, L/52
This medal was introduced on 1.9.39 but, unlike the former grades which had existed from its instigation in the year of 1813, was a new class to bridge the gap between the First Class and the Grand Cross. This award went on to capture the imagination of the German people and was used to great propaganda advantage by Dr Göbbels. In fact, there was a whole series of postcards, not unlike cigarette cards but much larger, which the German children and postcard collectors accumulated avidly. The cross is identical to the Second Class award with the exception of its size, which is 48mm by 48mm excluding the eyelet which, in this case, is flat to the cross and at the top of the upper arm and this eyelet allowed an unusual hanger to be put through it. This hanger has the appearance of a 'paper clip'. Through this is a neck ribbon of the same colours as those attached to the Second Class award but this ribbon measures 45mm.

The silver frame that surrounds the iron core is of real silver and varies in grade from .800 through to .950. This mark is usually found stamped beneath the eyelet on the reverse of the cross. This position sometimes has the maker's mark as well but this seems to be a more unusual occurrence.

The cross was bestowed for military leadership as well as individual acts of bravery. It has been estimated that it was necessary to have performed service that would have required the First Class Cross to have been bestowed a further five to seven times. As the war progressed, the level required for the bestowal also changed. It also mirrored the importance placed upon the military endeavour rendered to the State.

In the Luftwaffe the Knight's Cross was awarded on a points basis which has been described in the Iron Cross Second Class section and, in this case, about 20 points were needed for its bestowal. The change in the war periods and theatres of operations is amplified by the examples of Leutnant Egon Mayer who won the Knight's Cross for his twentieth aerial victory in 1941, compared to Oberleutnant Otto Kittle who had to shoot down his 123rd enemy plane before he was awarded the Cross in 1943. In the navy the calculation was made on a tonnage basis, with approximately 100,000 tons being required for the bestowal of the Cross. The Cross could be bestowed on all nationals fighting with or for the German forces. I have included two examples of awards to foreign volunteers, both from Belgium but representing the two ethnic groups which form that country.

Sturmann Remy Schrijnen of the 627th SS Volunteer Grenadier Division 'Langemarck' and Untersturmführer Jacques Leroy of 28th Volunteer Panzer Grenadier Division 'Wallonien'.

The number of Knight's Crosses awarded was approximately 7,318. Again the actual figure is slightly obscure because of the chaotic conditions prevailing at the end of the war. One good example of this is that of the award to Jacques Leroy. He had lost his eye and arm and was recovering in hospital when the award of his Knight's Cross was made on 20.4.45. He remustered with his unit, terribly wounded, to continue the fight but the prestigious award had not been bestowed upon him, nor had he received the preliminary citation and, worst of all, his name had not been entered on the roll of winners. It was not until 20.5.57 that the attestation was produced to prove his entitlement to the award by the divisional adjutant Roger Wastiau and it was reaffirmed on 8.12.73 by the famous SS leader and his commander, Leon Degrelle.

Although I am not covering citations in this book I have included the four for the different grades of the Knight's Cross of the Iron Cross as they have a special appeal to collectors.

The citation to the award came in two parts. The first part or preliminary award document, was also produced in two varieties and they were Gothic print and plain print. The actual wording also changed with the rise of the control of the armed forces by Hitler. The first type was printed as 'DER FüHRER and the high command of the fighting forces award [name]'. Secondly just 'DER FüHRER award [name]'.

At the top of both these types is a facsimile of the Iron Cross, then the title of the medal 'DAS RITTERKREUZ' and at the bottom the commanding officer's signature with the unit to which the commanding officer was attached and in the lower left-hand corner the stamp of the commander. At this point it is important to point out that Leroy did not receive either of these, nor did every recipient of these citations receive the full citation as I now describe.

The full citation is a beautifully produced document that consists of a vellum sheet on which a golden eagle is hand worked at the top, then the award wording in black ink and the rank of the recipient. The recipient's name follows in large letters which are executed in fire gilt. Beneath this is the grade of the Iron Cross followed by a facsimile of the Cross. Beneath this is the FüHRER HAUPT QUARTIER and the date of the award, followed by Hitler's full title and signature. It is considered that not all the award documents were personally signed by Hitler but in some cases a facsimile of his signature was employed.

Hitler organised a team of artisans, headed by Prof Gerdy Troost, to produce the award documents of this grade and above, as well as other important State documents. She was in overall charge of the manufacturing process while Franziska Kobell was in charge of the lettering, Frieda Thiersch the leather work and Franz and Hermann Wandinger were in charge of the gold lettering and other gold work.

The whole of the citation is encased in a red leather folder which is padded on the front binding. On the red leather is a gold embossed eagle. The inside of the cover is white and on the rear inner edge the gold inlaid name of the artist, Frieda Thiersch.

Another design of case was produced and this was intended for the presentation of the Knight's Cross citation to Generalfeldmarschalls. This consisted of a red leather folder with a similar gold eagle but in this case it was larger, and surrounded by a broad border, consisting of 14 boxes containing facsimiles of the Cross. These were surrounded by a maze design, which butted up to one another, giving a continuous appearance to the border. Indeed whether this design was ever presented is unknown but, considering the small number of Generalfeldmarschalls and the opportunity to inspect their personal files, it is probable that it was. However, so far none have come to light. The case in which these Crosses were presented was a plain black box which was oblong, with a black velvet base which had a recess for the cross to lie in, also a small slit at the top into which the 'paper clip' hanger fitted snugly. The portion above this was recessed to allow the neck ribbon to be accommodated lying horizontally across the box. The lid liner was of white satin.

An alternative case was produced at the beginning of the war, which comprised a large red leather box with a large gold hand embossed eagle on its lid. Around the edge of the lid was a thin gold border. Very few of these boxes were presented and a possible theory is that this type of box was awarded to Generalobersts and above and could have been awarded with the ornate citation case previously described. Generaloberst von Brauchitsch received his Knight's Cross on 27.10.39 in just such a box. He had become the head of OKH and CIC of the German army at Rundstedt's suggestion and the invitation of Hitler. Hitler would have preferred the avowed pro-Nazi Reichenau but Rundstedt suggested that 'that appointment would alienate the senior officer corps'. Not wishing to do this Hitler reluctantly appointed Brauchitsch. Always unhappy with this promotion, Hitler placed the blame on him for the failure to capture Moscow in 1941, dismissed him and assumed the post himself, thus becoming the first civilian to lead the German army. It is at this point that the wording on the citations changed as already has been described.

KNIGHT'S CROSS OF THE IRON CROSS WITH OAK LEAVES****

Known Makers: 12, 21, L12, L/13, L/19, L/50

On 3.6.40 to reward further acts of bravery, a small cluster of Oak Leaves was introduced and they were to be placed through the eyelet of the Cross where the 'paper clip' hanger had been. The Oak Leaves were not a conception of Hitler but had been created to honour the memory of Queen Louise of Mecklenburg-Strelitz, who was the wife of King Friedrich Wilhelm III and had died on 19.7.1810. The emblem was to serve as a separate and higher degree to the already existing Prussian Order, the Pour le Mérite. However, it was not until the introduction of the Iron Cross on 10.3.1813 that the Oak Leaves were authorised as a higher grade of the award. The use of oak leaves on Prussian orders goes back to at least the 'Order de la Sincérité of Brandenburg', (1705), which was redesignated the 'Order of the Red Eagle' in 1734. The Pour le Mérite, although instituted in 1667 as the Order of Generosity and later changed to the Pour le Mérite in 1740, did not become a purely military award until 1817. Therefore, it is entirely possible that the oak leaf device was used on the Order of the Red Eagle prior to its use on the Pour le Mérite.

As the Knight's Cross was an entirely new grade of the Iron Cross and was intended to fill the gap which had been left by the abolition after 1918 of the old military order, the Pour le Mérite, otherwise known as the Blue Max, it was a natural progression to adorn the Knight's Cross with an oak leaf cluster to denote further acts of valour or military leadership.

As the Oak Leaves were a commemorative device, we should consider their emblematic signification which has been explained as incorporating the important events and dates that occurred in the lives of Wilhelm and Louise. The central leaf had nine points to represent their nine children, five points on the left for their sons and four on the right for their daughters. At the base of the cluster of leaves, a Roman numeral 'X' was formed by the bottom edges of the middle leaf and the lowest points of the side leaves. This numeral, in combination with various numbers of points in the cluster, commemorated important dates in Louise's life. The numeral 10 added to the nine-pointed leaf resulted in nineteen, the day of her death. The total number of 24 leaf points in the cluster, added to the numeral 10 equals 34, the total years of her life. Louise was born on 10.3.1776. As a further interpretation, the 10 was also representative of her birthday, whereas the month of March was represented by the three leaves in the cluster. The 24 leaf tips represented the day of their marriage, 24.12.1793, while the numeral 10 represented the month, (December, from Decem meaning 10, was originally the 10th month). The

final combination of the seven points of the left leaf and the number 10 represented the 17 years they had lived together in Prussia. The symbolism of the centre lines of the leaves can be seen more clearly. The letter 'L' for Louise is formed by the middle and right leaves. The letter 'J' is formed by the central line of the middle leaf in conjunction with the uppermost point and the lower left edge of the leaf. This letter represents the month of her death, July.

The obverse comprises three oak leaves in a fan or cluster, one surmounting the other with a broad polished vein in the centre. The outer edges of the leaves are raised and polished also, while the tissue that comprises the inner parts of the veins of the leaves are recessed, pebbled and finished in matt silver. It measures 20mm by 20mm. The higher grades of the Iron Cross, ie from Knight's Cross with Oak Leaves upwards, were made by three firms, namely, Deschler & Sohn in München, Juncker in Berlin and Steinhauer & Lück in Lüdenscheid, with the 'diamonds' and 'Golden Oak Leaves' being made by another firm. The original dies were probably made by the firm of Deschler & Sohn in München, so the three firms would all produce identical examples. They were produced from real silver in grades from .800 to .950, which were stamped on the reverse of the cross. The reverse can be slightly dished or concave with a piece of silver wire running around, similar to that of the 'paper clip' hanger. This is neatly secured to the reverse, a good point to distinguishing a reproduction. Also the ends of the wire are neatly rounded on the original award pieces. The silver content mark is usually stamped on the left-hand side of the reverse, and sometimes the maker's mark is stamped on the right. But this again is more unusual. One very rarely encounters Oak Leaves with flat backs and just the silver content stamped .900. These are very rare and desirable. The actual piece illustrated depicts the reverse of a rare flat backed Oak Leaf cluster, bearing the silver mark .900. This piece was contained in the Grand Cross case, which housed the Grand Cross and was removed from Reichsmarschall Hermann Göring's hunting lodge by a British intelligence officer. The Cross was acquired together with several Knight's Cross citations from the officer concerned by Adrian Forman. There were 890 awards made and this, unlike the other figures for the Iron Cross series, is an exact one.

The citation was produced, like the former one, in vellum. This version did not have the Iron Cross drawn upon it, but just had the designation 'DAS EICHENLAUB'. The outer cover in this form was of white calf skin, again padded but instead of the gold stencilled eagle this has a gilded metal eagle fixed on to it.

The box in which the Oak Leaves were presented was either a small black box with velvet base with a slit in which to hold the award clip, or a similar box, slightly longer, with a small compartment recessed above the badge to hold a piece of Knight's Cross ribbon.

KNIGHT'S CROSS OF THE IRON CROSS WITH OAK LEAVES AND SWORDS****

Known Makers: 21, L/12, L/13, L/50
On 15.7.41 this award was introduced to reward continued acts of valour by the Knight's Cross recipients. The design is basically the same as that of the Oak Leaves but with a pair of crossed swords attached to the bottom of the cluster. The swords are at a 40° angle and it is this angle and the finish to the hilts and blades of the swords that distinguishes what is known as the awarded type, from the jewellers' or private purchase versions.

In the first type the sword hilts do not touch the blades of the swords. The reverse of the blades and the hilts of the swords are finished in the same way as that which is found on the obverse. In the jeweller's type the balls at the tips of the hilts touch the blades of the respective opposite sword. The reverse is unfinished. The badges are produced from real silver and can be encountered with silver grades ranging from .800 to .950. This again is stamped usually in the left-hand upper corner of the badge when viewing it from the reverse, with the maker's mark on the right. The jeweller's copy usually is found in .800 which is stamped in the position already described and very rarely has the makers mark. There were a total of 159 awards of this cluster.

The citation for this award became more exotic in that it was similar to the previous one, again with no Iron Cross motif but it had a metal gilded border which was patterned. The cover was white with a gilded metal eagle and had a gilded patterned border running round its edge. The box for the award was similar to the previous ones described.

Known recipients were:
GALLAND Adolf Generalleutnant, Luftwaffe 21.6.41; MÖLDERS Werner Oberst, Luftwaffe 22.6.41; OESAU Walter Oberst, Luftwaffe 15.7.41; LüTZOW Günther Oberst, Luftwaffe 11.10.41; KRETSCHMER Otto Fregattenkapitän, Kriegsmarine 26.12.41; ROMMEL Erwin Generalfeldmarschall, Heer 20.1.42; BÄR Heinrich, Luftwaffe 16.2.42; PHILIPP Hans Oberstleutnant, Luftwaffe 12.3.42; IHLEFELD Herbert Oberst, Luftwaffe 24.4.42; GRAF Hermann Oberst, Luftwaffe 19.5.42; MARSEILLE Hans-Joachim Hauptmann, Luftwaffe 18.6.42; GOLLOB Gordon M. Oberst, Luftwaffe 23.6.42; STEINBATZ Leopold Leutnant, Luftwaffe 23.6.42; KESSELRING Albert Generalfeldmarschall, Luftwaffe 18.7.42; BAUMBACH Werner Oberst, Luftwaffe 16.8.42; TOPP Erich Fregattenkapitän, Kriegsmarine 17.8.42;

SUHREN Reinhard Fregattenkapitän, Kriegsmarine 1.9.42; MüNCHEBERG Joachim Maj, Luftwaffe 9.9.42; HELBIG Joachim Oberst, Luftwaffe 28.9.42; EIBL Karl, Gen der Infanterie Heer 19.12.42; HUBE, Hans Generaloberst Heer 21.12.42; WILCKE Wolf-Dietrich, Oberst Luftwaffe 23.12.42; DRUSCHEL Alfred Oberst, Luftwaffe 19.2.43; BALCK Hermann Gen der Panzertruppe, Heer 4.3.43; DIETRICH Joseph SS-Obergruppenführer u. Generaloberst der Waffen-SS 16.3.43; GRAF STRACHWITZ Hyazinth Generalleutnant, Heer 28.3.43; MODEL Walter Generalfeldmarschall, Heer 2.4.43; LüTH Wolfgang Kapitän zur See, Kriegsmarine 15.4.43; GORN Walter Generalmajor, Heer 8.6.43; PELTZ Dietrich Generalmajor, Luftwaffe 23.7.43; LENT Helmut Oberst, Luftwaffe 2.8.43; SCHULZ Adelbert (also Adalbert) Generalmajor, Heer 6.8.43; RALL Günther Maj, Luftwaffe 12.9.43; HOTH Hermann Generaloberst, Heer 15.9.43; HARPE Josef Generaloberst, Heer 15.9.43; NOWOTNY Walter Maj, Luftwaffe 22.9.43; von GAZEN gen; GAZA Waldemar Maj, Heer 3.10.43; DIECKMANN August SS-Obersturmbannführer 10.10.43; von HUGE Günther Generalfeldmarschall, Heer 29.10.43; Graf von SCHWERIN Gerhard Gen der Panzertruppe, Heer 4.11.43; RUDEL Hans-Ulrich Oberst, Luftwaffe 25.11.43; HERMANN Hajo Oberst, Luftwaffe 23.1.44; Prinz zu SAYN-WITTGENSTEIN Heinrich Mai, Luftwaffe 23.1.44; BÄRENFÄNGER Erich Generalmajor, Heer 23.1.44;. von SAUCKEN DIETRICH Gen der Panzertruppe, Heer 20.2.44; BREITH Hermann Gen der Panzertruppe, Heer 21.2.44; BÄKE Franz Oberst, Heer 21.2.44; von MANTEUFFEL Hasso Eccard Gen der Panzertruppe, Heer 22.2.44; MAYER Egon Oberstleutnant, Luftwaffe 2.3.44; BARKHORN Gerhard Maj, Luftwaffe 2.3.44; GRIESBACH Franz Generalmajor, Heer 6.3.44; STREIB Werner Oberst, Luftwaffe 11.3.44; HEIDRICH Richard Gen der Fallschirmtruppe, Luftwaffe 25.3.44; SCHULDT Heinrich Generalmajor der Waffen-SS 25.3.44; POSTEL, Georg Generalleutnant, Heer 26.3.44; von WIETERSHEIM Wend Generalleutnant, Heer 26.3.44; von LEWINSKI gen; von MANSTEIN Erich Generalfeldmarschall, Heer 31.3.44; von KLEIST Ewald Generalfeldmarschall, Heer 30.3.44; BöRST Alwin Maj, Luftwaffe 6.4.44; KUPFER Dr Ernst Oberst, Luftwaffe 11.4.44; KREYSING Hans Gen der Gebirgstruppe, Heer 13.4.44; JORDAN Hans Gen der Infanterie, Heer 20.4.44; PRIESS Hermann Generalleutnant der Waffen-SS 24.4.44; BRANDI Albrecht Fregattenkapitän, Kriegsmarine 9.5.44; HEILMANN Ludwig Generalmajor, Luftwaffe 15.5.44; REINHARDT Georg-Hans Generaloberst, Heer 26.5.44; NIEMACK Horst Generalmajor, Heer 4.6.44; KöNIG Alfons Oberst, Heer 9.6.44; WITTMANN Michael SS-Hauptsturmführer der Waffen-SS 22.6.44; DIETL Eduard Generaloberst, Heer 1.7.44; PRILLER Josef Oberst, Luftwaffe 2.7.44; LANG Friedrich

Plate 46 Obverse Iron Cross First Class 1939 Bar - Variation 1.

Plate 47 Reverse Iron Cross First Class 1939 - Variation 1.

Plate 48 Obverse Knights Cross of the Iron Cross.

Plate 49 Reverse of Knights Cross in the Iron Cross showing the standard form of silver marking used upon an award piece.

Plate 50 Formal document for the Knights Cross awarded to Ferdinand Schneider-Kostalski.

IM NAMEN
DES DEUTSCHEN VOLKES
VERLEIHE ICH
DEM HAUPTMANN
FERDINAND
SCHNEIDER-KOSTALSKI
DAS RITTERKREUZ
DES EISERNEN KREUZES

FÜHRERHAUPTQUARTIER
DEN 9. JULI 1941
DER FÜHRER
UND OBERSTE BEFEHLSHABER
DER WEHRMACHT

Plate 51: Obverse Knights Cross of the Iron Cross with Oak Leaves.

Plate 52 Knights Cross of the Iron Cross with Oak Leaves. Close-up of the obverse of the Oak Leaves.

Plate 53 Reverse of the Oak Leaves showing from the left: flat-backed with a .900 silver mark; semi-dished with .900 silver and L/50 maker's marks and semi-dished stamped with .800 and L/19.

Plate 54 Knights Cross with Oak Leaves and Swords.

Plate 55 Close-up of the obverse of the clusters showing the relationship of the swords' hilts to their blades.

Plate 56 Close-up of the reverses showing, from the left: the swords being finished, marked .900 and 21; the swords hilts attached to the blades, marked .800 and the swords separated from the hilts, marked .800.

Maj, Luftwaffe 2.7.44; HARTMANN Erich Maj, Luftwaffe 4.7.44; LüTTWITZ Frhr. von Smilo Gen der Panzertruppe, Heer 4.7.44; DORR Hans SS-Obersturmbannführer der Waffen-SS 9.7.44; HACKL Anton Maj, Luftwaffe 9.7.44; STAHEL Rainer Generalleutnant, Luftwaffe 18.7.44; TOLSDORFF Theodor Generalleutnant, Heer 18.7.44; BAYERLEIN Fritz Generalleutnant, Heer 20.7.44; STEINHOFF Johannes Oberst, Luftwaffe 28.7.44; FEGELEIN Hermann Generalleutnant der Waffen-SS 30.7.44; SCHNAUFFER Heinz-Wolfgang Maj, Luftwaffe 30.7.44; Von SCHULZ Fritz Generalleutnant, der Waffen-SS 8.8.44; STEINER Felix Gen der Waffen-SS 10.8.44; FRIES Walter Gen der Panzertruppe, Heer 11.8.44; BüHLIGEN Kurt Oberstleutnant, Luftwaffe 14.8.44; MAYER Dr Johannes Gen der Infanterie, Heer 23.8.44; HAUSSER Paul Generaloberst der Waffen-SS 26.8.44; MEYER Kurt Generalmajor der Waffen-SS 27.8.44; Ritter von GREIM Robert Generalfeldmarschall, Luftwaffe 28.8.44; SCHöRNER Ferdinand Generalfeldmarschall, Heer 28.8.44; WISCH Theodor Generalmajor der Waffen-SS 28.8.44; BAUM Otto SS-Oberführer, Waffen-SS 2.9.44; KROH Hans Generalmajor, Luftwaffe 12.9.1944; WEGENER Wilhelm Gen der Infanterie, Heer 17.9.44; NORDMANN Theodor Maj, Luftwaffe 17.9.44; RAMCKE Bernhard-Hermann Gen der Fallschirmtruppe, Luftwaffe 19.9.44; von KNOBELSDORFF Otto Gen der Panzertruppe, Heer 21.9.44; MAUSS Dr Karl Generalleutnant, Heer 23.10.44; ZIEGLER Werner Oberstleutnant, Heer 23.10.44; FESSMANN Fritz Maj, Heer 23.10.44; RECKNAGEL Hermann Gen der Infanterie, Heer 23.10.44; EDELSHEIM Reichsfreiherr von Maximillian Gen der Panzertruppe, Heer 23.10.44; K LLNER Hans Generalleutnant, Heer 23.10.44; MUMMERT Werner Generalmajor, Heer 23.10.44; WURMHELLER Josef Maj, Luftwaffe 24.10.44; HOHN Dr Hermann Generalleutnant, Heer 31.10.44; von OBSTFELDER Hans Gen der Infanterie, Heer 5.11.44; BAADE Ernst-Günther Generalleutnant, Heer 16.11.44; SCHULZ Karl-Lothar Generalmajor, Luftwaffe 18.11.44; KITTEL Otto Oberleutnant, Luftwaffe 25.11.44; BöSELAGER Frhr. von Georg Oberstleutnant, Heer 28.11.44;. WEIDLING Helmuth Gen der Artillerie, Heer 28.11.44; HARMEL Heinz Generalmajor der Waffen-SS 15.12.44; HERR Traugott Gen der Panzertruppe, Heer 18.12.44; REINHARDT Alfred-Hermann Generalleutnant, Heer 24.12.44; PEIPER Joachim SS-Standartenführer, Waffen SS 11.1.45; KRüGER Walter Gen der Waffen-SS 11.1.45; KRETSCHMAR Wolfgang Oberst, Heer 12.1.45; RENDULIC Dr Lothar Generaloberst, Heer 18.1.45; WENGLER Maximilian Generalmajor d.R., Heer 21.1.45; NEHRING Walther K. Gen der Panzertruppe, Heer 22.1.45; HOGEBACK Hermann Oberstleutnant, Luftwaffe 26.1.45; RUDORFFER Friedrich Maj, Luftwaffe 26.1.45; KIRCHNER Friedrich Gen der Panzertruppe, Heer 26.1.45; MüLLER Friedrich-Wilhelm Gen der Infanterie, Heer 27.1.45; DöRNER Helmut SS-Oberführer und Oberst der Schutzpolizei, Waffen-SS 1.2.45; REINERT Ernst-Wilhelm Oberleutnant, Luftwaffe 1.2.45; WALTHER Erich Generalmajor, Luftwaffe 1.2.45; SACHSENHEIMER Max Generalmajor, Heer 6.2.45; von RUNDSTEDT Gerd Generalfeldmarschall, Heer 18.2.45; von MüLLER Dietrich Generalmajor, Heer 20.2.45; SCHULZ Friedrich Gen der Infanterie, Heer 26.2.45; HEINRICI Gotthard Generaloberst, Heer 3.3.45; LEMM Heinz-Georg Oberst, Heer 15.3.45; KUMM Otto Generalmajor der Waffen-SS 17.3.45; HARTMAN Walter Gen der Artillerie, Heer 18.3.45; BOCHMANN Georg SS-Oberführer, Waffen-SS 30.3.45; JüTTNER Arthur Oberst, Heer 5.4.45; von OPPELN-BRONIKOWSKI Hermann Generalmajor, Heer 17.4.45; DER Helmuth Generalmajor, Heer 18.4.45; SCHROER Werner Maj, Luftwaffe 19.4.45; BATZ Wilhelm Maj, Luftwaffe 21.4.45; BLASKOWITZ Johannes Generaloberst, Heer 25.4.45; NIEHOFF Herman Gen der Infanterie, Heer 26.4.45; BEHREND Hermann-Heinrich Generalmajor, Heer 26.4.45; DECKER Karl Gen der Panzertruppe, Heer 26.4.45 WEIDINGER Otto SS-Obersturmbannführer, Waffen-SS 6.5.45; WISLICENY Günther-Eberhardt Obersturmbannführer der Waffen-SS 6.5.45; STADLER Sylvester SS-Oberführer, Waffen-SS 6.5.45; BITTRICH Wilhelm Gen der Waffen-SS 6.5.45; GR SER Fritz-Hubert Gen der Panzertruppe, Heer 8.5.45; MEINDL Eugen Gen der Fallschirmtruppe, Luftwaffe 8.5.45; THIEME Karl Oberstleutnant, Heer 5.45; von LüTTWITZ Frhr. Heinrich Gen der Panzertruppe, Heer 9.5.45; HIZFELD Otto Maximilian Gen der Infanterie, Heer 9.5.45; BREMM Josef Oberstleutnant, Heer 9.5.45; YAMAMOTO Isoroku Grandadmiral, Imperial Japanese Navy 27.5.43

KNIGHT'S CROSS OF THE IRON CROSS WITH OAK LEAVES, SWORDS AND DIAMONDS*****

Known Makers: K (K in a circle = Klein)

15.7.41 saw the introduction of this grade. The basic design was as the Oak Leaves and Swords but was produced hollow so that each stone fitted into a hole. This enabled the light to shine through and enhance the fire of the diamonds. The Oak Leaves had a more pear shaped appearance with the swords below them, as in the former design. The hilts and handles of the swords were beset with diamond chippings. The first awards were produced in Paris by the firm of Tiffany's. The first German made pieces were produced in platinum but this was later changed to silver. The weight of the stones was, on average, 2.7ct but as each of these awards was individually made and not all by the same jeweller, that is to say the same craftsman each time let alone the same firm, the appearance of the individual clusters varies quite considerably. The jewellers' copies of this award are also varied, again for the same reasons. The example I examined was produced in .800 silver, the stones being recessed into the oak leaves, the swords' hilts did not meet the blades and the hilts were set with chippings. The back was flat and was, in fact, a plate fixed exactly to the edges of the reverse of the oak leaves. This was very neatly done and required a good jeweller's glass to notice the join.

There were 27 known recipients: MOLDERS Werner Oberst 6.7.41; GALLAND Adolf Generalleutnant 28.1.42; GOLLOB Gordon Maj 30.8.42; MARSEILLES Hans-Joachim Hauptmann 2.9.42; GRAF Hermann Oberst 16.9.42; ROMMEL Erwin Generalfeldmarschall 1.3.43; LUTH Wolfgang Kapitän zur See 9.8.43; NOWOTNY Walter Maj 19.10.43; SCHULZ Adalbert Generalmajor 14.11.43; RUDEL Hans-Ulrich Oberst 1.3.44; STRACHWITZ Hyazinth Graf Generalleutnant 15.4.44; GILLE Herbert Otto SS-Obergruppenführer und Gen der Waffen-SS 19.4.44; HUBE Hans Generaloberst 20.4.44; KESSELRING Albert Generalfeldmarschall 19.7.44; LENT Helmut Oberstleutnant 31.7.44; DIETRICH Joseph SS-Oberstgruppenführer und Generaloberst der Waffen-SS 6.8.44; MODEL Walter Generalfeldmarschall 17.8.44; HARTMANN Erich Maj 25.8.44; BALCK Hermann Gen der Panzertruppe 31.8.44; RAMCKE Bernhard-Hermann Gen der Fallschirmtruppe 20.9.44; SCHNAUFER Heinz-Wolfgang Maj 16.10.44; BRANDI Albrecht Fregattenkapitän 24.11.44; SCHöRNER Ferdinand Generalfeldmarschall 1.1.45; von MANTEUFFEL Hasso Eccard Gen der Panzertruppe 8.2.45; TOLSDORFF Theodor Generalmajor 18.3.45; MAUSS Dr Karl Generalleutnant 15.4.45; von SAUCKEN Dietrich Gen der Panzertruppe 9.5.45.

The lettering of the citation is produced in fire gilt and is superbly finished throughout. Again, it has a border of stamped gilded metal but in this instance, the design is more ornate. The outer case comes in three colours, blue for the Luftwaffe, darker blue for the navy and morocco for the army. The eagle is gilded metal but in this case the swastika is studded with small diamonds. The outer metal frame is once more gilded and the design is fretted out to allow the colour of the leather to show through the holes. This document is, in my opinion, one of the most attractively designed of any of the documents produced for any grade of medal during the period of the Third Reich. The presentation box was again the same as the one for the former types of the 'add on' awards to the Knight's Cross.

KNIGHT'S CROSS OF THE IRON CROSS WITH GOLDEN OAK LEAVES, SWORDS AND DIAMONDS*****

Known Makers: K (K in a circle = Klein)

On 1.1.45, to reward probably the most unusual flying personality of any country, Hitler introduced the highest grade of 'add ons'. The original idea for the formation of this grade was that it should be limited to 12 recipients but at this late time in the war, events overtook actions and only one award was rendered. That was to Oberst Hans Ulrich Rudel. His score of kills was so impressive, as was the amount of missions that he flew, which comprised 2,530 but it is estimated that he flew a few more than this. The later missions that he flew were with only one leg, as his other leg had been amputated after a crash.

The badge is identical to the diamond award, except that it was produced in 18ct gold by Godet & Sohn of Berlin and it is reported that they manufactured six examples of this award. More than two were definitely made, as Rudel had two examples in his possession which had been awarded to him at the end of the war. In correspondence with him, he did not make it clear why he had two examples. One story is that Hitler gave him one set and Göring gave him the other, feeling that Rudel was his greatest ace and it was his prerogative as Reichsmarschall of the Third Reich and CIC of the Luftwaffe, to present Rudel with this decoration. Göring had personally decorated Rudel with the Air-to-Ground Operational Flying Clasp with Diamonds, in April 1944 when he had completed his 2,000th mission.

He also stated that he did not receive a citation for the award but that it was promised to him when it was finished and in the fullness of time. The badge was presented again in the same small black box in which the other 'add ons' were awarded.

STAR OF THE GRAND CROSS*****

Known Makers: Rath

Little is known of this award and it is considered to be but a prototype. An example of this star was found in Austria at the end of the war. It consists of an eight-pointed breast order, with an Iron Cross First Class surmounting the star. Each arm, or ray, is formed on the outer edge by a row of dots, with the centre portion of the rays rising at the middle. The rays widen from the centre where the Iron Cross is positioned, then reduce to a point where they radiate from that centre. The reverse is plain, save for four rivets holding the cross to the star. The hinge is raised and is of the same type found on the reverse of Breast Stars of the Eagle Order. The pin is of a hand

57

59

58

60

42

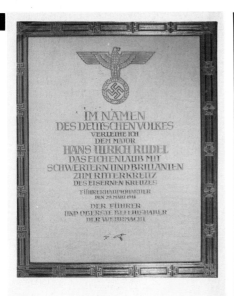

drawn type and underneath this pin is found the hand engraved maker's name, Rath of Munich. The Star is gold plated and highly polished. It has been stated that only one example has been encountered and the description of this Star is from that example, which now resides in the West Point Museum in America. However, I have encountered two other examples one of which I have had the opportunity to examine and believe to be original. It varies slightly from that described.

The case in which the badge was found is a large, red leather, hard hinged case, with a gold eagle embossed on its lid. There is also an embroidered wire version of this Star. Little is known of this particular piece and it is reported that there are other examples of it in existence. The originality and reason for it are unknown to this author.

Plate 57   Oak Leaves, Swords and Diamonds.

Plate 58   Oak Leaves, Swords and Diamonds variation.

Plate 59   Oak Leaves, Swords and Diamonds Dress Copy constructed from three parts and stamped '10' on the reverse.

Plate 60   Document cover for the citation for the Knights Cross with Oak Leaves, Swords and Diamonds— the swastika is studded with small diamonds.

Plate 61   The citation presented to Hans Ulrich Rudel.

Plate 62   Golden Oak Leaves, Swords and Diamonds, presented to Hans Ulrich Rudel.

Plate 63   Star of the Grand Cross of the Iron Cross.

GRAND CROSS OF THE IRON CROSS*****

Known Makers: L/12

This cross was instituted on 1.9.39 and is identical in every respect to the Iron Cross Second Class, save for its size which is 63mm by 63mm. It was suspended from a neck ribbon which is correspondingly larger than that of the Knight's Cross ribbon and is 57mm wide. Originally the silver rim surrounding the iron core was to have been changed to one of gold but this idea was stillborn and the medal was produced with a silver one, as in the case of the Grand Crosses of 1813, 1870 and 1914. The 1939 Grand Crosses were constructed using the standard .800 silver sheeting used for the rims of the Knight's Crosses and malleable iron plate of the same grade, though of thicker material, probably 3.5mm for the centre plate. All the components were die stamped and submitted to the identical process used for manufacturing the lower grades of crosses, using the older traditional method of construction.

The only recipient of the Grand Cross was Hermann Göring and he received it for the Luftwaffe's success in the Battle of France and that of the Low Countries in 1940. The award was rendered for those services on 19.7.40.

The original award was lost when Göring's house was destroyed in a bombing raid on Berlin, but he had a number of copies most of these being made by the firm of Godet & Sohn of Berlin. It is also reported that he had one copy

Plate 65 The citation for the Grand Cross of the Iron Cross.

Plate 64 Obverse Grand Cross of the Iron Cross.

made with a platinum rim. The truth of this story is unknown but his love of medals and regalia would not bring one to disbelieve the story. Another story was that he had one made with an onyx core. All the stories that surround the Reichsmarschall's eccentricities are possible, being borne out by the fact that he had an exact copy of his wedding sword made, which had been presented to him by the Luftwaffe as a recognition of the esteem in which they held him. In order to identify one example from the other he had the contours of the grips changed and had it made lighter.

The citation was similar to that of the one with diamonds but in this case his title and name were much larger, possibly to match the stature of his figure!

The outer case was a magnificent work of art. The eagle was again holding a swastika which was set with diamonds. The frame that went around the case was again similar to that found on the diamond case but was set with 30 red stones. Whether these were rubies or garnets is not known. Round the red stones were set eight diamond chips, giving in total 240 diamond chips. The presentation box was of red leather, with a black velvet base with a recess in which the cross was held. The inner liner was of white satin.

4. Decorations for Valour and Merit

ROLL OF HONOUR CLASP: ARMY****

Known Makers: Capital 'K' in a circle.

On 30.1.44 Hitler instigated this clasp to reward members of the army and Waffen-SS who had been entered on the 'Honour Roll of the German Army'. This roll had been started in July 1941 to record the honourable and heroic deeds carried out by its members. No tangible evidence of an entry on the roll existed. This badge filled the purpose of being an outward show of inclusion on the honour roll. It comprises a finely gilded and stamped wreath of oak leaves, with a ribbon and tie at its base and a large square swastika in its centre. The badge is finely executed and gives a definite three-dimensional appearance. The wreath measures 24.5mm across and is formed of five bunches of oak leaves on either side, comprising two and three bunches respectively. The width of the wreath is 5mm at the widest point and this tapers to the apex where the two sides meet with a single oak leaf, tip to tip. At the base, the bow is full and forms the base of the badge itself with a width of 21mm. The height of the badge from the base of the ties to the tip of the apex is 26mm. The swastika is of the non-mobile type and stands proud of the top of the wreath. The legs of the swastika have a fine indented line running round the whole of the emblem. The swastika itself produces two forms of this badge and they are namely the one in which the swastika is separately attached to the wreath by the tips of its forearms and then soldered, while the other form is die struck as a one piece striking. Both pieces look superficially identical but can be differentiated by the void between the swastika and the wreath at the attachment points. The reverse takes the outline exactly in negative of the obverse, being stamped in the latter form while the swastika is flat in the former. It has four pins for attachment on the reverse, to enable it to be secured to a piece of Iron Cross ribbon, Second Class. Approximately 4,556 awards of this clasp were rendered at the end of hostilities, making it a considerably rare award.

The recipient had already to be in the possession of the Iron Cross First and Second Class. The clasp was worn on the ribbon of the Iron Cross Second Class at the second buttonhole of the uniform. If the recipient already held an Iron Cross Second Class bar, he only wore the Roll of Honour Clasp.

From the collector's point of view, the smallness of its size, and the way that it was attached to the tunic, has made this a very difficult award to obtain.

It was contained in a small, black, oblong box, with cream flocked base on which the badge sat, with the ends of the Iron Cross ribbon being tucked underneath the bed that produced the base. On some examples of the bed, the maker's mark for Richard Klein is encountered embossed

66

Plate 66 Obverse of the Roll of Honour Clasp- Army.

67

Plate 67 Reverse of the Roll of Honour Clasp- Navy on the left, showing the four needle pins and in contrast, the three (4) flat pins of the Roll of Honour Clasp- Army.

45

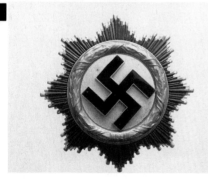

into the corner. This comprises a capital 'K' in a circle with three inverted chevrons in a further circle beside the first. The lid lining was of white silk.

ROLL OF HONOUR CLASP: NAVY****

Known Makers: Capital 'K' in a circle.

On 13.5.44 Grandadmiral Dönitz instituted the naval version of the Honour Clasp to recognise those members of the navy who had been entered on 'The Honour Roll of the German Navy', which had been opened in February 1943.

In this case the badge is produced from a single stamping but the gilt wreath is slightly larger, measuring 26mm across. The oak leaves comprising the gilded wreath are continuous and are made up of 15 individual bunches of irregular design, measuring 3.5mm across. The central motif is an anchor surmounted by a swastika. In this case, the swastika is mobile and also has the fine recessed line running round the edges of the legs. The field beneath the base of the anchor and the wreath should not normally be voided. The reverse takes the negative design of the obverse, being stamped. It has four fine prongs to attach it to the Iron Cross Second Class ribbon. It was worn in the same manner as that described for the army type, with the same provisions.

It was awarded in a black oblong box. In the case of this badge, the box's base was blue flocked and the lining was white silk. There are no exact estimations of the number awarded of this type of honour clasp but it is the hardest of the three clasps to obtain for one's collection.

ROLL OF HONOUR CLASP: LUFTWAFFE***

Known Makers

The first recorded instance of this Clasp being awarded was 5.8.44. Göring, in his inimitable way, did not want to be outdone by the other two services and belatedly introduced the Honour Roll of the German Air Force in 1944. Again the badge was a gilt metal wreath of oak leaves which, in this case, had a rough appearance taking the outline of the oak leaves as the border, thus the inner and outer edges of the oak leaf wreath gave a ragged appearance. There are six bunches of three leaves on either side, meeting tip to tip at the apex and, at the base, are two acorns protruding upwards into the central portion of the badge. The wreath measures 24.5mm and the width of the leaves is 3.5mm. In the centre is a flying Luftwaffe eagle, clutching a swastika in its talons. The reverse is the negative of the obverse, being stamped, with four lugs for attachment to the Iron Cross Second Class ribbon. It was worn in the same manner and with the same provisions as the other two clasps.

Plate 68 Obverse of the Rolls of Honour Clasp-Navy

Plate 69 Obverse of the Roll of Honour Clasp-Luftwaffe.

Plate 70 Obverse of the German Cross in Gold.

However, all members of the Luftwaffe who had been awarded the goblet or salver of honour, as well as those who had received the picture of the Reichsmarschall in silver frame, automatically received the clasp. It is possible that over 30,000 Clasps were rendered during the period of the war, this number making it quite a common award.

It was presented in a black oblong box, with an off-blue flocked base and white silk lid liner.

GERMAN CROSS IN GOLD***

Known Makers: 1, 4, 20, 21, 134

This breast star was introduced on 28.9.41 and was to recognise the bravery of the fighting forces above that which was required for the bestowal of the Iron Cross First Class but not up to that required for the award of the Knight's Cross. It was a useful award in that it could be bestowed upon a Knight's Cross winner, if he had not already won it, to show further appreciation of his valour. This is borne out by the example of the award of this cross to Max Simon, who had received the Knight's Cross in October 1941 and was awarded this medal at the end of 1943. Equally, it could be awarded from the Iron Cross First Class if it had not been enough to warrant the Knight's Cross. The idea that this was an intermediate award of the Iron Cross grading is erroneous. In fact, it was really a half-way house, running in tandem to the Iron Cross. The award could only be presented by the CIC army, navy or Luftwaffe or, in the case of a member of a senior staff, by the chief of the armed forces high command. On 22.4.45 Hitler gave permission for army group and independent army commanders to award the German Cross in Gold, Honour Roll Clasps and Iron Cross First and Second Class to members of their staff. It was also permitted to present the German Cross in Gold to officers of Axis military units if they already possessed the Iron Cross First Class. The star was designed by Prof Klein and consisted of a large enamelled Swastika in black, which was outlined in silver. This was on a silver field around the edge of which ran a thin red line. Adjacent to this line is a wreath in gold made up of laurel leaves wound round with silk ties. At the base is a box with the year of instigation, '1941', impressed into it. From this wreath emanate rays which cover the eight points of the star. These rays are chemically oxidised black. Beneath this is the silver back plate, which takes the outline of the edge of the badge and the rays which have already been described but it slightly protrudes from the rays, giving the badge the overall effect of a three dimensional appearance.

The construction of the award is one of the most complex undertaken by the designer and is formed from eight pieces. The star is formed from five distinct pressings and the pin, hinge and hook from a further three. The back plate has the outline of the rays on the eight points and a flat central panel with holes drilled at 3, 6, 9 and 12 o'clock respectively. This plate measures 63mm. Placed on to this is a similar plate with two further slots cut just inside the circle holes at 9 and 3. This plate measures 59mm. On to the central field is placed a circular disc with holes in the corresponding places to the second star plate. This plate has two lines of brick-red enamel with the central field being finished in a satin-finished silver. The plate measures 41mm. The next piece to be added is the swastika, that has two pins at 9 and 3 o'clock and measures 21.5mm. The two pins are located through the second and third pieces and are bent over, thus holding the body of the star together. It is this method of construction that allows the swastika to move. Whether or not this was intentional to help with damage is unknown. Master jeweller Keith Thompson, having disassembled a piece, found the oblong slots incongruous to the design of the star and viewed that they could have acted as a form of shock absorber. The wreath measures 39mm and has four pins which are placed through the holes and peened over into open-holed rivets on the reverse of the backplate.

The reverse is slightly convex with four open rivets. Above the upper one is an oblong recess into which is placed the hinge and below the lower one is an elliptical recess, into which is placed the hook. The pin is of the broad blade type and usually has the maker's stamp applied. This can be on either the upper or lower face. The eight pieces were produced from tombac or cupal. Early award pieces had a back plate with no recesses and the hinge and hook were placed directly on to it. The rivets also were of a ball type. The overall weight was much heavier as well. It is also found in another variety which has six smaller ball rivets and is known as the Austrian type. There are two forms of this, the first having six ball rivets in two vertical lines of three, the second has the six ball rivets placed in the six points of the star, on the left and right side. It has a massive hinge, pin and hook which in some cases have the maker's mark on it and the better examples are found with the maker's number 1, 4 or 21. There is also a five rivet piece which has one round post in the centre of the back plate. The manufacturer of this type is, as yet, unknown. The number of badges awarded was 24,204, of which the army received 14,639, Kriegsmarine 1,481, Luftwaffe 7,248, SS and Police 822 and foreigners 14.

The star was worn on the right breast pocket of the uniform. The box in which the medal was awarded was a square black one, with a black velvet base and white silk lining. Round the side of the upper lid was a fine gold embossed line to represent the grade of the award.

GERMAN CROSS IN GOLD CLOTH VERSION AIR FORCE BLUE**

GERMAN CROSS IN GOLD CLOTH VERSION NAVY BLUE****

GERMAN CROSS IN GOLD CLOTH VERSION FIELD GREY**

Known Makers

On 5.6.42 the embroidered version of the German Cross in Gold was authorised. This badge was produced purely for 'in the field use' and comprises a black silk embroidered Swastika, outlined in gold wire on a white silk field, bordered by a gold wire cord. This has the metal wreath that had been used in the construction of the metal badge, fixed to the backing. Round the outer edge of the wreath is another circle of gold wire, from which emanate embroidered rays with white tips. The backing of the badge on to which the embroidery and metal wreath are applied, is in the corresponding colours of the various branches of the services referred to in this section. The award was worn sewn on to the right breast pocket of the uniform.

This form of the decoration was intended for combat personnel who functioned in enclosed areas which could cause damage to the enamelled swastika. Also the size of the metal star caused the potential risk in enclosed areas of being caught on projecting parts of operational equipment.

GERMAN CROSS IN SILVER***

Known Makers: 1, 4, 20, 21, 134

This medal is exactly the same as the German Cross in Gold save for the wreath which, in this case, is silver and it was instigated on the same date as the former medal, 28.9.41. This badge was rendered for the conduct of the war and for significant acts of leadership that furthered the war effort rather than that for bravery and, again, fitted nicely into the War Merit Cross series. Those receiving the German Cross in Silver had to have the War Service Cross First and Second Class with Swords. For these award criteria and for these reasons, the medal is much rarer in this form than the gold version. Contrary to popular belief both grades could be worn together but this was a most unusual occurrence.

The reverse normally has four ball rivets but there is encountered a six ball version known as the Austrian type. However the six ball rivets are smaller in this version. 1,114 badges were awarded: army 874; navy 105; Luftwaffe 65; SS and Police 70.

The box again was identical to the one previously described but with a silver line running

round the side of the lid to denote the grade of the award.

GERMAN CROSS IN SILVER CLOTH VERSION AIR FORCE BLUE****

GERMAN CROSS IN SILVER CLOTH VERSION NAVY BLUE****

GERMAN CROSS IN SILVER CLOTH VERSION FIELD GREY****

Known Makers

This badge was produced purely for 'in the field use' and comprises a black silk embroidered swastika outlined in silver wire on a white silk field, bordered by a silver wire cord. This had the metal wreath used in the construction of the metal badge, fixed to the backing. Round the outer edge of the wreath is another circle of silver wire from which emanate embroidered rays with white tips. The backing of the badge on to which the embroidery and metal wreath are applied is in the corresponding colours of the various branches of the services referred to in this section. The institution date of the award is unknown.

WAR MERIT MEDAL*

Known Makers

For neatness of collecting, I have put this medal out of chronological order of instigation but I hope the reader will forgive this foible. The medal was designed by Richard Klein of Munich and was introduced on 19.8.40. It comprises of a round medal with a facsimile of the War Merit Cross Without Swords on the obverse and on the reverse 'FUR KRIEGS VERDIENST 1939'. The medal was made of bronze and was usually very well produced.

It was introduced for the reward of civilians who were aiding the war effort. It was also conferrable upon non-Germans engaged in Germany's war effort, although this was changed on 15.5.43 with the non-Germans being awarded the Eagle Order Medal either in the bronze or silver class. The medal was suspended from a ribbon comprising of stripes made up of red, white, broad black with a red central line, white, red. A further interesting ribbon has been discovered by Bob Sevier of the Cracked Pot. This was accompanied by a variation Mothers Cross ribbon and two Danzig pieces. The Mothers Cross is described later in the book. This ribbon comprises a 28mm band made up of a 3.5mm blue edge stripe, 3.5mm red stripe, 2.5mm white stripe and a 9mm central black stripe. The purpose of this ribbon is unknown but has been premised as the original ribbon intended for this award. A further suggestion is that it was for awards in the Danzig area.

The container in which the badge was issued was either a blue, brick-red or buff packet with the name printed on to the front in black.

WAR MERIT CROSS SECOND CLASS BRONZE WITHOUT SWORDS*

Known Makers: 4, 14 (in square), 18, 19, 34, 43, 45, 56, 57 (in oblong box), 101, 113, Jakob Bengel

The medal takes the form of a 49mm Maltese Cross. The crosses were die struck and produced from a variety of materials, mainly zinc, that had a bronze wash applied but in some cases the crosses were struck from bronze. These are considered very scarce. The Maltese Cross has a border round its edge, with the field between these borders being pebbled. The centre of the cross has a stylised oak leaf wreath with a tie at the top and bottom. The wreath measures 16mm across. In this, on the obverse, is a raised swastika and in a matching position on the reverse is a raised '1939'. The field behind both this reverse and obverse design is plain. At the upper arm of the cross is an eyelet with a ring through which the ribbon was suspended. The ribbon, in the case of the 30mm band, has stripes of 4mm brick-red, 4mm white, 14mm broad black, 4mm white and 4mm red. This combination of colours is the reverse of those employed for the Iron Cross 1939.

On 18.10.39 Hitler introduced a range of crosses which also include a similar series with swords. The relationship and orders which governed the award and production of them will be described here so that repetition in each section does not become too commonplace. Hitler required a series of awards to replace the non-combatants version of the Iron Cross but in doing so he wished to enlarge on the method of rewarding the recipients, because he realised, due to his own experiences in WW1 and those gained in the Spanish Civil War, that the scope of that grade of the Iron Cross would not fully cover the modern requirements of a fully mechanised war.

The award was to be also presented to civilians, as well as military personnel who performed outstanding service in the furtherance of the war effort, centring around bravery and service not in direct connection with military combat. For this purpose the crosses came, in all grades, with and without swords. The version without swords was awarded for service in the furtherance of the war effort and those with swords for bravery not directly connected to front-line activities. This bravery, in fact, could be of a much higher standard than that required in the front-line, considering that most of these recipients would not have been fired up by the smell of battle.

Originally Hitler had decreed that neither of the grades of the War Merit Cross, that is to say First and Second Class, with or without swords, could be worn with the corresponding grade of the Iron Cross. This regulation was rescinded on 28.9.41 and allowed the wearing of all the grades of both types with the relevant grades of the Iron Cross but below or behind it in precedence of wear.

It was necessary to have had the Second Class awarded before the First Class could be rendered, but in exceptional cases, both grades could be conferred upon the recipient together. The War Merit Cross could be awarded to a firm or company, for example a munitions factory or shipyard. These came under the German Labour Front and were organised along military lines. The German Labour Front was responsible for this type of award, having awarded Golden Flags as emblems of the efficiency of an individual company since 1.9.36. The firm's flag could have an emblem attached to it to show that it and its workers had received a factory citation. The flag comprised a silk red banner, with the emblem of the DAF, a large black cog wheel, in stylised form in the centre. On this centre, which is white, is a Swastika. The flag is fringed with silver fringing and in the right-hand upper corner a silver bullion War Merit Cross First Class is embroidered.

It is estimated that 1,591,567 crosses were awarded during the period of WW2. It was presented in a buff, blue or brick-red packet, with the name and class of the cross printed on the front.

WAR MERIT CROSS FIRST CLASS SILVER WITHOUT SWORDS**

Known Makers: 3, 3 (in a square box), 4, 8 (in a square), 15, 19, 50, 52, 56, 62, 65, 84, L/11, L/15, L/52, L/58, L 15

This cross was introduced by Hitler on the same date as the former. It is identical in design but the obverse is finished in a silver wash. The reverse is plain and silver washed as well but has a large pin and hook construction. Often the maker's number is stamped in the centre of the obverse. The quality of the badge varies quite tremendously as does the material in which it is produced. This can range from real silver usually .800 standard, through to pot or monkey metal.

One interesting recipient of this grade was William Joyce, 'Lord Haw-Haw', who received this cross for his propaganda broadcasts in September 1944. It is estimated that 91,239 awards of this cross were rendered during WW2. The box in which it was awarded, considering the number of awards, is of remarkable quality and is black simulated leather, with a black inside lower base with a slit to allow the badge

Plate 71   Reverse of the German Cross in Gold showing the recessed hinge and hook and two of the four doughnut rivets.

Plate 72   Reverse of the German Cross in Gold showing the six ball rivets known as the 'Austrian' type, with the variation of hinge, hook and pin. It is also interesting to note the name and Feldpost number engraved.

Plate 73   Obverse of the German Cross in Gold Cloth version- navy-blue.

Plate 74   Obverse of the German Cross in Silver.

Plate 75   Reverse of the German Cross in Silver showing four ball rivets and the variation pin, hing and hook.

Plate 76   Obverse of the War Merit Medal.

Plate 77   Reverse of the War Merit Medal. This example has the variation ribbon.

Plate 78   Obverse War Merit Cross Second Class Bronze Without Swords.

Plate 79   Reverse War Merit Cross Second Class Bronze Without Swords.

Plate 80   Obverse War Merit Cross First Class Silver Without Swords.

Plate 81   Reverse War Merit Cross First Class Silver Without Swords. Note the two different styles of pin, hinge and hook attachment.

76

77

78

79

80

81

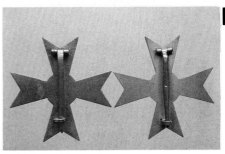

hinge to be accommodated. The upper inner lid lining is off-white satin or silk. The top of the outer lid of the box has either the silhouette of the badge or a representative copy of the badge, stencilled into it.

WAR MERIT CROSS FIRST CLASS SILVER WITHOUT SWORDS: SCREW BACK***

Known Makers: L/58

The hinge in this case is exchanged for a screw post and large screw cap similar to that found on the Iron Cross First Class. The domed plate is sometimes marked. In these cases the award boxes were recessed to accommodate this method of production.

WAR MERIT CROSS, KNIGHT'S CROSS SILVER WITHOUT SWORDS*****

Known Makers: 1, L/13

This award takes the basic design of the War Merit Cross Second Class but is larger, measuring 54mm across the arms and the oak leaf wreath measures 18mm. The width of the arms of the cross is 3mm. It was usually produced in genuine silver, with the silver grade ranging from .800 through to .950 but in some examples the cross is but silver-plated and these examples just have the maker's number on the lower arm. The upper arm has an inverted V attached to it, with three lines on each arm and with an eyelet at its apex. It is very important at this point to dispel a theory that has been in existence for some time, that this version came with only a plain hanger. It is, in fact, found with both ribbed and plain varieties; not only that, they are not all as long as one another. Also, in the case of the plain type the inverted 'V' is also plain to match the hanger. Through this eyelet is a ribbed hanger which supports the cross on the neck ribbon. As with all Knight's Crosses it was worn around the neck. The ribbon comprises a 46mm band formed from stripes of 4mm red, 4mm white, 22mm broad black, 4mm white and 4mm red. For the examples of the cross that were awarded, the ends of the ribbon were turned over into a triangle with a length of minute ribbon at each end to act as ties to secure the ribbon around the neck of the recipient. This is a new and very interesting point. If one had a short neck, one required a shorter hanger for comfort. If one had a number of neck decorations, General Otto Stapf for example had both the Knight's Cross of the Iron Cross and the Knight's Cross of the War Merit Cross with Swords, the hangers had to be adjusted for the comfort of the wearer, for there was no undress version for wear for either of these orders. This was also the case of the earlier Pour le Mérite,

which a number of staff officers had won in WW1 and had to wear with their WW2 counterparts.

The criteria for the award were that it was a prerequisite for a recipient already to hold the War Merit Cross First and Second Class and that any recommendation had to be forwarded through the OKW or state minister to the Reichschancellery where it was personally approved by Hitler.

On 19.8.40 this cross was introduced to reward the high achievements of the civilian population, civil service and political formations, to encompass military personnel and was for outstanding service in the furtherance of the war effort but not directly connected to combat. Great ceremony was employed with the award of the Knight's Cross decorations and the recipient was usually accompanied at the ceremony by a Knight's Cross winner. The Knight's Cross of the War Merit Cross ranked above the German Cross in Silver but below the Knight's Cross of the Iron Cross. Only 48 awards were rendered of this decoration, which made it very prestigious in the eyes of the Nazi hierarchy. Hitler in fact, circulated a letter from his headquarters on 27.8.43, outlining the criteria for award and the philosophy surrounding it and directed that 'prominent party comrades' were not to be honoured with this decoration. A definite jibe at Reichsmarschall Hermann Göring who had coveted the award of the Knight's Cross of the War Merit Cross with Swords. David Littlejohn suggests that this statement, 'prominent party comrades not to be honoured with this decoration', was made because Hitler had The German Order in mind for the 'top brass' of the party. We know from Albert Speer that Hitler wanted to reward Himmler with something but could not make up his mind just what. Speer threw out hints that he himself would not be unappreciative of a decoration! He thinks Hitler intended to see just what each of the top people had contributed to victory, once Hitler had won the war and then start giving out the German Order in various grades. The dead had already made their contribution, that is why, Littlejohn suggests, it was mainly dead party comrades who received the rare Order, thus the recommendations for the awards proposed for Gauleiter Koch and Stadtsminister Backe were refused or, more politely, withdrawn. In one case the cross was awarded in both forms to Reichsverkehrsminister Julius Dortmüller, who received it on 19.9.43 and was awarded the cross with swords on 24.7.44. Conjoined with the award was often a secondary prize as was the case with Dr Theo Morell who held the post as Hitler's personal physician. He received Germany's only electron microscope in conjunction with his award.

It has been believed that 118 awards of the cross without swords were rendered. However, the actual number is 48, as shown by the list of recipients. Not only that but not all the recipients have been officially recognised in the form of gazetting. This non-public announcing was to ensure the anonymity of the recipient and the work in which he was involved. This was also common in the awarding of British decorations, thus other awards may come to light.

Known recipients:

HAHNE Franz 20.5.42; THOMSEN Hans 25.5.42; DAVIDSHöFER Christian 5.6.43; HOLTMAYER Johannes 5.6.43; KRAUCH Carl 5.6.43; ROHLAND Walter 5.6.43; SAUR Karl Otto 5.6.43; SAWATZKI Albin 5.6.43; WERNER William 5.6.43; RAHN Rudolf 22.6.43; DORPMüLLER Julius 19.9.43; DEGENKOLB Gerhard 20.9.43; PIER Mattias 20.9.43; SCHIEBER Walter 20.9.43; SCHIRNT Kurt 3.10.43; SAUERBRUCH Ferdinand-Ernst; WOLF Ludwig 21.10.43; GRIMM Fritz-Wilhelm 7.12.43; AMBROS Otto 1944; BüTEFISCH Heinrich 1944; RICKHEY Georg Johannes 1944; WURSTER Karl 1944; MORELL Theodor 24.2.44; DOHRN Hermann 10.8.44; HASSENPFLUG Werner 12.8.44; HILDEBRANDT Hubert 12.8.44; PEUCKERT Rudi Werner 12.8.44; TIMM Max 12.8.44; DILLI Gustav 14.8.44; HAYLER Franz 16.8.44; ARPS Willi 24.8.44; ESAU Abraham 22.9.44; KOHNERT Hans-Joachim 30.9.44; BEHRENS Gustav 1.10.44; BLOEDORN Wilhelm 1.10.44; HECHT Kurt 1.10.44; HUBER Reinhold 1.10.44; PFLAUMBAUM Walter 1.10.44; GANZER Karl-Richard 15.9.44; ZSCHIRNT Kurt 3.10.44 (accredited with the award twice); LINNEMEYER Werner 12.10.44; LIPPISCH Alexander 12.10.44; MESSERSCHMITT Willy 12.10.44; ECKHARDT Alfred 7.12.44; BERTRAM Richard Wolfgang Paul 26.12.44; DARGEL Paul 15.1.45; SCHELP Fritz 20.2.45; BOHRMANN Otto 21.2.45.

It was presented in a blue box, with an inside black velvet base, which has a round recess into which the cross and hanger fit. The upper part of the box above this recess is indented to accommodate the neck ribbon.

WAR MERIT CROSS, KNIGHT'S CROSS GOLD WITHOUT SWORDS*****

Known Makers

This last and highest grade of the order was, to all intents and purposes, identical in every respect to the silver grade except that it was produced only in real silver and the cross itself was then gold plated. The silver grade was stamped on the bottom of the lower edge of the V of the lowest arm of the cross.

On 13.7.44 Albert Speer and Hitler discussed the necessity of the introduction of a higher grade of the Knight's Cross of the War Merit Cross with and without swords. It has been stated that the awards were introduced on 13.10.44; however Dr Klietmann gives the introduction date as 8.7.44. Other sources state that this grade was not formally introduced at all.

It is believed that Speer personally had this grade produced by having existed crosses gold plated. Only two crosses are known to have been awarded and this occurred on 20.4.45 when Speer personally invested Franz Hahne and Karl Otto Saur.

It was presented in a blue box similar to the one formerly described for its counterpart.

WAR MERIT CROSS, SECOND CLASS BRONZE WITH SWORDS*

Known Makers: 4, 14 (in square), 18, 19, 34, 43, 45, 56, 57 (in oblong box), 101, 113, Jakob Bengel

This cross was instituted on 18.10.39 by Hitler and is identical in every respect to its non-combatants counterpart with the exception of the addition of swords which pass through the quadrants of the cross. These swords are broad bladed and double edged, of the Roman centurian or military design. This cross was awarded for bravery which occurred not in the face of the enemy. It is estimated that 6,134,950 awards were conferred during the period of WW2.

It was presented in a packet which was either blue, brick-red or buff, with the name of the order and its derivation printed on the front.

WAR MERIT CROSS, FIRST CLASS SILVER WITH SWORDS**

Known Makers: 3, 3 (in a square box), 4, 8 (in a square), 15, 19, 50, 52, 56, 62, 65, 84, L/11, L/15, L/52, L/58, L 15

This cross is identical to its non-combatants counterpart, with the exception that the swords were added to the cross through the quadrants of the arms of the cross. The reverse of the swords are plain, as is the rest of the obverse of the cross which had only, in some instances, the maker's number stamped in the centre.

This cross was awarded for bravery which occurred not in the face of the enemy, and it is estimated that 483,603 awards of this cross were rendered during the period of WW2.

It was presented in a black box, with a black base liner which had a slit to accommodate the pin as in the previous types. The lid liner was of white satin while the box top had either a silhouette or facsimile of the cross stencilled on to it in silver.

Plate 82 Obverse War Merit Cross Knights Cross Silver With Swords.

Plate 83 Reverse War Merit Cross Knights Cross Silver Without Swords.

Plate 84 Obverse War Merit Cross Second Class Bronze With Swords.

Plate 85 Reverse War Merit Cross Second Class Bronze With Swords.

Plate 86   Obverse War Merit Cross Second Class
Bronze With Swords, this example being Spanish
made.

Plate 87   Reverse War Merit Cross Second Class
Bronze With Swords. The fields of the arms of the
cross and the swords are plain. This example being
Spanish made. The wreath is a separate piece
applied.

Plate 88   Obverse War Merit Cross First Class
Silver With Swords.

Plate 89   Reverse War Merit Cross First Class
Silver With Swords. Note the deterioration in quality
of production as well as the pin, hinge and hook
assembly.

WAR MERIT CROSS, FIRST CLASS SILVER WITH SWORDS: SCREW BACK***

Known Makers: L/58
The pin in this case was substituted by a screw post and screw plate similar to that found on the Iron Cross First Class. The domed plate is sometimes marked. In these cases the award boxes were recessed to accommodate this method of production.

WAR MERIT CROSS, KNIGHT'S CROSS SILVER WITH SWORDS*****

Known Makers: 1, L/13
This cross was identical to its non-combatants counterpart, as was its date of institution, save that it had the swords added. The cross was produced in genuine silver with the grade from .800 through to .950. Sometimes the maker's mark is situated on the lower arm of the cross in the recess of the V, as in the former described position.

This order was intended for award to military, administrative personnel and civilians who had served bravely in combat or in the direction of the war but not where an award of the Knight's Cross of the Iron Cross would be warranted. It was necessary for the recipient to have been awarded the War Merit Cross with Swords First and Second Class. The award ranked in precedence over the German Cross in Silver but below the Knight's Cross of the Iron Cross.

It is estimated that 211 of these Knight's Crosses were awarded during the period of WW2. However, not all recipients of the award were gazetted. This was to protect the anonymity of the recipient and the work in which they were engaged. Such was the case of Dr-Ing Ernst Blaicher, who was awarded the cross on 15.11.43 for his work in tank production. A further bestowal which was not gazetted, is to Oberstleutnant Othmar Wolfan who was on the staff of Kommandierender General der Deutschen Luftwaffe in Finland, who was recalled from Finland in the closing days of the war to Berlin to receive an important post and decoration. His niece asserted that he received the award and then went into Russian captivity for his troubles.

It was contained in a box that has already been described.

Known recipients were:

von BOETTICHER Friedrich 27.5.42; von GABLENZ Carl August Freiherr 25.8.42; LEFFLER Kurt 4.10.42; RITTER Ernst 4.10.42; WITZELL Karl 5.10.42; DEL Günter 17.10.42; LIEBEL Willy 27.11.42; REMY Karl 7.12.42; von UNRUH Walter 1943; PLIEGER Paul 10.5.43; DORSCH Xaver 13.5.43; BRUGMANN Walter 14.5.43; JACOB Alfred 4.6.43; HINKEROHE Joseph 5.6.43; SCHMID Karl 5.6.43; GEHRCKE

Rudolf 27.7.43; WAHLE Carl 3.8.43; DALUEGE Kurt 6.9.43; NEUBACHER Hermann 7.9.43; BENOIT Wilhelm 13.9.43; SEXTEL Anton 13.9.43; GANZENMüLLER Albert 19.9.43; HANDLOSER Siegfried 23.9.43; HEINEMANN Erich 23.9.43; KUBE Wilhelm-Richard Paul 27.9.43; KöRNER Helmuth 3.10.43; REINHARDT Fritz 3.10.43; RITTER Julius 6.10.43; BLAICHER Ernst 15.11.43; KüHL Bernhardt 16.11.43; ENNSBERGER Alois 28.11.43; GOUDEFROY Erich 7.12.43; BIERSCHENK Ernst 7.12.43; HELLENTHAL Remigius 7.12.43; KINDERVATER August 7.12.43; RABITZ Friedrich 14.12.43; WEISE Erich 16.12.43; HENRICI Hans 1944; KURZ Eugen 1944; MARTINI Wolfgang 1944; RIEDEL Walter 1944; THIEL Walter 1944; SCHRADER Rudolf January 1944; KLASING Ernst 28.1.44; von HELLDORF Wolf Heinrich Graf 10.2.44; SCHACH Gerhard 10.2.44; HOELCK Klaus 21.2.44; NAGEL Jakob 21.2.44; WOLF Karl 21.2.44; SCHULZE Wilhelm 25.2.1944; WAGNER Hermann 25.2.44; MüLLER Ernst 28.2.44; BROM Rochus 7.4.44; POGGEMEIER Friedrich 7.4.44; POLZIUS Wilhelm 7.4.44; MERKER Otto 28.4.44; FINCKH Eberhard 11.5.44; NEUBERT Georg 28.4.44; LANDSKRON Franz 11.5.44; SCHULZE Kurt 15.5.44; DENNIS 16.5.44; FISCHER Richard 22.5.44; FRYDAG Karl 22.5.44; HEYNE Hane 22.5.44; KESSLER Philipp 22.5.44; LAGENOHL Max 22.5.44; LüSCHEN Friedrich 22.5.44; GEBHARDT Karl Franz 31.5.44; BACMEISTER Adolf 31.5.44; GUTZEIT 31.5.44; TöNNIS 31.5.44; GEILENBERG Edmund 1.6.44; TIZ Arthur 1.6.44; HENNE Willi 2.6.44; KITTEL Walter 4.6.44; RöMER Wolfgang 4.6.44; SCHLEGEL Hans 4.6.44; de FRESSE Karl 9.6.44; LEEB Emil 14.6.44; NIKOLAUS known as Claus Selzer 20.6.44; BöHMCKER Johann-Heinrich 21.6.44; ERDMANN Kurt 21.6.44; LEYERS Hans 24.6.44; SCHINDLER Max 24.6.44; STUDT Erich 24.6.44; BECK Emil 11.7.44; DORPMüLLER Julius 24.7.44; KNEPPER Gustav Heinrich 26.7.44; REIFFERSCHEIDT Franz July 1944; SCHüRER Friedrich 24.7.44; OTTE Carlo 9.8.44; DOHRN Hermann 10.8.44; SCHüTTE Ernst-Wilhelm 10.8.44; BRAUWEILER Max 12.8.44; von PAPEN Franz 15.8.44; VOLKMANN Reinhardt 17.8.44; VORWALD Wolfgang 17.8.44; WEISS Karl 22.8.44; von SEIDEL Hans Georg 31.8.44; WEBER Friedrich September 1944; RIEDEL Klaus September 1944; STAPF Otto 9.9.44; KEHRL Hans 23.9.44; KREUZ Lothar 24.9.44; PEHLE Heinrich 1.10.44; MüLLER Josef 12.9.44; BOCHRINGER Gustav 6.10.44; WALTER Paul 6.10.44; BASTIAN Max 12.10.44; von BRAUN Werner 28.10.44; DORNBERGER Walter 28.10.44; DEGENKOLB Gerhard 29.10.44; ROHLAND Walter 29.10.44; SAUR Karl Otto 29.10.44; SCHIEBER Walter 29.10.44; VEESENMAYER Edmund 29.10.44; JüTTNER Hans 30.10.44; OHNESORGE Karl-Wilhelm 1.11.44; SCHMERBECK 1.11.44; WERNER Rudolf 1.11.44; COLS-

MANN Erwin 4.11.44; KöSTRING Ernst-August 4.11.44; NAGEL Wilhelm 4.11.44; OSTERKAMP Herbert 7.11.44; HUSS Fritz 10.11.44; ENGEL Johannes 11.11.44; BERGER Gottlob-Christian 15.11.44; KALTENBRUNNER Ernst 15.11.44; MüLLER Heinrich 15.11.44;. POHL Oswald 16.11.44; WURSTER Eugen 17.11.44; PREIçLER Fritz 18.11.44; CHRISTIANSEN Carl 19.11.44; PFAUSER Anton 20.11.44; KEHRL Hans 27.11.44; WAEGER Kurt 27.11.44; GERWIG Heinrich 28.11.44; SCHAEDE Hans-Joachim 28.11.44; BEKURTS Karl 5.12.44 KELCHNER 5.12.44; MALZACHER Hans 5.12.44; WEISSENBORN K. 5.12.44; BüRGER Walter 7.12.44; GRIES Wilhelm 7.12.44; MAUTERER Arthur 7.12.44; WIENS Günther 7.12.44; WOLFF Albert 7.12.44; HOFFMANN 7.12.44; HöLZER Peter 7.12.44; KIDERZATER August 7.12.44; KOMP Karl 7.12.44; KOSER Johann 7.12.44; LAMMERTZ Maximilian 7.12.44; MALDAKER Gustav 7.12.44; RöCHLING Hermann 17.12.44; HINRICHS Hermann 20.12.44; KISSING 20.12.44; von HANEKEN Hermann 21.12.44; PFROGNER Anton 21.12.44; SCHMEIDLER Herbert 21.12.44; THOLENS Hermann 21.12.44; WINKELMANN Otto 21.12.44; LOIBL Ludwig 23.12.44; BERTRAM Richard Wolfgang Paul 26.12.44; EWERT Walter 26.12.44; FUCHS Werner December 1944; KORTE Hermann 31.12.44; SCHÄFFER Emil 31.12.44; GOHRBANDT E. 1945; De la CAMP Bürkle 1945; KAMMLER Hans 1945; SCHRöDER 1945; SCHWARZ 1945; WASSNER 19.1.45; LINDAU Erwin 1.1.45; BACKENKöHLER Otto 3.1.45; von FRIEDEBIURG Hans Georg 17.1.45; WENNEKER Paul Werner 17.1.45; MAçNER 19.1.45; MARZECHA Walter 25.1.45;- KOEPKE Jacob 28.1.45; WACHTEL Max 31.1.45; EISENBECK Martin 2.2.45; KR MER February 1945; MALSI Georg 1.1.45; WALTER Helmuth 6.2.45; MöCKEL Helmut 11.2.45; WARLIMONT Walter 15.2.45; KIRSCH Ludwig 20.2.45; METZGER Julius 20.2.45; SCHOLL Wilhelm 20.2.45; ZECHMANN Heinrich 20.2.45; AGARTZ Friedrich 21.2.45; ENGELHARDT Conrad 24.2.45; KORRENG Augus 25.2.45; WEIGELT Johannes-Kurt 25.2.45; KOHNLHAUER Erich March 1945; DETMERING Rolf 16.3.45; REUSCHEL 28.3.45; KETTLER Kurt April 1945; GREUL Emil 20.4.45; HAMBERGER Wilhelm 20.4.45; KUNZE Heinz 20.4.45; STREIT Bernhardt 20.4.45; SCHWARZ Friedrich 28.4.45; FANGER Paul 30.4.45; KüPFMULLER Karl 30.4.45; BüRKNER Leopold 2.5.45; SALMAN Otto 2.5.45

WAR MERIT CROSS, KNIGHT'S CROSS GOLD WITH SWORDS*****

Known Makers
This award is identical to the Knight's Cross of the War Merit Cross with Swords. The cross was produced in genuine silver, from grade .800 through to .950 which was gold plated. The silver mark was situated in the lower arm in the underside of the V of that arm, as was the maker's stamp. As has already been stated, on 13.7.44 Speer brought to Hitler's attention the necessity for a higher grade of the Knight's Cross of the War Merit Cross. It has not yet been proved that any awards of this grade of the cross have been made although a considerable number of crosses were produced.

It was housed in a blue box as previously described.

Plate 90 Obverse War Merit Cross Knights Cross Silver With Swords.

Plate 91 Reverse War Merit Cross Knights Cross Silver With Swords.

5. Luftwaffe Award Badges 1933-45

AIRCREW BADGE****

Known Makers: CJJ

This badge comprises an oval wreath formed of oak leaves on the right and laurel leaves on the left. It is surmounted by an eagle holding a swastika in its talons. On the reverse is a horizontal pin. The badge comes in two types, the first and possibly the more common, is in nickel silver. The eagle is riveted by three ball rivets, one through each wing of the eagle into the wreath and one through the swastika. The pin is of either a broad blade or a thin needle type. The badge can be totally devoid of any maker's mark or has the Juncker's trade mark, 'CJJ' in the box. It is believed that there are approximately only eight known examples of this type.

The second type is made of aluminium, with the eagle sweated on to the wreath. In this version the wreath and eagle are die stamped. The reverse is formed with two holes, one at either end of the badge. In the holes are countersunk the hinge mounting and the hook mounting. The pin in this type is of a thin needle type.

There is a cloth version of this badge which comes in cotton thread, white cotton for the wreath and black cotton for the eagle. The fletching on the eagle's wings is picked out in white cotton.

The box for this badge is blue, with a blue velvet base and blue silk lining.

The introduction of this badge into service is a little difficult to determine and understand, as is its role in the following order. The known references give its introduction as 1933 and that it had been used for the reward of pilots and observers in the clandestine Luftwaffe or the qualified members of the German Air Sports Association. However, it gained official sanction on 1.4.34 and on 19.1.35 became the official Combined Pilots and Observers Badge. It became supplanted by the new version in November 1935 and was removed totally from circulation. However, the Luftwaffe Diary for 1942 for use by

Plate 92   Obverse Air Crew Badge.

Plate 93   Obverse Pilots Badge.

Plate 94   Reverse Pilots Badge.

Luftwaffe personnel as a form of text book, still shows the badge in the order of badges. This gives rise to the assumption of the principle that, like the Army Parachutists Badge, a new badge did not have to be re-sat for and the original could still be worn.

PILOTS BADGE**

Known Makers: A, B & NL, B.W.S. (within club emblem), C. E. JUNCKER, CEJ (in rectangular frame), JME, JMME, W. DEUMER.

The original instruction for this badge came on 27.5.35, although the badge was not brought into being by Göring until 12.8.35. On 27.11.35 the regulations publishing the exact specification for the badge were made public and were, an oval, slightly convex, silver-plated wreath, the right half of laurel and the left half of oak leaves. This is the opposite of the Aircrew Badge. The raised surfaces of the wreath are highly polished. At the base of the wreath there is a three band tie and, on the viewer's right, nine bunches of three oak leaves overlapping one another. At each joint are two acorns, one on either side. On the opposite side are nine bunches of three laurel leaves with two berries at the joint, one on either side of the central leaf's point. The wreath is 53mm by 42mm with a width of 8mm. It has an eagle in flight mounted upon it, oxidised and old silver-plated, clutching a swastika in its claws. The wings are finely detailed, as are the head and body. Normally, the gap between the legs is solid but in the case of the badges produced in aluminium, this area is generally voided. Occasionally, the portion between the legs is voided on the early nickel silver versions as well. The wingspan of the eagle can vary between 64mm and 67mm, due to the form of manufacture as well as the individual producer. On the reverse the eagle is riveted to the wreath on each side by two small ball rivets which change in style with the different methods of manufacture. There is a

vertical hinged pin which is soldered on. This badge was found in nickel silver or aluminium and as the war progressed, pot metal or monkey metal. I consider the most desirable badges of this type to be the thin wreath, nickel silver and aluminium types produced by C. E. Juncker.

The badge was awarded upon completion of the flying training and when the pilot received his flying licence and citation.

Dr Heinrich Doehle gave the institution of the badge as 26.3.36 and this has been widely considered as the official date of introduction. This poses the intriguing question 'What was the design of the Pilots Badge from 12.8.35 to 26.3.36?' There are two versions of the cloth badge which correspond to the officers and NCOs, taking the form of the metal badge but embroidered in relief. The wreath is worked in silver, the eagle in oxidised silver, and the swastika in dull aluminium thread. The NCOs' version is identical but executed in cotton thread. The badge was worn on the left upper pocket of the service uniform or flying jacket. It was issued in a blue box with the badge designation stencilled in gold block letters on its lid.

PILOTS BADGE: VARIATION****

Known Makers

In this case the wreath is round and consists of oak leaves on the right and laurel leaves on the left, as in the case of the standard badge. The base has a ribbon comprising three parts. The apex has a number of small berries and the overall quality of the striking is indistinct. The eagle

Plate 95   Obverse Round Pilots Badge. This form is thought to be that awarded to female members of the Luftwaffe.

Plate 96   Reverse Round Pilots Badge.

95

96

59

is mounted at the top of the wreath at approximately ten to two and was identical to that found in the standard Pilots Badge. The appearance of the swastika is in a similar position to that found in the standard Pilots Badge but is more dominant in the design of this badge. The space above the eagle's wings is reduced to a gap so that the apex of the wreath and the wings of the eagle nearly form a straight line. The reverse is quite different in that the wreath is semi-dished and the eagle held on by two ball rivets, as in the former badge but at the top. The hinge is of the barrel type with a pin and large hook at the bottom.

All the examples that I have encountered follow this form of construction, giving rise to the possibility that it was produced by one manufacturer.

The reason for this variation is unclear. One theory that has been put forward is that it was to recognise jet pilots who were being trained and came into service at the closing stages of the war. I highly discount this theory. In a letter to me, David Littlejohn has expanded on it thus 'The easiest, cheapest and most logical way to get an aircraft from the factory to the front line squadron, which is to add it to its strength, is to fly it there. But it would be a crazy waste of good combat trained pilots to get one of them to fly as a sort of "bus driver" from factory to front. The result, at least so far as the RAF was concerned, was to employ civilian pilots. These were either chaps too old to be on active service but who, pre-war, had been civil pilots, or women. This was known as the ATA (Air Transport Auxiliary) and the pilots were known as 'ferry pilots'. Now I cannot imagine that Germany did not have its equivalent of the ATA and my guess is that this is what this badge is for, civilian pilots working for the Luftwaffe, not actual Luftwaffe trained aircrew. I have been told by a reliable source that there was even a bullion version of this badge with the round wreath'. John Angolia in *For Führer and Fatherland Vol 1* amplifies this by stating 'Knight's Cross winner Wilhelm Joswig did not get his military licence until 1943, thus was not awarded the Pilots Badge until that time, yet he flew military aircraft from 1939 on his civilian licence'. In fact, researchers seem to prove that this badge was indeed intended for women pilots employed by the Luftwaffe and was introduced in c1943. The women were employed in transporting aircraft to various destinations within Germany and delivering aircraft to regrouping points ready for collection by front line pilots. They undertook aircraft testing and evaluation and, in some cases, were actually test pilots as in the case of Hanna Reitsch.

Another conclusion is that this design was not taken up by the Luftwaffe.

COMBINED PILOTS AND OBSERVERS BADGE***

Known Makers: A, B & NL, B.W.S. (within club emblem), C.E.JUNCKER, CEJ (in rectangular frame), JME, JMME, W.DEUMER, L/64

On 26.3.36 this badge was introduced to replace the older Aircrew Badge and takes the format of the former badge but the eagle is bright silver and the wreath are gilt. The high parts of the gilt wreath are polished, while the indentations are matt. This badge is again found in aluminium and later in the war, pot or monkey metal. The quality of these badges varies widely from a purely silvered and gilded Pilots Badge, to a super struck and silver-plated and gilt plated example.

The badge was awarded on completion of both the pilots and observers courses and was presented with licence and certificate. On 31.7.44 regulations prescribed that the award could be rendered providing that the intended recipient had held the Pilot Observers qualification certificates for a minimum of one year.

In special cases the badge was authorised to be awarded to foreigners in recognition of special services rendered to the Luftwaffe. An honorary presentation of this badge was normally made to foreign attachés upon their return to their home duty station.

The cloth version was again identical to the pilots form but with the colours conforming to the metal badge. The officers' version was again executed in silver and gold bullion while the NCOs' version was in cotton.

The badge was to be worn on the left breast pocket and after 1936 could be worn on the political uniform as well as the military one.

The box is blue with blue silk lining and blue velvet base with the title stencilled on to the top in gold lettering.

COMBINED PILOTS AND OBSERVERS BADGE IN GOLD WITH DIAMONDS*****

Known Makers: Rudolf Stübiger

This award was conceived during the summer of 1935 with the first bestowal taking place on 11.11.35. It is interesting to note that both the inception and first presentation predate the introduction of the Combined Pilots and Observers Badge, which was introduced on 26.3.36. Furthermore, the badge was produced in Austria by the Viennese jeweller, Rudolf Stübiger. The construction is unique with the whole of the badge being hand produced.

The wreath is cast and then hand finished in the same design as that employed on the Pilots Badge. The wreath measures 52.5mm by 41.5mm with a width of 7.5mm. The general appearance of the eagle differs from that of the Pilots Badge with the wings being enlarged, the wingspan measuring 65mm while the depth of the left wing is 12mm and the right, 15mm. The eagle is constructed to allow the stones in the wings to have light coming from behind, enhancing the fire of the diamonds. The edges of the feathers are all slightly pebbled as is the outside of the swastika. This measures 12mm across and the individual arms are 3mm wide. The upper parts of the wings are highly polished, which compliments and enhances the appearance of the fletching. The general appearance of the eagle is larger and the legs are spread with a gap between them. The legs of the eagle are finely detailed. There are 36 diamonds in the right wing and 31 in the left. A total of 19 are inlaid in the eagle's body. 18 small diamonds are inlaid in the arms of the swastika. The whole of the eagle's frame is constructed in platinum while the wreath is made of 22 ct real gold.

The reverse of the wreath is flat and has a matt finish with a thin barrel hinge at the apex. The pin is of a thin, needle type and is retained in a unique holder acting as a safety catch.

The eagle has a 3mm flat frame running round the edge of the wing and the body, which is employed to strengthen the structure of the eagle. The wings have a strut of similar construction running across them, which is covered by the wreath. On to this is attached a screw post which fits through individual holes drilled in the wreath, securing the eagle to the body of the wreath. The eagle is held on to the wreath by two massive screws.

In correspondence with the firm of Rudolf Stübiger, his son indicated that they produced 70 of these badges. On the first of these badges only the shop number was scratched on the reverse of the badge in the position of the hinge. After 1938, when Austria became part of the Greater German Reich, they placed their logo on the reverse of the eagle. This information gives one a good clue to the period and therefore the person to whom a badge was possibly awarded.

This badge was possibly the most exciting flying badge of any country. Apart from its obvious beauty, the rarity and the people to whom it was awarded, notably Herman Göring himself, it also rewarded some of the bravest of the Luftwaffe pilots. The first award of the badge was presented to the chief of the Luftwaffe GeneralStaff, Generalleutnant Wever, on 11.11.35 and led to the award of 55 other persons.

The known recipients were: ANTONESCU Ion; DöNITZ Karl; HIMMLER Heinrich; BALBO Italo; DIETRICH Sepp; HARTMANN Erich; von BLOMBERG Werner; FRANCO Francisco; HARLINGHAUSEN Martin; von BRAUCHITSCH Walter; GALLAND Adolf; HORTY Miklos; BAUMBACH Werner; GöRING Hermann; JESCHONNEK Hans; ODENSCHATZ Karl; Ritter von GREIM Robert; KORTEN Günter; BAUR Hans; FRAFF

Hermann; KELLER Alfred; von BELOW Nicolaus; GOLLOB Gordon; KESSELRING Albert; CHRISTIANSEN Friedrich; von GABLENS; KAMMHUBER Josef; KASTNER; PARANI; STUDENT Kurt; LOHR Alexander; PELTZ Friedrich; TRETTNER; LENT Helmut; PFLUGBEIL; UDET Ernst; LOERZER Bruno; ROMMEL Erwin; VALLE; Baron von MANNERHEIM Carl Gustav Emil; RAMCKE Bernard; WEVER Walther; MöLDERS Werner; von RICHTHOFEN Wolfram; REITSCH Hanna; MUSSOLINI Benito; SKORZENY Otto; Gräfin von STAUFFENBERG; MILCH Erhard; SPERRLE Hugo; NAURISIL Frederick; NOWOTHY Walter; STUMPFF Hans-Jurgen.

Many misbeliefs have been constructed around the award of the Combined Pilots Badge with Diamonds and the reason why some of the officers had been awarded the badge.

The Combined Pilots and Observers Badge was authorised to be awarded in special cases to foreigners in recognition of special services rendered to the Luftwaffe. An honorary presentation of this badge was normally made to foreign attachés upon their return to their home station. It is interesting to note that one of the first honorary awards of the badge was to Benito Mussolini, who was awarded the badge in April 1937. The citation clearly states that it was for, 'Das Goldene Flugzeugführer und Beobachter-Abzeichen' (The Golden Pilot and Observer Badge). However, Angolia has stated that this citation was for the Combined Pilots Badge with Diamonds. The Combined Pilots Badge with Diamonds was conferred upon Mussolini on 28.9.37 by Göring, who personally pinned it to his tunic. Andrew Mollow, in a letter to Guns, Weapons & Militaria in December 1981 entitled, 'Mit or Mitout Diamonds?', said 'In pointing out the error in Chris Ailsby's article on the Order of the German Eagle, David Littlejohn has contributed to a basic misunderstanding which exists concerning the Luftwaffe Pilot/Observer Badge. David Littlejohn refers to the Pilot/Observer Badge in Gold and Diamonds awarded to Benito Mussolini in September 1937. Whereas most postwar publications on German orders and medals refer to only two classes or categories of this badge, I believe there were three.

'The basic badge with silver eagle on an upright gilt metal wreath was awarded to Luftwaffe aircrew on successful completion of their flight training.

'As a special personal award, Göring introduced sometime in 1935 a Pilot/Observer Badge in Gold and Diamonds. This badge was awarded to prominent members of the Luftwaffe, most or all of whom had been at one time or another qualified pilots.

'The third class of this badge was a version in which both the eagle and wreath were in solid gold. This badge Göring awarded to foreign heads of state such as King Boris of Bulgaria and Benito Mussolini and a very few eminent Germans such as the Reichsführer of the SS, Heinrich Himmler.'

This poses an interesting question as to whether there was such an animal as the Golden Pilot and Observers Badge and was it upgraded to the diamond award, as those named eventually received the award with diamonds and was this form used to reward friendly nations' politically appointed air personnel. As yet, a gold badge produced in gold has not been observed.

The criterion for the award was that each recipient must be the holder of a pilot's licence. This pilot's licence could have been either in the civil form, to encompass single-engined aircraft and even to have allowed the consideration of the holder of a glider pilot's licence. This would have qualified them for the badge. This explains the entitlement of the badge for some of the more unusual bestowals namely, Himmler and Dietrich. It is also believed that Dr Fritz Todt was a recipient of the award but this has yet to be fully confirmed. Upon the death of the holder, the badge had to be returned to Göring's personal office. This was the case with Gen Korten who was mortally wounded in the bomb plot attempt of 20.7.44. After his death, the badge was not immediately returned and Göring's office was most indiscreet in requesting its return before his body was cold in its grave.

Hansen-Nootbar recalls one argument between Dönitz and Göring which ended when Göring unpinned the diamond studded pilots decoration from his exquisite uniform and handed it to Dönitz who, to the delight of the officers watching them, unpinned the U-boat decoration from his own service blue jacket and handed it to Göring. It was a typically nimble and appropriate response.

Von Puttkamer gives a shorter version of this episode in his memoirs, implying that from then on Dönitz made his way successfully with Göring. One is left wondering about the incident. Was it the force of Göring's personality and intelligence or the aura of his power and the long established position he held in the Nazi hierarchy or loyalty to the Führer perhaps, that caused Dönitz to respond as he did and humour and get along with the Reichsmarschall in public, while privately regarding him as a national disaster. For, when he and Hansen-Nootbar were alone they referred to Göring as, 'the grave digger of the Reich' or 'the fat one'. Whether this symbolic gesture actually constituted the award of the two badges to the two personages is doubtful but undoubtedly Dönitz was awarded the badge. It is less likely that Göring received the Submarine Badge with Diamonds from Dönitz.

The box for this decoration is uncertain and it is considered that it was just a jewellers case which transported the badge to the award ceremony.

GLIDER PILOTS BADGE: FIRST TYPE****

Known Makers: C. E. JUNCKER

On 8.7.40 the firm of Wilhelm Ernst Peekhaus submitted their design for this badge. It was approved on 16.12.40 and was produced by the firm of C. E. Juncker of Berlin. It consists of a wreath of oak leaves made up of eight bunches of three leaves on either side, the edges of the leaves forming the inner and outer edges of the wreath. They meet tip to tip at the apex with a swastika at the base. There are the two forms of swastika. The fields between the arms of the swastika are either solid or voided. The height of the wreath can vary between 55mm and 57mm with the width of the badge being 42mm. The wreath is finished in a silver wash with the highlights being polished.

On the wreath is a soaring eagle, flying from left to right, which is finished in oxidised old silver colour. The design of the eagle is elegant with a well defined head positioned over the forward thrusting wing. There are subtle differences in the eagle the most significant being in the wings' fletching and the line of the trailing wing. The width of the wings is 53mm and the depth of the body from claw tips to the top of the wings varies from 15mm to 16mm.

The reverse is flat and the eagle is held on to the wreath by two ball rivets, one through each wing tip. The rivets can also be a small, flat type. At the apex is a hinge which can be either a barrel or ball type. The latter has a needle pin countersunk. The former has a needle pin with a shepherd's crook bend. At the base is a 'C' form hook. The reverse of the eagle is flat with a matt finish that is oxidised from light-grey to nearly black.

However, as the war progressed the quality of the badge deteriorated, not so much in the stamping of the individual wreath and eagle, but the fact that the eagle is sweated on to the wreath. The badge is made in nickel silver or aluminium and then zinc, pot or monkey metal. The badge was awarded on completion of a glider pilots training and was issued with a citation and pilots licence. The cloth versions of this badge were produced for both officers and NCOs in the manner described in the Pilots Badge section. It was worn on or a little below, the left breast pocket of the tunic.

It was presented in a blue box, with blue satin liner and velvet base, with the name stencilled in silver on the lid.

FLIERS COMMEMORATIVE BADGE****

Known Makers: L/11, C. E. JUNCKER

This badge was introduced on 26.3.36 and consisted of a wreath of oak leaves meeting at the apex tip to tip with a swastika at the base. The wreath on either side of the swastika comprises seven bunches of oak leaves formed irregularly from either two or three leaves positioned randomly in the wreath. The jagged edges of the leaves form the inner and outer edge line to the wreath. The badge measures 54mm by 42mm with the width of the wreath being 7mm at its widest point. The swastika is found in the two forms with either the field between the lower arms being solid or voided. Unlike most flying awards this badge is struck in one piece. The centre of the badge consists of an eagle perched on a rock, with its wings furled downwards and looking to the left. The field between the eagle's legs, leg and tail in some badges is voided. In this type the eagle has a more three-dimensional appearance with the legs being of a more pronounced design, as is the fletching on the body and wings. The whole badge is of a smoked appearance with polished highlights, while the eagle and rock are of a darker, matt-grey colour.

The reverse is flat with a barrel hinge, needle pin and 'C' form hook that can either be placed on a plate and soldered to the badge or soldered directly to the badge.

It is found produced in nickel silver, aluminium, zinc and pot or monkey metal.

The badge was to reward both active and reserve personnel who had served as fliers during WW1 for four years flying service, had been discharged from flying duties after 15 years service or had been invalided out of the service as a result of an air associated accident. In the event of a person being killed in the course of his flying duties, the badge was awarded to the next of kin. This badge is one of the rarest of all the flying awards of this period and again was produced in both cloth versions which are, in turn, very rare.

The metal badge was presented in a blue box in the same manner as before.

ANTI-AIRCRAFT WAR BADGE*

Known Makers: A, W.H., BREHMER, C. E. JUNCKER

On 19.7.40 the firm of Wilhelm Ernst Peekhaus submitted a metal badge to the air force ministry for their approval. This consisted of a wreath of oak leaves with a block at the base. The oblong box at the base has a raised, central spine and from either side of the box is the top portion of a single oak leaf. From these, on either side, emanate eight bunches of three leaves, the central one taking prominence over the two lower ones. The serrated edges of the leaves form the inner and outer edge lines of the wreath. Surmounting this wreath is a flying Luftwaffe eagle clutching a swastika, which is sweated on to the wreath at the apex, which has two semi-circular protrusions to accommodate the emblem. The central design of the badge is made up of an 88mm anti-aircraft gun. This gun is pointing upwards and to the right, breaking the wreath. The field between the edge of the wreath, gun plinth and breech block can be found in various ways, solid, semi-voided or completely cut out. The height of the badge from the base to the top of the eagle's wings is 63mm and 45mm across the badge. The width of the wreath is 6mm. The eagle's wings measure 40mm.

The reverse is flat with a vertical needle pin, hinge and 'C' form hook. There are a wide variety of assemblies employed in the construction of this design of badge. The earliest badges were constructed in nickel silver or, very rarely, aluminium. However as the war continued the badge is found in zinc, pot or monkey metal.

The badge was approved and instituted on 10.1.44. The criteria for the award was that it was to be awarded on a points basis. Sound locaters and searchlight crews were also eligible for the award. One point for each detection was awarded, 16 points being required for the award of the badge. The criteria for the anti-aircraft batteries were:

- Shooting down an aircraft unaided: four points.
- Shooting down an aircraft aided by another crew: two points
- Five unsuccessful engagements with enemy targets.
- Three actions where an aircraft was downed.
- Any single act of bravery or merit which occurred in the course of air defence.
- Three successful ground engagements against ships, tanks or fortifications.
- A battery commander became eligible for the award when half of his company had been awarded this badge.

The badge was awarded either in a blue box as described before, with the title stencilled on its lid in silver, or in a paper packet with just the badge name printed on it.

GROUND COMBAT BADGE*

Known Makers: M.u.K.5, G.H.Osang, GB, RK, GWL

This badge was designed by Prof von Weech of Berlin. It comprises a wreath of oak leaves with a tie at the base. From each side of the tie is a single half oak leaf and from these emanate seven bunches of three leaves. The central leaf nearly obliterates the two beneath it. The bunches meet tip to tip at the apex of the wreath and the serrated edges of the leaves make up the outer and inner edge line of the wreath. The central upper portion has a black massed cloud. The clouds are separated from the wreath on either side and the apex, by three voided areas. These vary in size with the different forms of production. Sur-

Plate 97 Obverse Combined Pilot and Observer Badge.

Plate 98 Reverse Combined Pilot and Observer Badge.

Plate 99 Obverse Combined Pilot and Observer Badge in Gold with Diamonds.

Plate 100 Reverse Combined Pilot and Observer Badge in Gold with Diamonds.

Plate 101 Obverse Glider Pilots Badge First Type. Note the badge on the left has a semi-segmented swastika and the wreath has a less pronounced profile, while the badge on right has a solid swastika and pronounced profile. Both eagles display subtle differences.

Plate 102 Reverse Glider Pilots Badge First Type. Note variation in rivets as well as the hinge, hook and pin assembly.

Plate 103 Obverse Fliers Commemorative Badge.

Plate 104 Reverse Fliers Commemorative Badge.

Plate 105 Obverse Anti-Aircraft War Badge.

Plate 106 Obverse Ground Combat Badge. The eagle on the left-hand badge is of thin pressed metal, while that on the right is a solid stamping. The cloud formations demonstrate subtle differences in each badge.

Plate 107 Reverse Ground Combat Badge. Note that on the left there is a single rivet while on the right there are three. The hinge, pin and hook construction are worthy of consideration.

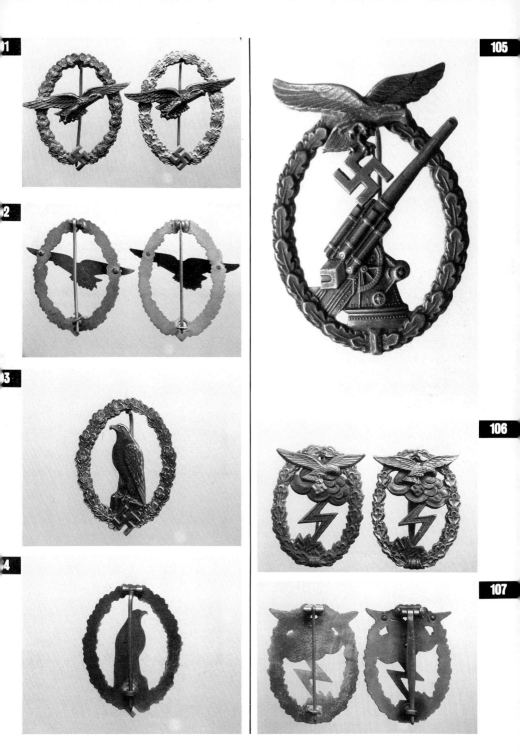

65

mounting this is a Luftwaffe eagle. This is struck into the design of the badge and forms a base for a separate identical additional eagle. This is usually a separate piece that is pressed out or a solid struck piece which is then riveted to the badge. From the cloud is a bolt of lightning with an arrow tip striking the ground formed by a number of jagged points representing mountains. The lightning bolts symbolise striking power coming from the air.

The badge measures 56mm by 43mm and the eagle has a wingspan of 41.5mm. The height of the eagle from the top of the wings to the lower tip of the swastika is 21mm. The width of the wreath varies between 7 and 7.5mm.

The reverse of the badge is flat and can have a variety of hinges. These fall into three distinct types. The first is a conventional hinge that is let into the back of the badge and then has a piece of the badge turned over at each end. This is similar to the type of hinge encountered on the 75 and 100 Tank Battle Badges. It usually has a broad bladed, bellied pin. The second type is a conventional hinge which can be of any construction, soldered directly on to the reverse of the badge. The third form has an integral hinge cast into the badge during the manufacturing process. These two types have needle pins held by a barrel attachment, or the shepherd's crook method. The hook is normally of the 'C' form attached to the badge by means of a plate or by being recessed into the body of the badge. The last type of hinge usually has the integral hook cast in, in manufacture. The eagle can be held to the reverse of the badge by three small domed rivets, two domed rivets or one flush rivet.

This badge was instituted on 31.3.42 to reward the members of the German Air Force who were engaged in military operations in support of the German armed forces. These units consisted of 22 divisions and were known as 'The Luftwaffe Replacement Army'. One of the most famous parts of this army was the Hermann Göring Division. The control was vested in the hands of Hermann Göring himself until July 1944.

If an army award badge such as the General Assault Badge, Infantry Assault Badge or Tank Assault Badge had been awarded previously to the institution of this badge, it was to be exchanged for this badge.

The criteria for the award were:
● Being involved in three engagements on different days.
● Being wounded in one of the actions for which this badge could have been awarded.
● To have been awarded a decoration in one of these actions.
● A Luftwaffe member killed during an action was automatically awarded the badge.

Members of parachute units and assault gun units were authorised to receive the badge pro-vided they fulfilled the same qualifications, with the proviso that they were on three separate combat days.

There was a cloth version of this badge in bullion for officers and presumably in cotton for NCOs. However this badge in the bullion format is extremely rare, as is the cotton version, which this author has not yet encountered.

The badge was awarded in either a blue box with silk liner and velvet base, the base is sometimes encountered in a form of brushed cardboard, or in a paper packet with just the badge's derivation printed on it.

GROUND COMBAT BADGE: 25 CLASS*****

Known Makers: Usually Unmarked
On 10.11.44 the higher grades were introduced. All the four types were slightly larger than the unnumbered type and comprised an oak leaf wreath with a flattened bottom. It is interesting to note at this point that unlike the army numbered assault badges which were in two distinct designs, one for 25 and 50 and the second for 75 and 100, these badges were identical for all grades. The lateness in the war obviously dictated economies and therefore a standardisation of the badge.

With this series of badges extreme caution has to be exercised when one is tempted to buy. They are extremely rare and few genuine examples are known to exist. Although the design of the badge is very similar to the unnumbered badge, there are a great number of subtle differences. The base of the wreath has an oblong box measuring 10mm by 8mm, into which is fixed a plate 8mm by 6mm with a raised 1mm edge line. On to the recessed field is placed the Arabic numerals, '25'. The line and figures are finished in gold while the field is blackened. From either side of the box emanate the tip of an oak leaf over a single leaf. From these, on either side, are seven fans of three oak leaves reducing slightly in width until they meet at the apex, tip to tip. The wreath is finished in a silver wash.

The central, upper portion of the inner wreath is made up of clouds but, in this case, they do not have the three voided areas found on the unnumbered form. It has a lightning bolt striking the ground. The bolt head or arrow is smaller, as is the jagged ground area. The aforementioned portions are all matt blackened. The flying Luftwaffe eagle is incorporated across the wreath and over the clouds. The portion of the eagle over the clouds is recessed to allow the superimposed eagle to be recessed into the body of the badge. This eagle is a solid striking and has a dull silver wash applied over it. The badge measures 58mm by 45 mm, with the eagle's wingspan being 41mm.

The reverse of the badge is flat with a hinge, pin and hook as found in the first type of the

66

unnumbered badge. There are three ball rivets, placed in a wide downward pointing triangle, which hold the eagle to the body of the badge. The whole of the reverse, to include the pin, is blackened with an enamelled matt paint.

As with the assault badge with the army and the Waffen-SS, there was a great need to reward the achievements of the Luftwaffe ground forces. The numbers in the box represent the number of ground engagements with which the recipient was credited. Again, members of the parachute units and assault gun units were authorised to receive the numbered badges. Until now there has been doubt as to whether any of these badges were awarded. There is at least one occasion when the 25 class badge was definitely bestowed and the actual example is used in this illustration. It was awarded to an Unteroffizier of the 7/Flakregiment II on 20.4.45. It is also thought that he went on to receive the badge in the 50 class.

DAY FIGHTER OPERATIONAL FLYING CLASP: BRONZE CLASS**

DAY FIGHTER OPERATIONAL FLYING CLASP: SILVER CLASS**

DAY FIGHTER OPERATIONAL FLYING CLASP: GOLD CLASS***

Known Makers: RK, B.S.W., R.S & S, S & S, F. & BL, M.KUNSTOFF, BSW (within a clover leaf), BWL (within a clover leaf), BWS, BWS (within a clover leaf), JMME & SOHN

As the air war progressed, it was felt that the Luftwaffe personnel should be rewarded for their flying activities and service in the air by a special badge. This badge was to be an outward expression of the flying service that they had achieved.

The badge takes the form of a round wreath of laurel leaves with a swastika at its base. From either side emanate seven bunches of three leaves that have two laurel berries, one on either side of the central leaf at each joint. They meet tip to tip at the apex with four berries. In varying manufacturers, these four berries can change to three or two. This is not an omission but a variance in the die. The height of the wreath is 21mm with the width of the leaves being 3.5mm. On each side of the wreath is a sprig of oak leaves which is formed by two rows of three leaves, one of two and a single leaf at the outer edge. There are two holes forming the voids between the stalks of the leaves at the point where the leaves join the wreath. These holes can be in a variety of forms and in some cases they are omitted altogether. They tend to form a weakness in the structure of the bar and from a design point of view, serve no good purpose. The length of the bar, from tip to tip, is 76mm with the width of the sprig at its widest point being 13mm. The central motif superimposed on the centre, was to be a device of the individual badge. This device was made in silver or white metal, which was blackened and riveted on to the badge. The silver overpiece was the same design as the badge underneath. In later war badges the silver over-piece is often omitted due to restrictions on the availability of scarce materials. This leaves just the rivet hole in the centre of the device.

The reverse of the badge is flat. The reverse of the wreath in some cases can be recessed, leaving a cartwheel effect. There are a number of ways the barrel hinge can be attached to the reverse. Some have a hinge let into the reverse and then have the badge turned over the two edges or soldered directly to the reverse. Normally the pin is a flat broad blade with a belly but in some cases this has a ribbed effect. Needle pins are unusual and normally found on late war, inferior badges. The hook is of the 'C' type that can be recessed into the badge on a circular plate, soldered to a plate and then fixed to the badge or just soldered directly on to the badge.

This badge was introduced on 30.1.41. It was designed by Prof von Weech of Berlin and consists of a winged arrow pointing upwards. The reverse has a horizontal pin and usually the maker's mark. The pin is either flat or fluted and the quality is very good. The composition of the badge is from nickel silver through to pot metal. The overall colour of the badge represents the grade or class. Thus the bronze class was for 20 operations, silver for 60 and gold for 110 operations. As the war progressed it was decided to introduce a series of pendants to hang below the wreath. This pendant takes the form of a little star with a little sprig of three laurel leaves projecting from each side. The star has a raised central pellet with eight larger raised rays emanating from it. The star is 12.5mm high and the length of the bar is 36mm. The date of institution of this device or Anhanger, was 26.6.42. In this case the pendant represents 500 missions above the 110 of the original badge. As the war continued it became obvious that this was confusing, so on 29.4.44 a simpler method of numbering was introduced. Thus the pendants were modified to a panel in which the number of missions was struck, these numbers were in gold ranging from 200 through to 2,000. The field behind the numbers is blackened and the outside of the box has the same laurel sprigs on either side. The box is 7mm high and the length of the bar is 38mm. There was a cloth version for officers in bullion and presumably cotton thread for NCOs.

The badge was issued in a blue box with a cream base, with the badge type stencilled in gold on the lid.

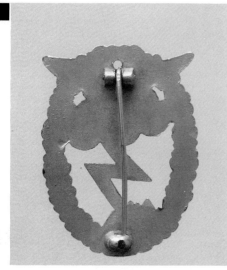

Plate 108 Reverse Ground Combat Badge. Note this badge has an integral hinge and hook assembly.

Plate 109 Obverse Ground Combat Badge-25 Class. This badge has been photographed beside a standard Ground Combat Badge to illustrate the differences in the wreath and cloud formation.

Plate 110 Reverse Ground Combat Badge-25 Class. Note that this has a three rivet construction hinge, hook and pin assembly similar to that employed on the basic badge.

Plate 111 Obverse Day Fighter Operational Flying Clasp-Silver Class.

Plate 112 Reverse Flight Clasp illustrating the standard method of production and the attachment of the pendant.

Plate 113 Obverse Reconnaissance Operational Flying Clasp-Gold Class with Flower Pendant.

Plate 114 Obverse Reconnaissance Operational Flying Clasp-Bronze Class. Note the variation in design.

Plate 115 Reverse Reconnaissance Operational Flying Clasp-Bronze Class. Note the variation in the method of construction.

Plate 116 Obverse Long Range Night Fighter Operational Flying Clasp-Gold Class with Flower Pendant.

113

114

115

116

RECONNAISSANCE OPERATIONAL FLYING CLASP: BRONZE CLASS**

RECONNAISSANCE OPERATIONAL FLYING CLASP: SILVER CLASS**

RECONNAISSANCE OPERATIONAL FLYING CLASP: GOLD CLASS**

Known Makers: RK, B.S.W., R.S & S, S & S, F. & BL, M.KUNSTOFF, BSW (within a clover leaf), BWL (within a clover leaf), BWS, BWS (within a clover leaf), JMME & SOHN
This badge was also introduced on 30.1.41, to reward the reconnaissance air-sea rescue and meteorologists of the Luftwaffe. It took the form of a wide eyed eagle looking to the left. I find this badge most appealing and possibly one of the best examples of contemporary design, being very stylised. Again, the mission requirements for the bronze class were 20, silver 60 and gold 110 missions. Again there was confusion in the case of the star pendant, as it represented 300 missions in the case of air-sea rescue and meteorological squadrons and 250 missions in reconnaissance squadrons. This confusion was terminated, after 28.4.44, by the introduction of numbered pendants.

The badge was awarded in a blue box with cream base liner and gold lettering giving the type on the lid.

LONG RANGE NIGHT FIGHTER OPERATIONAL FLYING CLASP: BRONZE CLASS**

LONG RANGE NIGHT FIGHTER OPERATIONAL FLYING CLASP: SILVER CLASS***

LONG RANGE NIGHT FIGHTER OPERATIONAL FLYING CLASP: GOLD CLASS***

Known Makers: RK, B.S.W., R.S & S, S & S, F. & BL, M.KUNSTOFF, BSW (within a clover leaf), BWL (within a clover leaf), BWS, BWS (within a clover leaf), JMME & SOHN,
With the increase in bomber activity by the RAF during the night, there was a need to reward the night fighter squadrons who intercepted and destroyed the incoming bombers, so on 14.8.42 a new flying clasp was introduced. This takes the form of the previous one with a round wreath of laurel leaves, with a swastika at its base and sprigs of oak leaves on either side.

This time it has an arrow pointing downwards and the wreath is blackened in each grade to represent the darkness of the night. Again the number of missions for bronze with black wreath were 20, silver with black wreath 60 and gold with black wreath 110. In this case the star pendant represents 250 missions.

Again the badge was awarded in a blue box with a cream flocked base, the title being stencilled on the lid.

SHORT RANGE NIGHT FIGHTER OPERATIONAL FLYING CLASP: BRONZE CLASS**

SHORT RANGE NIGHT FIGHTER OPERATIONAL FLYING CLASP: SILVER CLASS**

SHORT RANGE NIGHT FIGHTER OPERATIONAL FLYING CLASP: GOLD CLASS***

Known Makers: RK, B.S.W., R.S & S, S & S, F. & BL, M.KUNSTOFF, BSW (within a clover leaf), BWL (within a clover leaf), BWS, BWS (within a clover leaf), JMME & SOHN
With the increase in air activity over occupied Europe, there was a need to reward the night fighter squadrons and again on 14.8.42 a new clasp was introduced. It is identical to the former clasps, with a wreath of laurels with an oak leaf sprig on either side. In this case also the wreath is blackened in all grades but the swastika is polished to show the colour of the grade. The central device is a winged arrow pointing upwards. The missions were 20 for bronze, 60 for silver and 110 for gold, with the star pendant representing 250 missions.

The badge was awarded in a blue box with cream flock base.

AIR TO GROUND SUPPORT OPERATIONAL FLYING CLASP: BRONZE CLASS***

AIR TO GROUND SUPPORT OPERATIONAL FLYING CLASP: SILVER CLASS***

AIR TO GROUND SUPPORT OPERATIONAL FLYING CLASP: GOLD CLASS****

Known Makers: RK, B.S.W., R.S & S, S & S, F. & BL, M. KUNSTOFF, BSW (within a clover leaf), BWL (within a clover leaf), BWS, BWS (within a clover leaf), JMME & SOHN
With the war in Russia taking a terrific toll on men and machinery, a new form of air war was

devised and this needed a special badge to reward the fliers who had so successfully damaged the Russian armour. So, on 20.4.44, a new clasp was introduced for these tank busters which, as in the former badges, comprises a laurel wreath with a swastika at its base and an oak leaf sprig on either side. The central device of this badge is a pair of crossed swords which have a double edge, central fuller, straight quillon and triangular pommel.

Again the number of missions required for the badge were, bronze 20, silver 60 and gold 110. As with the other clasps the star pendant, as described earlier, was attached to represent additional flights above the 110 required for the gold class. As the change from the star pendant to the box showing the number of flights and the intro-duction of the badge were within 17 days of each other, it is unlikely that you will encounter this badge with the star pendant which would have represented 400 missions but with the pendant with just the numbers. Because of the lateness of the introduction of this badge, this is a rare award and much rarer with a pendant attached.

It was awarded in a blue box with a cream base, with the type stencilled on the lid in gold.

Plate 117   Obverse Short Range Night Fighter Operational Flying Clasp-Gold Class with 1300 pendant.

Plate 118   Obverse Air to Ground Support Operational Flying Clasp-Gold Class with 300 Pendant.

117

118

6. Naval War Badges 1939-45

U-BOAT WAR BADGE FIRST WORLD WAR***

Known Makers

With the growth of importance of submarine warfare in WW1, the Kaiser belatedly instituted a War Badge in January 1918, to denote submarine personnel. This comprises an oval badge with laurel leaves running round its rim, surmounted by an Imperial crown. The base of the wreath is decorated with crossed ribbons. Through this oval badge is a submarine that had been used in WW1. This badge was to be worn in WW2 and could be worn in conjunction with its WW2 counterpart.

Dönitz wore this badge with great pride, in conjunction with his diamond version. Incidentally, this WW1 badge had no revised award status and was unusual in award badges of the Third Reich, as promotion through the classes of medals and badges usually required the recipient to receive the new award in its Third Reich form. For example, a pilot in WW1 who was an operational pilot in WW2 did not wear his first badge but the modern 1935 version. Notable exceptions to this were pilots and observers of the old Imperial Austrian Air Force who held those qualification badges. Upon the incorporation of the shrunken Austria into the greater Reich, those personnel who were recalled to the colours were allowed to fly on their original awards. However, the flying awards of the Austrian Republic which had been created after WW1 were banned.

Plate 119 Obverse U-Boat War Badge First World War.

U-BOAT WAR BADGE: FIRST TYPE**

Known Makers: Schwerin, G.W.L, R.K.

Hitler reinstituted the Submarine War Badge on 13.10.39. The badge was similar to that of the WW1 issue, except that the Imperial crown was substituted by the Third Reich emblem of the eagle and swastika, with the U-Boat being modified to a more modern type. The badge is oval and comprises a wreath of laurel leaves with a cross ribbon tie at the base. On either side are seven bunches of three leaves. The inner and outer edges of the wreath do not take the outline of the leaves. At the apex is an open winged eagle whose wings run between the two arms of the laurel bunches. The wings have four lines of fletch on each side while the body of the eagle has a small chest surmounted by a small head facing to the viewer's left. It clutches a small swastika in its talons. This can have the fields between the arms either voided or solid. Across the lower part of the badge is a submarine facing to the viewer's left. The badge measures 48mm across and is 39mm high from the base of the wreath to the top of the eagle's head. The wingspan is 31.5mm and the swastika measures 7.5mm across the tips. The construction of the badge varied due to war conditions. The best examples are of very high quality being struck in brass, with a very fine detail to the badge and segmented arms to the swastika.

The reverse is flat and on the back of the submarine in this type is usually found the maker's mark of Schwerin & Sohn of Berlin. Also on this type is a broad pin, with laid down hinge at the top and large hook at the bottom. The poorer quality badges were produced in pot metal with a needle pin, again with the maker's mark being stamped on to the reverse. The pot metal, which was gilded, quite often deteriorates to give a rather unpleasant appearance. The badge was designed by Paul Casberg of Berlin.

The CIC of the Navy, Grandadmiral Dr h.c. Erich Raeder, announced the introduction of the badge on 13.10.39 in Berlin where he stated 'I herewith order the institution of the Submarine War Badge for crew members of submarines in the Navy. The badges will be presented by the commanders of the submarines. The badge can be presented to all officers, NCOs and crew members who serve on submarines directed against the enemy and who prove themselves'.

The criteria for the award were:

- To have been involved in a particularly successful mission.
- To have completed or participated in more than three missions.
- To have won a bravery decoration in one of these missions, even if it was the first.
- To have been wounded on a mission, again even if it was the first mission or wound.
- The badge with citation was rendered to the next of kin of those lost at sea in a U-Boat due to enemy action.

The badge was to be worn on the service jacket, blue and white jacket, blue and white mess jacket, pullover and blue and white shirt, on the

Plate 120 Obverse U-Boat War Badge-First Type. Note the thin chest of the eagle and the form of the laurel leaves that make up the wreath.

Plate 121 Reverse U-Boat War Badge-First Type. This badge has been customised by the original recipient.

Plate 122 Obverse U-Boat War Badge-First Type variant. Note the heart shaped chest of the eagle and its wing profile. The laurel leaves of the wreath have a more pronounced form and the U-Boat has a deep water line, large deck gun, conning tower and flag. In this form the swastika is sometimes segmented.

Plate 123 Reverse U-Boat War Badge-First Type variant.

left side like the WW1 Submarine Badge. It was to be worn during duty and off duty hours.

The badge was awarded in a variety of manners. The brass high grade badges were usually awarded in a black, hinged box, with a black or blue velvet base, with a white silk lid lining. The poorer quality badges were awarded in paper packets. These are quite rare as they were seldom saved after the award ceremony.

There was provision for a cloth version of the badge and it came in two versions. Those for enlisted men and NCOs is gold cotton on a blue felt backing and the officers' version of the U-Boat Badge was not bullion embroidered. Perhaps a few one-off examples may exist of gold bullion which is worked on to a felt padded badge but these would be purely private purchase items. The type for officers was woven in Bevo style in gilt wire, on a blue silk oval backing. Both of these forms could be sewn on to naval uniforms but from the lack of availability of examples and

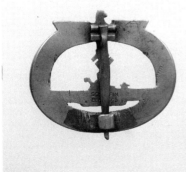

photographs of them in wear, it seems they must have been very unpopular with crew members.

U-BOAT WAR BADGE: FIRST TYPE: VARIATION**

Known Makers: F.O.
There are three or four slight variations in the production of the U-Boat War Badge but I have, for convenience, condensed them to two. The first badge is normally known as the Schwerin type and the second type, I have attributed to the French form of manufacture. The type which I have designated as this variant has three main characteristics separating it from its Schwerin counterpart. The first is in the design of the eagle's chest which has a pronounced heart or shield shape surmounted by bold symmetrical fletching. The second point to notice is that the laurel leaves which produce the wreath are more pronounced, the tips of those laurel leaves giving the impression of being worn. The central vein of each leaf is also more pronounced. The third point of reference is that of the submarine and there are a number of identifying points but they can be codified down to the deck gun, flag, conning tower and water line. Some of the finer quality badges have a segmented swastika but these are quite rare.

The reverse is plain with a horizontal hinge, hook and pin. The hinge is a rolled form of barrel and soldered directly on to the badge at the viewer's right. The needle pin is held to the hinge with the shepherd's crook form of attachment. The hook is of the 'C' type soldered directly to the reverse of the badge. The maker's mark is found in raised capital letters, 'F.O.' for Friedrich Orth. The badge measures 48.7mm across and is 39.6mm from the base to the top of the eagle's head.

Being but a variation, the criteria for award and method of wear are identical to those already described.

U-BOAT WAR BADGE WITH DIAMONDS A+B TYPES****

Known Makers: Schwerin
A special U-boat badge was produced to be awarded to particularly successful commanders. This badge followed the design of the standard award but had a separate swastika set with nine brilliants. This was placed on to the swastika incorporated into the design of the badge. The size of this swastika varied with manufacture and has been described as the 'A' and 'B' types. The 'A' type represents the badge as first awarded and the 'B' type was issued sometime in late 1942. The precise date of the change and the reasons for it are at present unclear. The firm that produced both types was Schwerin of Berlin.

The 'A' type badge was produced in tombac which was either gold-plated or fire gilded and on to the swastika of the badge was placed a swastika whose top point rests on the lower chest of the eagle and the bottom point is positioned on top of the conning tower of a type VII U-boat. This massive swastika is finely hand crafted from solid silver with burnished edges and raised and beaded individual grounds, each being bordered by a raised line in the form of a square, into which is set a rose-cut simulated stone or white sapphire set by four claws, one in each corner. The swastika is 13mm in diameter and 2mm in thickness. The badge measures 48mm in width and 38.5mm in height from the base of the wreath to the top of the eagle's head and is 3mm thick.

The reverse shows clearly the swastika applied over the cut out swastika of the badge. The holes that are drilled to allow the light to pass through, thus enhancing the fire of the brilliants, are reamed out to maximise the effect and its reverse is matt finished. The badge itself is flat with a large pin and hinge construction and a 'C' form hook soldered directly to the bottom of the badge. The maker's name, in indented capital letters, is on the reverse of the U-boat in two lines 'SCHWERIN, BERLIN 68'. On the two examples of this type I have examined, there is visible a claw line on either side.

The 'B' type badge is, to all intents and purposes, the same as the 'A' type badge but is struck in unmarked solid silver that is fire gilded. The swastika, applied to the badge in the same manner, is formed in the same way but has a diameter of 8.5mm and is inset with nine small rose-cut diamonds. The badge has similar measurements and reverse to that encountered on the 'A' type.

There is another version of this award badge which so far is unique. The wreath is a finer type. The eagle has a heart-shaped chest with broad fletching and its legs are separated to hold the swastika. This is set with nine rose-cut diamonds which are set directly into the arms of the swastika. The reverse is semi hollow with a thin square pin which has the silver content .800 stamped into it and the maker's mark L/21. In the example that has been examined, this is in a square which has been double-struck. This badge is of particularly high quality and was produced by the firm of Foerster & Barth. Few of these badges are known to exist and whether or not they were awarded or produced by that firm as prototypes for consideration for acceptance by the naval high command, is unknown.

To have qualified for the badge the recipient had to be a holder of the Knight's Cross of the Iron Cross with Oak Leaves. The 28 commanders who qualified and received this award are listed:
BRANDI Albrecht Fregattenkapitän U617, U967;
LUTH Wolfgang Kapitän zur See U138, U181;
RETSCHMER Otto Fregattenkapitän U99;

SUHREN Reinhard Fregattenkapitän U564; TOPP Erich Fregattenkapitän U552; BLEICHRODT Heinrich Korvettenkapitän U48, U109; von BULOW Otto Korvettenkapitän U404; EMMER-MANN Carl Korvettenkapitän U172; ENDRASS Engelbert Kapitänleutnant U46, U567; GUGGEN-BERGER Freidrich Kapitänleutnant U81; GYSAE Robert Korvettenkapitän U98, U177; HARDE-GEN Reinhard Korvettenkapitän U123; HART-MANN Werner Kapitän zur See U37, U198; HENKE Werner Korvettenkapitän U515; LANGE Hans-Gunther Kapitänleutnant U711; LASSEN Georg Korvettenkapitän U160; LEHMAN-WIL-LENBROCK Heinrich Fregattenkapitän U96; LIEBE Heinrich Fregattenkapitän U38; MOHR Johann Korvettenkapitän U124; MUTZELBURG Rolf Kapitänleutnant U203; MERTEN Karl Frei-drich Kapitän zur See U68; SCHEPKE Joachim Kapitänleutnant U100; SCHNEE Adalbert Korvet-tenkapitän U201; SCHOLTZ Klaus Kapitän zur See U108; SCHUTZE Victor Kapitän zur See U103; SCHULTZE Herbert Korvettenkapitän U48; THOMSEN Rolf Kapitänleutnant U1202; PRIEN Gunther Korvettenkapitän U47.

This prestigious award was not a government or Reich award but one which was purely from the commander of the navy.

It has been reported that Reichsmarschall Göring received a badge in acknowledgement for his award to Grandadmiral Dönitz of the Com-bined Pilots Badge with Diamonds and this event is described in the section concerning that award. Whether or not a formal bestowal of the U-Boat Badge with Diamonds followed this occurrence is unknown. The award would have been made begrudgingly by Dönitz, as it contra-vened his intended award criteria for this badge. In correspondence with me, Dönitz stated he had no recollection of receiving the Combined Pilots Badge with Diamonds or the German Order which he had also supposedly been awarded by Hitler.

The badge was rendered in a protective black or exceptionally dark blue box, which is hinged with a press-stud holder. The base of the box has a raised plinth on which the badge sits. Through this plinth is a slit to take the pin. In the case of the Schwerin badge that I examined, the lining was of a very dark blue but it was black velvet in the case of the Foerster & Barth badge. The lid liner in both was of white satin but neither had the maker's name or logo stencilled on to them.

U-BOAT COMBAT CLASP: BRONZE CLASS***

U-BOAT COMBAT CLASP: SILVER CLASS****

Known Makers: Ausf/Schwerin/Berlin 68

These two badges are identical except for the colour applied to them. In the case of the bronze badge, the colour is applied to the badge and arti-ficially patinated. The silver badge has a form of silver plating that is then frosted, with the high-lights gently polished. The silver plating often lessens the distinction of the design of this badge, filling the fine die striking and diminish-ing the crispness of its lines. The badge com-prises a small U-Boat Badge measuring 30mm by 24mm, with an eagle with downswept wings at the top of the laurel wreath. The wings of the eagle follow the line of the wreath. The ribbon ties at the base of the wreath are replaced by crossed swords, indicating the combat worth of the decoration. These are broad bladed with a double edge and central fuller. The handles have four lines making up the grip, round pommels and broad straight quillons. From either side of the swords, which themselves rest on an unadorned field, are five bunches of three laurel leaves. The inner and outer edges of the wreath formed by them do not follow their line but have solid, symmetrical ones. The central badge or wreath is flanked on either side by oak leaves, consisting of three rows with two leaves in each row. The upper and lower rows have smaller oak leaves. The length of the badge measures 76.5mm and the width of the leaves is 15mm. The badge is gently bowed along its length to allow for a comfortable fit to the chest.

The reverse is flat with an integral hinge and a 'C' form hook recessed into the body of the badge, with a circular mark that is then moulded up to the stem of the 'C'. The pin is of a large conflagration and goes horizontally across the badge, usually from right to left. The structure of the pin is usually fluted. The maker and original designer of the badge was Peekhaus and the logo is found on the reverse of the badge in raised capital letters on either side of the central wreath.

On 15.5.44 the high command of the navy introduced the U-Boat Combat Clasp in Bronze. This was done to follow and come in line with, the army and the Luftwaffe. It was to commemo-rate and recognise greater courage performed by the U-Boat service. When one comes to consider that something close to 90% of crews of U-Boats were lost at sea and that the personnel of those boats were all volunteers, it brings one to con-sider the bravery and valour that this decoration was instituted to commemorate. On 24.11.44, a silver grade was introduced for further acts of

Plate 124 Obverse U-Boat War Badge with Diamonds by Schwerin. Note this badge was awarded to Kaptain zur See Wolfgang Luth.

Plate 125 Reverse U-Boat War Badge with Diamonds showing the maker's mark in two lines and the swastika plate carrying the diamonds surmounting the integral swastika of the badge.

Plate 126 Obverse U-Boat War Badge with Diamonds by Schwerin with small swastika. Note: This was awarded to Kapitän Zur. See Klaus Scholtz.

Plate 127 Obverse U-Boat War Badge with Diamonds variant by Foster & Barth. The stones in this badge are genuine diamonds as opposed to brilliants.

Plate 128 Reverse U-Boat War Badge with Diamonds variant showing the maker's stamp on the pin, L/21.

Plate 129 Obverse U-Boat Combat Clasp-Bronze Class.

Plate 130 Reverse U-Boat Combat Clasp-Bronze Class.

Plate 131 Obverse Destroyers War Badge-First Type.

Plate 132 Reverse Destroyers War Badge-First Type. Note the badge on the left has a horizontal needle pin and the maker's mark S.H.U. Co. in raised capitals, while that on the right has the broad bellied pin which is stamped 4. The long upper hook is unusual as it appears to have not been cropped to the correct length. However at least two badges like this have been observed.

Plate 133 Obverse Destroyers War Badge-Second Type.

Plate 134 Reverse Destroyers War Badge-Second Type.

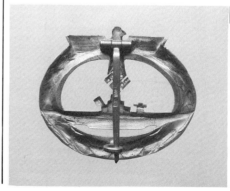

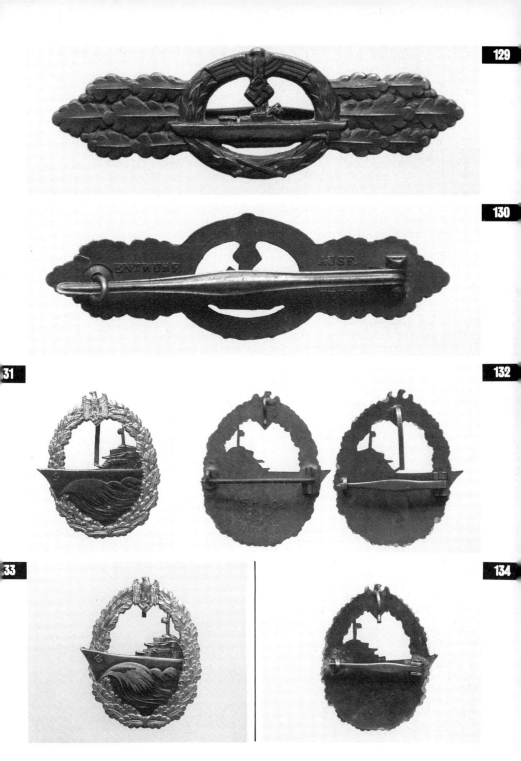

129

130

131

132

133

134

77

valour and a gold version of the badge was produced. There was no authorisation for the gold class but it may, in due course, come to light. No recorded examples of the gold class are known.

The exact details of the criteria for the award of either of these badges is uncertain and on corresponding with Admiral Dönitz about the matter, he replied that it was 'to be something of the greatest bravery'. Award was determined by the recommendation of the U-boat commander. He was to take into account the number of trips the members of his crew had undertaken and the danger encountered in the prosecution of each sortie. The personal bravery of any crew member was also taken into account. In effect therefore the criteria could vary with each U-boat engagement. Actual award was not made until each recommendation had received the personal approval of Grandadmiral Dönitz. The clasp was to be considered as having the equivalent value of the War Merit Cross First Class with Swords. It was worn on the upper left breast above the ribbon bar.

It was awarded in a plain paper packet with the name printed on the front. The silver class was sometimes awarded in an oblong blue card box, with a blue flock lining.

DESTROYERS WAR BADGE: FIRST TYPE**

Known Makers: 4, 4 (in square), 14, FO, JFS, Schwerin, S.H.u.C.o, W

The badge consists of an oval wreath of oak leaves with a crossed ribbon tie at the base. Each arm of the wreath meets at the apex with a small closed winged eagle positioned between them. The wreath has two leaves emanating horizontally, one from either side of the ties. Above each horizontal leaf is the tip of a single leaf and from this formation, on either side, are six bunches of two leaves irregularly positioned and crowned by a single leaf that touches the outer edge of the eagle's wing. The outer edge of the wreath takes the line of the jagged edges of the individual leaves. A destroyer comes through the wreath with its superstructure joining the inner edge of the right-hand side of the wreath and its prow breaking the left-hand side. Beneath the prow is a large bow wake, indicating that the destroyer is travelling at high speed in a heavy sea. The wreath is gilded and the ship and sea are an oxidised dark black silver, with some of the highlights being brightly polished. The badge measures 54mm from the base to the top of the eagle's head and 45mm across the badge from the tip of the prow to the opposite side of the wreath. The wreath itself is 7mm wide.

The reverse is plain and slightly concave and this badge can have a variety of hinges and hooks. When the pin construction is horizontal, there is usually a small hook positioned behind the eagle's body at the top of the badge. This is employed to hook through a small cotton eyelet on the tunic to maintain the badge in an upright and secure position. The reverse is blackened and the maker's name can be encountered in raised capital letters, as can the logo of the individual firm.

The designer of the badge was Paul Casberg of Berlin and it was first produced in bronze and then later, due to war constraints, in zinc or pot metal.

A cloth version was authorised for wear on the dark blue uniform and consisted of the badge produced in all gold thread on a dark blue wool.

On 4.6.40 this badge was introduced by Grandadmiral Erich Raeder, on the demand of the Oberbefehlshaber der Kriegsmarine during the battle of Narvik. This badge was initially to reward the crews under the command of Commodore Bonte involved in the battle. It was awarded in conjunction with the Narvik Shield, and was a separate distinction from the Shield.

In an order dated 22.10.40, award and authorisation for the wear of the badge was extended to crew members of other destroyers or vessels that could be described as such and comprised torpedo boats and E-boats. Following the initial singular awards for participation in the battle of Narvik a crew member needed to meet the qualifying requirements before he could receive the award.

The criteria for the award were:
- To have been wounded.
- To have served on a ship sunk by enemy action.
- To participate in three separate engagements with the enemy.
- To complete 12 operational sorties without enemy action.
- To have performed an heroic action for which no other decoration had been awarded.

The badge was worn on the lower left breast of the naval uniform, underneath the Iron Cross First Class or similar award.

In the early days of the war it was presented in a blue box with blue velvet base and white silk lid lining and later, in a plain paper packet which can be found in the usual three or four colours, with the name printed in black on the front.

DESTROYERS WAR BADGE: SECOND TYPE**

Known Makers: Mourgeon (Paris)

This badge was produced in France and is very similar in design to its previously described German counterpart, with the notable exception that it has the variation oak leaf pattern leaves comprising the wreath of this badge, as do the other badges of this type of French production. In this version the ship, which is in the form of a destroyer, is more finely worked and the detail is more greatly enhanced. The eagle surmounting the badge is identical to the one in the former. The badge measures 54mm from the base to the tip of the eagle's head and 44.5mm from the tip of the prow to the outside of the wreath, while the wreath measures 8mm at its widest point.

The reverse has the French style pin, hinge and hook. The hinge comprises of two parallel pieces of thin metal that have a semicircular outer end, while the inner ones are flat and held apart by a vertical small piece that doubles up and acts as a rest for the pin. The two parallel pieces of metal are drilled and have a large headed brass pin placed through them to act as a pivot for the pin. The pin is a flat bellied one that tapers to the point. The hook is of the 'C' form soldered directly to the reverse of the badge. The pin, hook and hinge are placed on the badge in a horizontal configuration and at the top is placed a hook that is employed to fit through a loop sewn on to the tunic that holds the badge securely to the uniform. The reverse of the badge is slightly concave and flat and finished in a black oxidised finish that is treated over the pin assembly. Whereas on a number of these badges that comprise the French type of German naval award the negative imprint of the obverse is found in the reverse, it is not noticed on this type. The badge was worn in the same relative position on the naval tunic as that described in the previous badge.

The award criteria for this badge is identical to that already described. The container in which these badges are encountered is a buff box which comprises a separate bottom and lid with the corners stapled together. The badge inside is found wrapped in tissue paper.

MINE SWEEPERS, SUB-CHASERS AND ESCORT VESSELS WAR BADGE*

Known Makers: A, AS, AS (in triangle), R.K., Schwerin, W (in a circle), WH
This badge takes the form of a chemically blued silver water spout rising from the waves of the sea, with the outer edge being formed by a wreath of laurel leaves. The inner and outer edges of the wreath take the line of the leaves which form it. The bottom has a tie formed in three raised lines, with four acorns positioned one at each corner. From the tie emanate seven bunches of two oak leaves that are positioned irregularly to form the wreath, with a single oak leaf at the apex. Each juncture of bunches is punctuated by a pair of acorns, one on either side of the wreath.

This is surmounted by a broad winged eagle clutching a swastika in its claws. The badge mea-

sures 54mm from the base to the top of the eagle's head. The width of the badge is 43.5mm and the width of the wreath is 7.5mm. The eagle's wingspan is 28mm. Another version of this badge has measurements of 56mm, 45mm, 8mm and 30mm.

On the reverse is a large pin which is usually vertical but it is encountered in the horizontal position. The horizontal form has a hook behind the eagle which helped to fix the badge to the uniform through a small cotton stitch. This had the double effect of keeping the badge flat to the tunic at the top and should the pin have become open and free from the tunic, the badge hung from this cotton loop. Usually these horizontal pins are of the thin needle type. Most badges carry the maker's logo or address on the reverse and are finished with a silver backing while others, usually of a later production, are gilded.

The quality of these badges varies. The highest quality badges are formed of brass, finely detailed with a segmented swastika, the wreath being finely gilded and the water spout, and in some examples the sea waves, silver-plated, the waves being then chemically blued or blackened. The lesser quality examples are of zinc, pot or monkey metal which were poorly struck with a very inferior finish.

A cloth version was authorised for wear on the dark blue uniform and consists of the wreath being executed in yellow cotton and the water spout and sea in silver cotton thread, all on a blue backing.

Grandadmiral Raeder directed Otto Placzek to create a special badge for mine sweepers. The badge was instituted on 31.8.40 for officers and ratings of the German Navy and its civilian Merchant Marine employed in its service. It was worn on the left breast of the service tunic, underneath the Iron Cross First Class or equivalent grade of award.

The criteria for the award were:
● When three operational sorties had been completed.
● If the recipient had been wounded during an operational sortie, even if it was his first.
● If the ship had been sunk due to enemy action.
● For exemplary conduct in the execution of his duties over a 6 month period.
● The completion of a specially dangerous mission in a mined area.
● A mission that comprised 25 days or more on escort duty.

The first award of this badge was made on 28.11.40. The award container varies widely to include a blue box with navy blue flocking base and silk lid liner, through to the paper packet which comes in various colours with the badge derivation printed on its front in black.

E-BOAT WAR BADGE: FIRST TYPE****

Known Makers: Schwerin

This badge was designed by Wilhelm Ernst Peekhaus of Berlin and was instituted on 30.5.41. The design of the badge consists of an oak leaf wreath which has a tie at the base and surmounting it at the top is an eagle clutching a swastika. It is interesting to note that the wings on this eagle are stubby. The tie is formed from a broad raised central spine with a small raised edge line on either side. From this emanate seven bunches of two oak leaves that are positioned in irregular order with a single acorn being positioned haphazardly at the junction of the leaves. Both the wreath and eagle are finely gilded. The badge measures 57mm from the base to the top of the eagle's head and 45mm across the badge. The wreath measures 7.5mm and the eagle's wingspan is 23.5mm, the height of the eagle and swastika being 14mm.

The main subject of the badge is an E-boat ploughing through the sea. The boat only comes to half-way through the wreath and is finished in silver. The sea is blue-black with the crests of the waves being burnished silver.

The reverse of the badge in the most desirable examples has a scolloped effect on the reverse of the E-boat and the reverse of the wreath is flat. On this form of manufacture the manufacturer's name and address is found in two lines, in small raised capital letters, 'SCHWERIN BERLIN 68'. It usually has a horizontal pin. When this is the case, a small hook can be found which helped to secure the badge to the uniform. It also can be found with a vertical pin construction and in this case the reverse of the badge is normally flat. Also, in rarer examples, the maker's address or logo can be found. The badge was worn on the left breast pocket, beneath the Iron Cross First Class or like award.

The criteria for the award were:
- 12 sorties against enemy vessels or installations.
- Outstanding leadership.
- A particularly successful mission.
- To have been wounded in the course of an action, even if this was the first.

The badge was usually presented in a blue box with a blue flock base, with white silk lid liner and the badge title stencilled in silver on the outer upper lid of the box. This badge was discontinued soon after its inception and therefore it is considered very rare.

E-BOAT WAR BADGE: SECOND TYPE**

Known Makers: AS, AS (in a triangle), R.K., R.S., Schwerin, W. E. Peekhaus

The wreath of this badge has a flatter base and the oak leaves are of a smaller and more delicate design. The tie has a more pronounced central spine and the two outer lines are wider and join the central spine with a very fine line. The eagle that surmounts the wreath is much larger and in comparison with the stumpy winged version of the First Pattern Badge, it has a longer wingspan. The swastika in this badge is found in two distinct styles, which can either be of a solid construction or cut out between the arms and it is placed beneath the inner edge line of the wreath.

The other main distinguishing factor to be found is that in this type the E-boat, which takes the form of a more modern boat, is cutting through a sea which comprises three distinct, low waves. This time the boat breaks the wreath so that the prow forms part of the outer edge design, while the bow wake breaks the outer edge of the wreath on the opposite side. The badge measures 60mm from the base to the top of the eagle's head and 53mm across the badge from the tip of the prow to the edge of the bow wake. The wreath measures 8mm and the eagle's wingspan is 36.5mm, with the height of the eagle and swastika being 20mm.

The reverse has the maker's logo or address on it with a horizontal or vertical pin. Again in the case of the horizontal pin the little hook is found at the top, which safeguarded the attachment to the tunic as previously described.

This is another badge designed by Wilhelm Ernst Peekhaus of Berlin but this time it was in conjunction with Korvettenkapitän Rudolf Peterson and the resultant design was introduced into service in January 1943. It was worn on the left breast pocket, underneath the Iron Cross First Class or like award.

The criteria for this award were identical to those of the previous two badges.

It was presented in a blue box with blue flock base and white silk lid liner, through to the paper packet in varying colours with the derivation of the badge printed in black on the front.

E-BOAT WAR BADGE: THIRD TYPE**

Known Makers: Mourgeon (Paris)

This badge is of the French constructed type with the distinctive wreath, eagle and swastika which surmount it. The badge is of the same general design as that of the E-Boat Badge First Type. The badge measures 55mm from the base to the top of the eagle's head and 41mm across. The width of the wreath is 7mm, the eagle's wingspan is 27mm, and the height of the eagle and swastika are 14mm.

The reverse is hollow struck and has the distinctive French pin, hinge and hook construction. The whole of the reverse is silvered.

The concept of German badges being produced in France is quite logical, considering that the

German navy was based right around the coast. This would enable the naval personnel to purchase the badges locally.

The criteria for this Award were identical to those of the previous two badges.

The container in which the badge was awarded was a buff box in two parts with the edges stapled together and the badge was wrapped in white tissue paper.

HIGH SEAS FLEET WAR BADGE: FIRST TYPE**

Known Makers: Adolf Bock, Schwerin, Friedrich Orth

This badge has as its central design the head on view of a German navy capital ship at full steam, ploughing through a sea and producing a bow wave. This is passing through an oak leaf wreath, with a large winged eagle at the top of the wreath. The base of the wreath has a ribbon tie in the form of an 'X' with an acorn in the upper and lower V formed by the tie and, on either side, are eight bunches of two oak leaves. The tip of each leaf has a single acorn that is positioned to the outer or inner edge of the wreath. The height of the badge from the base to the top of the eagle's head is 57mm and the width is 44mm, with the width of the wreath being 7mm. The eagle's wingspan is 31mm. The wreath is gilded and the ship and sea are dark oxidised silver, with some of the highlights being polished. Also, the gilt on the wreath tends to be absorbed, giving the appearance of having a silver wreath and this should not be confused with a variant type, that is to say a badge with a gold wreath and a badge with a silver wreath.

The reverse of the badge is flat with a dished effect behind the battleship. There are a number of types of hinges and pins, while the hooks are nearly always of the 'C' form. The reverse is blackened along with the hinge, pin and hook assemblies. The badges by Bock and Schwerin are of particularly high quality with heavy pins and quality hinge and hook construction, while those of Friedrich Orth tend to be of inferior quality, with a thin needle pin. In the case of this maker the hook is cast in with the badge and, as the badge gets older, this tends to crystallise. In this brittle state it is very prone to being broken off. A cloth version was authorised to be worn on the blue uniform and consists of a yellow cotton wreath and eagle, while the battleship and sea are worked in grey cotton with the highlights in lighter grey or off-white cotton thread.

This badge was introduced on 30.4.41 at the direction of Grandadmiral Raeder, who at the time was CIC of the navy, to recognise the sea actions in which the German navy had been employed against the British navy. The designer of the badge and principal maker, was Adolf Bock of Berlin. It was worn on the left breast pocket, underneath the Iron Cross First Class or like award.

The criteria for the award were:
● 12 weeks service on a battleship or cruiser.
● This could be reduced if the recipient had been wounded during the 12 week cruise.
● If the cruise had been successful.
● For service with the high seas fleet, but for which no other award badge could be given.

The award of the High Seas Fleet War Badge could be rendered upon the recommendation of the ship's captain and approved by a commodore or a rear-admiral.

The container in which the badge was awarded was a blue box with blue flock base and white silk lid lining, with the name of the badge stencilled in silver on the lid top, while the inferior quality badges were presented in a grey paper packet with the badge derivation printed on the front.

HIGH SEAS FLEET WAR BADGE: SECOND TYPE**

Known Makers: Mourgeon (Paris)

This badge is identical in all respects to that of the former badge, the difference being in the construction and in the fact that this badge was produced in France. The difference lies in the way that the wreath is produced. In this case the oak leaves are of a more offset pattern giving a rougher appearance to both the inner and outer edges of the wreath. The eagle has a rounder form of fletching to the underside of the wing and the actual wingspan of the eagle that surmounts the wreath is reduced. The badge measures 55mm from the base to the top of the eagle's head, the width is 41mm and that of the wreath 8mm. The eagle's wingspan is 27mm.

The reverse is semi-stamped and there is a horizontal hinge, pin and hook of the French style which has been previously described, with a hook mounted behind the eagle. Again this is to facilitate the badge's safety as well as appearance on a tunic. The reverse is finished in silver. This range of French badges are scarce and desirable.

The criteria for the award were identical to the previous badge. The form of container is similar again to the former in the fact that it is a buff box with the corners stapled together.

HIGH SEAS FLEET WAR BADGE WITH DIAMONDS*****

Known Makers

An example of the High Seas Fleet War Badge First Type was produced in solid silver .800 grade. The swastika in this badge is slightly

Plate 135 Obverse Mine Sweepers, Sub-Chasers & Escort Vessels War Badge.

Plate 136 Reverse Mine Sweepers, Sub-Chasers & Escort Vessels War Badge illustrating two forms of hinge, hook and pin construction.

Plate 137 Obverse E-Boat War Badge First Type.

Plate 138 Reverse E-Boat War Badge-First Type.

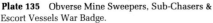

136

Plate 139 Obverse E-Boat War Badge-Second Type. Both badges are from the same manufacturer, however that on the left has no flag and mast. The rear deck is flat and finished with the silver coating.

Plate 140 Reverse E-Boat War Badge-Second Type.

Plate 141 Obverse E-Boat War Badge-Third Type.

Plate 142 Reverse E-Boat War Badge-Third Type.

Plate 143 Obverse High Seas Fleet War Badge-First Type.

Plate 144 Reverse High Seas Fleet War Badge-First Type.

enlarged and 14 rose-cut diamonds are set directly into this. The reason for the production of this badge is unsure but it is considered that it was produced to reward Knight's Cross winners with Oak Leaves when they had been engaged in naval activities which would have gained them the High Seas Fleet War Badge. This would have then logically come in line with the other diamond beset medals for the other branches of the naval service, that is to say the Submarine Badge with Diamonds, and E-Boat Badge with Diamonds, Mine Sweepers, Sub Chasers and Escort Vessels War Badge with Diamonds and Destroyers War Badge with Diamonds. However, no action from the German high fleet facilitated the award of the Oak Leaves to the Knight's Cross, so the award never became necessary. Thus the badge is still surrounded in uncertainty.

Plate 145 Obverse High Seas Fleet War Badge-Second Type.

Plate 146 Reverse High Seas Fleet War Badge-Second Type.

Plate 147 Obverse High Seas Fleet War Badge with Diamonds.

7. Army and Waffen SS War Badges 1939-45

INFANTRY ASSAULT BADGE: SILVER CLASS*

INFANTRY ASSAULT BADGE: BRONZE CLASS*

Known Makers: B.W.S. (within clover leaf), JFS, L.C.F., S.H.u.C.o., WH, L/56

Both types of this badge consist of an oak leaf wreath surmounted by a downswept winged eagle, clutching a swastika in its talons. Across the wreath, pointing from right to left, with the butt just breaking the lower edge of the wreath, is a Kar98 rifle with a fixed bayonet, the point of which extends past the edge of the wreath. The rifle sling forms a loop from the stock to the butt. The wreath comprises four single oak leaves on either side, with two acorns situated at the tip of each leaf. The tie at the base is formed by a piece of ribbon that is vertical and gives the impression of running behind the badge. On to the ribbon are placed five individual raised pellets. The general quality of the design and manufacture is of the highest and there were many manufacturers and similarly many techniques employed in the manufacture of this badge. Considering its liberal award, these badges have a most pleasing design.

I have been able to categorise the silver badges into two main types, solid reverse and hollow stamping. Both categories are of good quality and the silver plating shiny, with the highlights being silver frosted. The bronze version, on the other hand, tends to absorb its colour and does not have the same attractive appearance. The highlighted or leading edges of the badge tend to lighten and give it the appearance of being very well worn, although the metal surface may not show any indication of having been worn.

The pin construction is usually of a needle type and of a vertical nature. Screw backs, however, are encountered and are considered to be more unusual, although this scarcity does not tend to increase the monetary value of the badge in proportion.

The badge was designed by C. E. Juncker of Berlin under the direction of the OKH and was instituted in the silver form on 20.12.39 by Generaloberst von Brauchitsch. The bronze form was introduced on 1.6.40 and was to reward the

members of motorised infantry units. It was worn on the lower breast on all uniform tunics, however wear on the greatcoat was not authorised.

The criteria for the award were:

Silver Award:
- To have taken part in three or more infantry assaults.
- To have taken part in three or more infantry counter-attacks or the combination of this and the above.
- To have taken part in three or more armed reconnaissance operations.

148

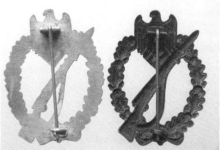

149

Plate 148 Obverse Infantry Assault Badge-Silver Class.

Plate 149 Reverse Infantry Assault Badge-Silver & Bronze Classes. Note the solid and hollow striking that can be encountered in either class.

- To have been engaged in hand to hand combat in an assault position.
- To have participated on three separate days in the restitution of combat positions.

Bronze Award:
- To have taken part in three or more motorised infantry assaults.
- To have taken part in three or more motorised infantry counter-attacks or the combination of this and the above.
- To have taken part in three or more motorised armed reconnaissance operations.
- To have been engaged in hand to hand combat in a motorised assault position.
- To have participated on three separate days in the restitution of the motorised combat position.

A cloth version of this badge was permitted and can be found on printed linen. The badge itself was usually presented in a simple paper packet, with the designation of the award printed on it.

SILVER TANK BATTLE BADGE*

Known Makers: A, AS, A.W.S. 1942, H (over stirrup), R.K., R.R.S., WM (within a circle), W, FRANK & REIF

This award consists of an oval wreath of oak leaves positioned between two tramlines that form straight edges to the wreath. At the base is a tie formed from an outer raised edge line that is convexed and between these two lines is a raised thicker, straight sided tie, that is slightly semi-circular. From this emanates five single oak leaves on either side. At the apex is an eagle with downspread wings, clutching a swastika in its talons. This form of eagle is commonly known as the army type. A tank passes through the wreath from left to right from the viewer's position. The tank's left-hand track obliterates the wreath and just breaks its outer line. The field beneath the tank is struck to represent a grass field.

The reverse of the badge can be found in three distinct types. The first type is flat and semi dished. The main portions of the badge of the second type are flat, while the reverse of the tank is slightly indented showing part of the outline. The third type is a die striking that shows the negative of the obverse. There are a number of methods by which the hinge and hook are attached to the body of the badge. In the first two forms a circular ball hinge can be found that is inserted into the body of the badge, as well as a more normal form of hinge that is inserted into a rectangle that then has the edges folded over. The pin, in all three styles, is normally of the thin needle pin type. The general construction and manufacture of this badge was of a very good quality but the finish of the plating deteriorated with the advance of the war. Early pieces were

Plate 150   Obverse Silver Tank Battle Badge.

Plate 151   Reverse Silver Tank Battle Badge. Observe the scollop and hollow striking.

silver-plated while later versions had a silver wash over their component metal, which was normally of a zinc alloy type.

The badge was designed by Ernst Peekhaus of Berlin and introduced on 20.12.39 by the order of Generaloberst von Brauchitsch and could be awarded to drivers, radio operators, gunners and tank commanders. It was worn on the lower left breast of all uniform tunics. However, wear on the greatcoat was not authorised.

The criteria for the award were:

● To have taken part in three armoured assaults on three different days.
● To have been wounded in an assault.
● To have won a decoration for bravery in an assault.

The badge was awarded in a simple paper packet which came in various colours, with the name printed on the front. One cautionary note is that the hollow striking has been very well copied as recently as 1992 and great scepticism must be employed when purchasing this scarcer form.

SILVER TANK BATTLE BADGE: 25 CLASS***

SILVER TANK BATTLE BADGE: 50 CLASS***

Known Makers: JFS, RK, GB

In June 1943 it was considered that the Tank Battle Badge did not properly recognise the competence of the long serving members of crews of the armoured forces. A new design was introduced to counteract this deficiency. This comprised an oval wreath of oak leaves with an army style eagle and swastika at the apex and an oblong box to replace the tie at the base. Fitted into this box was a further box with raised outer edge line and on to the recessed field, either the raised Arabic numerals '25' or '50' to represent the numbers of engagements undertaken by the recipient. Over the wreath is a tank whose tracks break the outer edge. This tank is a separate striking that is fixed to the wreath. The tank is coloured black, while the wreath has a silver wash applied.

There are three distinct types of manufacture of these badges and I have categorised them as a), b) and c):

a) The wreath has an outer and inner raised edge line and measures 6mm across. At the base is an oblong base with chamfered edges which measures 10mm by 8mm, with a further recessed box measuring 8mm by 6mm which has a 0.5mm raised outer edge line. The recessed field is blackened, while the raised numerals and edge line are finished in gilt. From the box, on either side, six single raised oak leaves that run inside the tramlines without touching them. At the tip of each leaf and positioned on either side, is a large single acorn. The uppermost leaf just touches the outer edge of the eagle's wing. This wingspan measures 20.5mm and 26mm from the tip of the swastika to the top of the eagle's head. The width of the swastika is 11.5mm. The area between the inner edge of the wing and the eagle's leg is voided. The whole of the body of the wreath is plated a silver colour over a zinc badge.

The tank is a separate stamping and fixed over the body of the wreath, so that the left track breaks the outer edge of the wreath. The tank is struck three-dimensionally and measures 41mm across its widest point. On the side of the turret there is an oblong observation plate formed by a stamped line.

The reverse is flat with a 'V' shaped indentation where the swastika is formed. The hinge is fixed by means of two slots at either end that are turned over to secure the base of the hinge to the body of the wreath. The hook is fastened to the base by a circular plate. The pin is of the broad blade, bellied type. There are two small ball rivets attaching the tank to the body of the badge. On the right-hand edge of the wreath can sometimes be found the makers marks of either the raised capitals 'JFS' in a raised square, or raised 'RK'. The badge is often encountered unmarked.

b) The wreath has the same measurements as a), as does the box at the base. The eagle's wingspan is 21mm and the swastika is 11.5 mm wide. The area between the inner edge of the wing and the eagle's leg is also voided. Through the wheel hub of the first small track wheel can be found the head of the rivet securing it to the wreath with a similar rivet at the base of the track guard on the other side of the badge. The tank is constructed in a similar manner and has the same measurements as a). The turret has the oblong observation plate but, in this case, the central field is recessed.

The reverse is hollow with a flat, semicircular area. The hinge is of the barrel type and soldered directly into a rectangular raised box. This rectangular box is nothing more than a guideline for the artisan to position the base of the hinge, thus making construction easier. The hook is of the 'C' type, soldered on to a circular plate that is fixed to the body of the badge just above the indentation of the numbered oblong box. The pin is of the needle type. There are two ball rivets positioned on either side of the semicircular area. The reverse of the tank shows more of the negative of the obverse than in a). This type of badge rarely shows any makers' marks, if any.

c) The measurements of this type are the same as the two former ones, the main difference being in the area between the inner edge of the wing and the eagle's leg. This is solid in this type. The swastika is slightly smaller, measuring 10.5mm. The turret has the oblong observation box and the central field is recessed.

The reverse is hollow, with the same semicircular area. The hinge in this type is a piece of thin metal that is bent over to produce the structure and then soldered to a rectangular box, which is then positioned directly on to the wreath. The pin is of the thin needle type that is bent over to form the method of attachment as well as to form a spring to hold the pin tight under the hook. This form of pin resembles a

Plate 152 Obverse Silver Tank Battle Badge-25 Class. Note the stamping of the eagle and swastika.

Plate 153 Obverse Silver Tank Battle Badge-50 Class. Note the voided areas between the eagle's body and wings.

Plate 154 Reverse Silver Tank Battle Badge-25 & 50 Classes. Observe the construction of the wreath and the variation in the form of riveting.

Plate 155 Obverse Silver Tank Battle Badge-75 & 100 Classes.

Plate 156 Reverse Silver Tank Battle Badge-75 & 100 Classes. These are the common reverses of both badges.

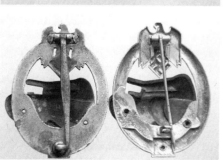

shepherd's crook. The hook is of the 'C' type that is soldered to an oblong plate, which is then soldered to the body of the badge and positioned above the recessed numeral box at the base. There are three open rivets, two positioned in the same relative places on the semicircular plate and one at the centre of the recessed rectangular box.

The reverse of the tank shows a deep, recessed negative of the obverse and, in line with the left-hand rivet on the semicircular plate, can be found the small, raised capitals, 'GB'.

There are many very slight variances in the obverse design of these three types but they are too small on their own to warrant in depth description but, conjoined, they produce three distinct types.

The badges were worn on the left breast pocket and each grade superseded the lower type, therefore, only one badge could be worn at any one time. The period of time for either the bronze or silver Tank Battle Badge counted together, thus if someone transferred from one form of mechanised armour to another, only one badge could be worn.

SILVER TANK BATTLE BADGE: 75 CLASS****

SILVER TANK BATTLE BADGE: 100 CLASS*****

Known Makers: RK, JFS

As the war progressed the need for even higher numbers of engagements to be recognised by the award became evident, giving rise to the inception of this badge. It takes a totally different style of design to that employed in the 25 and 50 class badges in that the oak leaves which form the outer edge of the wreath are cut out, so that both the inner and outer edges of the wreath take the line of the oak leaves, giving its outline a rough appearance. At the apex is a closed winged army style eagle, clutching a swastika in its talons. The base of the wreath is flatter, with an oak leaf spreading horizontally from each side of the oblong numeral box. These numerals are again Arabic and expressed as '75' and '100' and raised, while the field is recessed and blackened. The tank is silver and the wreath gilded.

Plate 157 Obverse Bronze Tank Battle Badge. This shows the differences in the design of the hollow struck compared to the scolloped and flat reverse types. This is to be extended to the study of the Silver Tank Battle Badge.

Plate 158 Reverse Bronze Tank Battle Badge. Note the hollow, scolloped and flat types. Again to be extended to the Silver Tank Battle Badge.

There are two distinct types of manufacture employed in the construction of these badges and I have categorised them as a) and b):

a) The wreath comprises of two horizontal oak leaves emanating one from either side of an oblong numeral box that measures 12mm by 9mm. This has a 1mm raised edge line. Into this is fixed a plate 9mm by 6.5mm with a raised 1mm edge line. The central field is recessed and on to this, in raised Arabic numerals, are the figures '75' or '100'. The width of the oak leaves and box, measured from the tip of each oak leaf, is 36mm. Rising from these horizontal leaves, on either side, is a single leaf followed by a bunch of two and this design is repeated once again to meet at the eagle's outer wing line. The first three leaf connections have two acorns, one on either side, while the upper leaf meets the eagle's wing without an acorn. The width of the wreath measures 7.25mm. The eagle has a wingspan of 20mm and the area between the inner line of the wings and the eagle's legs is voided. The eagle holds a swastika in its talons and this measures 10mm across. The height of the eagle and swastika is 23.5mm from the tip of the swastika to the top of the eagle's head. The height of the badge is 61mm from the base to the top of the eagle's head and the width across the badge, from the wreath to the edge of the tank track, is 50.25mm.

The tank is a separate piece fixed on to the body of the badge, so that the left-hand track just breaks the outer line of the wreath. The tank is not produced in as high relief as that in the lower grade badges but conforms to the same general design. The field upon which it is placed has a hammered area just above the oblong box and runs in a semicircle beneath the right-hand track. This field stands proud of the wreath and the oblong numeral box.

The reverse of the wreath is flat, with an oblong box at the apex. This has two lips, one at either end and under this is positioned the base of the hinge, with the lips turning over to hold the hinge. The hook is of the 'C' form, mounted on a plate that is then recessed into the body of the wreath at the base, with the edges being pushed over it to form a slight hump round the plate. The pin is of the broad blade type. There are two ball rivets that hold the tank to the wreath. On the right-hand side of the wreath can be found the makers' marks which are, in raised capital letters, 'JFS' in a square box or 'RK'. More often, the badges are found unmarked. The reverse of the tank shows a ghosted negative of the obverse.

b) The wreath in this type is similar to that found in a). The oblong numeral box measures 10.25mm by 8mm and the inner plate 8.25mm by 5.5mm, with each box having a raised 1mm edge line. The widths of the base and wreath are the same as for a), as are the dimensions of the eagle

159

160

161

162

Plate 159   Obverse Bronze Tank Battle Badge-25 Class. Note that this design should be extended in the Silver Tank Battle Badge-25 & 50 Classes.

Plate 160   Reverse Bronze Tank Battle Badge-25 Class. Note that this design should be extended in the Silver Tank Battle Badge-25 & 50 Classes.

Plate 161 |Obverse Bronze Tank Battle Badge-75 & 100 Classes. Observe the variation in the wreath, eagle and rivet in the 100 Class. This form of construction is encountered in the Silver Tank Battle Badge-75 & 100 Classes.

Plate 162   Reverse Bronze Tank Battle Badge-75 & 100 Classes. Note the wreath construction.

Plate 163   Obverse General Assault Badge.

Plate 164   Obverse General Assault Badge. Observe the voided swastika and area between the eagle's body and wings.

and swastika. The area between the wing and the eagle's leg in this case is not voided. The height of the badge is 59mm and the width across the badge from the wreath to the edge of the track is 49.25mm

The tank is a separate piece fixed on to the body of the badge so that the left-hand track just breaks the outer line of the wreath. The design of the tank is similar to that employed in a), however it is struck in lower profile. The main differences lie in the field beneath the tank, the hammered area being omitted and the field being lower than the wreath. At the centre of the hub of the second track wheel is a ball rivet, with a similar one beneath the track guard on the right-hand side.

The reverse of the wreath is hollow with a flat semicircular plate. At the neck of the eagle, where it meets the semicircles of the wing line, is an oblong box into which is placed a barrel hinge. At the base, above the recessed numeral box, is a 'C' form hook soldered on to a plate that is fastened on to the semicircle. The upper part of the plate is cut to the shape of the semicircle. The pin is of the needle type. There are two ball rivets on the semicircle and a further one at the centre of the recess of the oblong numeral box. The reverse of the tank shows a deep indentation of the negative of the obverse.

The badge was worn on the left breast pocket of the uniform and the higher number replaced the lower. The badge was presented in a simple paper packet in varying colours, with its name printed on the front. There were occasions when the badges were also presented in a plain brown cardboard box.

SILVER TANK BATTLE BADGE: 200 CLASS*****

Known Makers

Little is known of this badge or its recipients. I include a direct quote from *For Führer and Fatherland* Vol 1 by John Angolia 'This specimen bears a 200 device, is hallmarked on the reverse and is known to have been awarded in at least one case'. In conversation with the author, Angolia said that the recipient went into his shop and showed him the badge as well as the entry in his paybook, but was not prepared to part with the items. Gordon Williamson has located a former SS Panzer Jäge Hauptsturmführer who was also awarded the 200 Panzer Assault Badge. While I was at the Max Show in 1992 an American veteran, whilst viewing my exhibition, paid particular attention to the numbered awards. He informed me that I did not have a 200 Class and said that he had taken such a piece from a German in the closing days of WW2. Unfortunately, he was unprepared to send it to me for inspection and verification.

BRONZE TANK BATTLE BADGE*

Known Makers: A, AS, A.W.S. 1942, H (over stirrup), R.K., R.R.S., KWM (within a circle), W, FRANK & REIF

This award was introduced on 1.6.40 and was to reward and distinguish the crews of armoured vehicles other than tanks which comprised self propelled gunners and the like, the Panzer Grenadier personnel and the support units, including medical personnel who were engaged in rendering medical assistance to the battlefield wounded. The crews of armoured cars were also eligible for this award rather than the silver class. It is, in all respects, the same as the silver award and it is found in the same three production methods as with its silver counterpart except for its colour.

It was worn on the left breast pocket of the uniform and was presented in a paper packet which came in varying colours, with the badge type printed on the front.

BRONZE TANK BATTLE BADGE: 25 CLASS****

BRONZE TANK BATTLE BADGE: 50 CLASS****

Known Makers: JFS, RK, GB

This badge is again identical to the equivalent silver grades, except that in this case the wreath and the tank are finished in bronze. The reverses are also the same. It was presented in a paper packet in varying colours, with the badge type printed on the front.

BRONZE TANK BATTLE BADGE: 75 CLASS*****

BRONZE TANK BATTLE BADGE: 100 CLASS*****

Known Makers: JFS

This badge again is identical to the equivalent silver grades, except on this occasion the tank is bronze while the wreath remains gold. The reverses are encountered once again with the variations being the same as the equivalent silver grades. The badge was presented in a paper packet, with the type printed on the front.

BRONZE TANK BATTLE BADGE: 200 CLASS*****

Known Makers

This badge has to be proved to have existed, and is included to stimulate a positive response from the reader.

GENERAL ASSAULT BADGE*

Known Makers: FO, G.B., FRANK & REIF

The design of this badge consists of an oval disc measuring 53mm by 42mm and is 6mm wide. It has raised edge lines on either side which are indented by 1mm. The central field of the tramlines has a fine pebbling applied and over this is laid a wreath of oak leaves. At the base are a pair of acorns from either side of which run five individual oak leaves separated by a large acorn running to the centre of the badge at an angle. At the apex, the two leaves are unadorned by an acorn and there is a 3mm gap between the two tips. The central device is that of the army eagle clutching a swastika in its talons, this is then surmounting a bayonet and crossed grenade.

The reverse is either solid with a needle pin or it is found hollow stamped, again with a needle pin. A private purchase version was available with a screw back plate, that is to say it did not have the hinge and hook but these were substituted for a screw post. This type is quite rare.

A further type has appeared in the last couple of years and this has caused some concern as to its originality in collecting circles. The differences are in the reverse and can be best described as semi-hollow. The wreath is flat while the eagle, swastika, bayonet and grenade are hollow with flat, recessed fields. At the apex and base there are two semi-circular slots that have plates which are recessed into the wreath and are held by two rivets. On to the upper one is soldered a hinge and the lower a 'C' form hook. The pin is of the thin needle type that is held at the hinge by the shepherd's crook type of bend. At the centre of the eagle's field is the maker's mark, 'JFS' in a square. The badge is constructed of fine quality zinc that seems to have had no silver wash applied. It has been claimed that this type was found in relatively large quantities in a factory in Czechoslovakia. A badge of this description but without the maker's mark and finished with a fine silver wash, formed part of the collection that made up the brick library of the Kriegsmarine in Kiel. It was returned by Lt- Cdr Albert McRae, thus proving the existence of this type of badge if not the one with the maker's mark.

The badge was designed by the firm of Ernst Peekhaus of Berlin and was instituted by Gen von Brauchitsch on 1.6.40. It was originally intended as the Engineers Assault Badge, but was quickly redesignated to include members of the artillery, anti-tank and anti-aircraft units that served with the infantry and armour in the Cauxiliary role used in the conduct of the assault. As well as the original engineers, again medical personnel treating the battle field wounded were entitled to be awarded this badge. It was worn on the left breast of the tunic.

The criteria for the award were:
● The recipient must not be eligible for the Infantry Assault Badge, silver or bronze.
● To have taken part in three infantry or armoured assaults on three different days.
● To have taken part in three infantry or armoured indirect assaults on three different days.
● To have been wounded in either the second or third categories.
● To have won a decoration in either the second or third categories.

The badge was also awarded for the single-handed destruction of eight tanks and other armoured fighting vehicles up until the introduction of The Special Badge for Single-Handed Destruction of a Tank on 9.3.42.

The badge was presented in a plain paper packet which could be in varying colours, depending on manufacturer and availability, with the designation of the badge printed on the front. It has also been known for it to come in a lowly cellophane packet.

GENERAL ASSAULT BADGE: 25 CLASS**

GENERAL ASSAULT BADGE: 50 CLASS**

Known Makers: JFS, RK

As the war progressed, the need to upgrade the General Assault Badge became apparent, to recognise the military skills of the veterans. On 22.6.43 four new grades were introduced.

The design of the first two were identical except for the number in the box. It consists of a wreath of oak leaves similar to the unnumbered badge, which is silvered and measures 58mm by 48 mm, with a width of 7mm. At the base is a square box that measures 10mm by 8mm with a raised edge line. Into this is positioned another box, 8mm by 6mm that has a raised edge line and recessed field. On to this, in raised Arabic numerals is '25' or '50'. These are finished in gilt and the recessed field in black. The eagle is larger and very finely executed. Once again it is clutching a swastika in its talons and surmounts the crossed bayonet and grenade. The central motif that this comprises has a black oxidised finish. The motif is separate from the wreath and held on to it by four ball rivets.

There are two forms of manufacture employed in the construction of these badges. The obverse of both types are nearly identical to one another, with the real differences being encountered on the reverse. I have described these as a) and b):

a) The wreath has a flat back with two large protrusions into the central void at the top and two small ones at the base. Into the centre of these is placed a ball rivet that secures the central motif. The pin is of the broad blade type and the

92

hinge is held on to the wreath by part of the wreath being cut and then turned back on to the hinge. The hook is held in a ball at the base of the wreath. The makers' marks are usually 'RK' or 'JFS' in a box and can be found on the left-hand side of the wreath. The reverse of the eagle is flat, as is the grenade but the blade of the bayonet is slightly hollow.

b) The reverse of the wreath is hollow, with a barrel hinge, needle pin and 'C' form hook attached to a round plate that is soldered to the base of the wreath. The reverse of the eagle is formed hollow, as is the swastika, bayonet and grenade. This form of badge is nearly always unmarked.

The badge was worn on the left breast of the tunic.

There was a retrospective credit given for service in Russia that was accounted from the start of the Russian campaign on 22.6.41 and was accumulated as:

● eight months service equalled 10 actions.
● 12 months service equalled 15 actions.
● 15 months service equalled 25 actions.

GENERAL ASSAULT BADGE: 75 CLASS***

GENERAL ASSAULT BADGE: 100 CLASS*****

Known Makers: JFS, RK
These badges were introduced at the same time as the preceding badges, again to recognise the service of the combat veterans. The badges are identical except for the numbers in the numeral boxes. There are two forms of manufacture employed in the construction of these badges. While the obverses to all intents and purposes are identical, the main differences lie in the reverses. The description of the common obverse is that the badge consists of a wreath constructed of oak leaves but this time the edges of the leaves form the inner and outer edges of the wreath. The base of the wreath is flat with a numeral box at the centre measuring 10mm by 8mm and into this is positioned a plate, 9mm by 7mm, with raised edge line and a recessed field that has, in raised Arabic numerals, either '75' or '100'. The raised parts of the box and numerals are gilded while the recessed field is blackened. From either side of the box emanates a single oak leaf and from these, on either side, five further leaves that are separated by two single acorns, one on each side. The wreath measures 56mm by 49mm with a width of 7.5mm. The width across the base leaves and numeral box is 40.5mm. The wreath is indented to accommodate the central emblem of the eagle and swastika, surmounting crossed grenade and bayonet. The wreath is gilded while the central emblem is blackened. The eagle is larger than the unnumbered grade, with seg-

mented legs and the swastika it clutches being again slightly larger than in the unnumbered badge. The bayonet and grenades are crossed at a different angle to that of the 25 and 50 grade badges. This device is separate from the wreath and is joined to it by four ball rivets.

The reverses described can be broken down into a) and b):

a) The wreath is flat and has a broad pin. The hinge is attached to the wreath by the wreath being cut and then turned back on to the hinge fitting. The hook is held in a ball at the base of the wreath. The makers' marks are usually 'RK' or 'JFS' in a box which is to be found on the right side of the wreath. The reverse of the eagle and swastika is flat, while the crossed grenade and bayonet are slightly hollow. The emblem is held on to the wreath by four ball rivets running through the wreath which are usually of a silver colour.

b) The reverse of the wreath is hollow with a flat field and a raised portion where the obverse of the wreath has been recessed to accommodate the central emblem. It is at these recessed points that it is attached to the wreath by four ball rivets. At the apex of the wreath is a barrel hinge on its side and at the base a 'C' form hook on a round plate, that is soldered to the reverse of the recessed numeral box. The pin is of the thin needle type. The reverse of the eagle, swastika and crossed grenade and bayonet is hollow.

The badge was worn on the lower left breast of the uniform.

There was a retrospective credit given for service in Russia that was accounted from the start of the Russian campaign on 22.6.41 and was accumulated as:

● eight months service equalled 10 actions.
● 12 months service equalled 15 actions.
● 15 months service equalled 25 actions.

It was presented in either a paper packet or a lowly cellophane envelope.

SPECIAL BADGE FOR SINGLE-HANDED DESTRUCTION OF A TANK SILVER CLASS**

SPECIAL BADGE FOR SINGLE-HANDED DESTRUCTION OF A TANK GOLD CLASS****

Known Makers
On 9.3.42 a new badge was introduced to recognise the destruction of armoured fighting vehicles or tanks. Up until this time the Gen Assault Badge had been awarded for this act. This award was not for members of anti-tank units but for service personnel who destroyed a fighting vehicle single-handed. The award was made retroac-

Plate 165 Reverse General Assault Badges. Note the semi-hollow form with the recessed hinge and hook. This actual example formed part of the Kiel brick library presented to Lt Commander Albert McRae.

Plate 166 Reverse General Assault Badge. Note the hollow struck form.

Plate 167 Obverse General Assault Badge-50 Class.

Plate 168 Reverse General Assault Badge-25 & 50 Classes clearly showing the JFS trademark.

Plate 169 Obverse General Assault Badge-75 & 100 Classes.

Plate 170 Reverse General Assault Badge-75 & 100 Classes. Note the construction of the wreath on the left 75 Class. This form can be found in both grades.

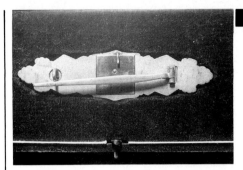

Plate 171   Obverse Special Badge for Single Handed Destruction of a Tank-Gold & Silver Classes.

Plate 172   Obverse Close Combat Bar-Bronze Class.

Plate 173   Reverse Close Combat Bar. Note the variation of hinge, hook and pin assembly as well as the method of attachment of the backplate. The upper and lower bars are from the same manufacturer.

Plate 174   Reverse Close Combat Bar-Gold Class as awarded by Hitler personally. Note the absence of makers or designers marks, the single central rivet and small hook.

tive to 21.6.41 to reward qualifying actions from the start of the campaign against the Soviet Union. By 18.12.43 there was a need to introduce a higher grade of the award, so the gold class was brought into being.

The silver grade comprises a Tiger 4 tank that measures 43mm by 18mm. The emblem is coloured black and placed on to a piece of silver ribbon measuring 33mm by 88mm. The band has an upper and lower 4mm black cotton thread stripe, indented from the edges by 2mm. The band is constructed of silver thread formed in two rows at the edges and 24 rows between the two bands of black cotton. The reverse shows a small oblong metal plate, through which are placed three pins which are bent over to secure the emblem to the silver ribbon. The whole of the reverse is then covered with a black cotton patch.

The gold class is identical to the silver class, save that the tank is an oxidised silver colour giving a faint, lightly gilded effect in the early awards. Subsequently, just the plain blackened emblem was applied. The band was produced in the same manner but in some cases the silver wire was changed for gold cellon as well as a gold bullion wire.

The criteria for the award were:
- Destruction was to be by means of a hand grenade, rocket grenade, satchel charge or any other similar hand held explosive.
- One silver emblem was awarded for each fighting vehicle destroyed.
- Four awards could be worn at any one time, being worn one directly above the other on the upper arm of the tunic.
- On the fifth award, the five badges were exchanged for one gold one.
- This process continued with one gold award having silver badges beneath it until the 10th badge was awarded, when the silver ones were replaced by another gold. This process continued with silver awards being given until the 15th and so on.

The greatest number of tanks destroyed by one man qualifying for the bestowal of the badge was 21. This was achieved by Oberstleutnant Günter

Viezenz. When the badge was presented it was normally pinned to the right sleeve of the uniform and later the recipient sewed it on. An entry was also made in his Wehrpass.

CLOSE COMBAT BAR BRONZE CLASS**

CLOSE COMBAT BAR SILVER CLASS**

CLOSE COMBAT BAR GOLD CLASS****

Known Makers: RS, FFL in three circles, JFS in a square box, Ausf. A.G.M. u K. CJ Juncker
The date of introduction of this badge was 25.11.42 and was instituted by Hitler as a visible token of achievement in hand to hand combat and was to be awarded in three grades. The designer of the award was W. E. Peekhaus of Berlin. The three bars are identical except for colour and are made up of a square box with a black back plate. There is an army styled eagle surmounting crossed bayonet and grenade. The square of the box is made up of two oak leaves on each side except for the top, where the eagle with outstretched wings replaces the oak leaves. From either side of the box, emanate two sets of arrowheads made up of lines. Surmounting these on either side are four oak leaves. Adjacent to each square where the oak leaves join are two small acorns on each side. The bar measures 98mm by 26mm taken at the widest part. The whole is slightly curved to give a good fit to the recipient's breast. The reverse is flat save for the designer's logo, which is usually found in two parts on either side of the back plate. On the left is 'FEC.W.E. Peekhaus, Berlin.', which refers to the Latin 'FECIT' (made by) but can be more accurately termed, 'designed by'. On the right is the maker's name or logo. The pin's hinge is an integral part of the badge. The pins are usually of the broad type and can be of a corrugated construction as well as flat.

There is another form of bar that is identical on the obverse but has, on the reverse, a single rivet holding the back plate to the bar and a small hook soldered to the top of the bar. The hinge is of the barrel type and let into the reverse. The hook is likewise let into the bar with a circular recess into which the 'C' form hook is positioned, attached to a round plate. This is the type that Hitler presented personally and it has been stated that approximately only 50 were awarded. He considered that this was the highest infantry decoration and reserved the right to award the gold version personally. This was formalised on 26.3.45 when the OKH announced that Hitler had reserved the right to personally present the Close Combat Bar in Gold as the highest infantry decoration and on 30.8.44 decreed that those who were to be awarded the gold class were automatically to receive the German Cross in Gold.

This he did for the first time on 27.8.44, when he awarded 14 officers of the army and Waffen-SS at his headquarters. By the end of the war, only 538 awards of the gold bar had taken place to the ground forces who qualified. This can be further broken down into individual categories as: 100 to Mannschaftsdienstgrade, 303 to Unteroffiziersdienstgrade and 135 to Offiziersdienstgrade. The bar was worn above the ribbon bar and this was to show the high esteem in which the award was held. There are two forms of cloth version of the clasp and these are a simple screen version on cotton and an embroidered form which has been encountered in bronze and silver.

The criteria for the award, where the combat days were to be counted from 1.12.42, were:
- To have been engaged in hand to hand combat when supported by armour.
- A bronze bar required 15 days of close combat, which could be reduced to 10 days if he had been wounded.
- A silver bar required 30 days which could be reduced to 20 days if he had been wounded.
- A gold bar required 50 days which could be reduced to 40 days if he had been wounded.

For service in Russia a retrospective credit was introduced from 22.6.41 with a service ratio of:
  a) Five combat days being represented by eight months service.
  b) 10 combat days being represented by 12 months service.
  c) 15 combat days being represented by 15 months service.

It was awarded in a plain paper packet with the name printed on the front. As the war progressed this paper packet was replaced by a lowly cellophane one. In the case of the gold class these were awarded in a black hard hinged case with a white satin lid liner and a recessed black velvet base. The case was held together by a press-stud.

ARMY BALLOON OBSERVERS BADGE: BRONZE CLASS****

ARMY BALLOON OBSERVERS BADGE: SILVER CLASS****

ARMY BALLOON OBSERVERS BADGE: GOLD CLASS*****

Known Makers: Unmarked
The German Army and Waffen-SS made extensive use of observation balloons during WW2. The balloons, manufactured by Riedinger of Ausburg, used a design that resembled the British barrage balloons. The balloons, known as Fesselballon, were 34m long, 9.87m in diameter, and

were filled with 1,400cu m of hydrogen (Wasserstoffgas). Suspended below this gas-filled bag was a small two-man basket into which three observers (Ballonbeobachter) could be accommodated at a squeeze. The normal operating height was 3-500m, with a maximum operational altitude of around 2,000m. Observers either made visual observation or used large plate cameras to produce photographic panoramas for artillery planners.

The balloons were operated by Ballonbatterie, each with two balloons, attached to artillery observation battalions (Beobachtungsabteilung). Some of the batteries were motorised and could manage a road speed of up to 45km/h. They could have a complement of up to six trucks each carrying 28 hydrogen cylinders and others carrying 11 tonne winches and 7mm cable to control the balloons in flight. The observers were easy targets for aircraft and ground fire and required special ground support as well as that of the Luftwaffe. Protection for the vulnerable balloons was provided by four 20mm flak cannon attached to each battery. During the early war years when the Luftwaffe had air superiority, especially in the east, this technique of spotting proved to be very effective but no less dangerous.

At least two independent balloon batteries, 101 and 102 existed. Balloon batteries were used near Sedan in 1940 and thereafter were in action on the Eastern Front. One such example was on the Narva Front where war correspondent Reinsberg of 23rd Waffen-SS Division 'Nederlands' photographed the observer with his captive balloon in action. The OKH had realized the hazardous nature of their deployment and by the end of 1944 they had been withdrawn from use.

The badge was introduced on 8.7.44 by the OKH to recognise the bravery and proficiency of the balloon observers. The badge was produced by a firm in Dresden and consisted of a wreath of oak leaves with two acorns at its base, surmounted by a closed winged army eagle. This eagle looks to the viewer's right and the beak is joined to the wing, giving a bearded effect to the eagle. There are five leaves on either side of the wreath with one or two acorns where the leaves join. The height of the badge from the two acorns at the base to the top of the eagle's head, is 58mm and 41.5mm wide. The width of the wreath is 8mm. The centre is a balloon which, as previously described, looks like a barrage balloon, on which is a Balkan cross.

The reverse is a negative of the obverse with a small barrel hinge attached to the swastika, a 'C' form hook soldered directly to the top of the wreath, at the base and a needle pin. The quality of the striking of this badge is of the highest order. The gauge of the metal is fairly thick and therefore makes the badge quite heavy. The quality of the badge cannot be justifiably recognised by photographs in reference books.

The award of the badge was based on the recommendation of any one of the following officers, the officer in command of the troop, commander of the artillery unit or commander of a balloon observer unit.

The criteria for the award were on a points basis:

- Bronze Class 20 points.
- Silver Class 45 points.
- Gold Class 75 points.

The actual accumulation of points is a little obscure. However, points were awarded for degree of difficulty. Having to parachute from the balloon during the course of the mission earned the observer 10 points. The award of the bronze and silver badge is confirmed but the gold award seems not to have been given. The recipient of a gold award must have been either slightly insane or have had a death wish! This is one of the most difficult badges to obtain.

175

176

Plate 175 Obverse Army Balloon Observers Badge-Bronze Class.

Plate 176 Reverse Army Balloon Observers Badge-Gold Class.

8. The Wound Badge

WOUND BADGE WW1 BLACK CLASS*

WOUND BADGE WW1 SILVER CLASS*

WOUND BADGE WW1 GOLD CLASS**

Known Makers

These awards comprise a wreath of laurel leaves that has a bow at the base with seven bunches of three leaves on either side, with two laurel berries at each joint. The only difference is the colour of each grade. The steel body of the black award is painted with black enamel paint, the silver award is silver-plated and the gold is of poor quality gilding. The badge measures 42mm by 39mm. Crossed swords are superimposed on to the central pebbled field. A German steel helmet is superimposed over the swords.

The reverse shows the negative of the obverse. It has a hinge and hook, which can be an integral part of the edge of the badge, that is folded over, with a needle pin. Other forms of construction and materials were employed. These included the badge being struck in genuine silver with a fine pin, hinge and hook assembly, as well as a solid back plate being fixed to the reverse outer edge of the badge, so that it took on the appearance of a solid stamping. Both these forms are very rare and were presumably a private purchase option.

At this point it is important to note that there are approximately five types of the obverse and many unofficial varieties. The study of the Wound Badge is a field all on its own and *German Wound Badges* by William E. Hamelman should be consulted for an in depth study. From the general history of the awards of the Third Reich, these badges were a permitted award that was incorporated into the line of progression of the awards of the Third Reich form. The badges were worn on the left side of the tunic or jacket.

The German Emperor and King of Prussia, Wilhelm II introduced these awards on 3.3.18. He voiced his opinion in the regulations that 'Ich will den Dienste des Vaterlandes Verwundeten als Besondere Anerkennung ein Abzeichen Verliehen' (I will give to those wounded in the service of the Fatherland, a badge of special recognition).

The criteria for the award were:
- Up to two wounds: Black Award.
- Three to five wounds: Silver Award.
- One wound resulting in the loss of hand, foot, eye or causing deafness: Silver Award.
- Five or more wounds: Gold Award.
- One wound resulting in total disability, permanent blindness or loss of manhood: Gold Award.

The award was made retrospective from 3.3.18, thus covering wounds suffered during the whole period of WW1. On 11.3.18 the King of Bavaria,

Plate 177 Obverse Wound Badge WW 1 Silver Class & Prinzen Size Gold Class.

Plate 178 Reverse Wound Badge WW 1, Black Silver & Gold. Note the variation in pin, hinge and hook assembly as well as .800 silver stamping on the pin of the upper badge.

Plate 179 Obverse Wound Badge WW 1. This piece is of Nazi construction and features a variation steel helmet and swastika suspension appending it to an Iron Cross Second Class 1914 ribbon.

Plate 180 Obverse Spanish Wound Badge in Silver & Gold. Note the variation in the swastikas.

Plate 181 Reverse Spanish Wound Badge in Silver & Gold. Note the hollow striking and the solid form.

Plate 182 Obverse Spanish Wound Badge in Silver. Note the cut-out design and screw plate.

Plate 183 Reverse Spanish Wound Badge in Silver.

Plate 184 Obverse Wound Badge 1939 Gold Class.

Plate 185 Obverse Wound Badge 1939 Black Class. Note this is the hollow struck form which gives rise to a slightly different profile to the swastika.

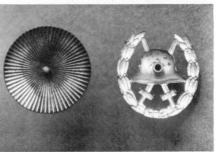

Ludwig III, gave permission for the badges to be received by Bavarian troops under the same criteria. However, in regulations issued on 3.6.18 the Bavarian War Ministry declared that the Wound Badge was not a decoration but an award. The enabling order was expanded on 8.7.18 by the German supreme command to encompass German colonial troops and Askaris in German service.

With the abolition of the monarchy and the abdication of the Kaiser on 9.11.19, everything was temporarily changed. However, the Iron Cross and Wound Badges continued to be awarded retrospectively right up to 1925. An edict dated 7.3.25 brought an adjustment to the issuing of orders, medals and war badges and the continued awarding of WW1 decorations was halted.

Some unorthodox designs were employed after this edict and one such piece that demonstrates the ingenuity of designers is a standard badge produced from a very fine striking more closely resembling the so called 'Spanish Type'. It was produced from bronze that was artificially patinated. At the apex of the wreath is an integral protrusion forming an eyelet through which is placed a jump ring attached to a small swastika with a similar protrusion to its lower leg. In turn, the swastika has a stirrup over its upper arm through which is placed a further jump ring attached to a ribbon ring, through which is placed a length of World War 1 Iron Cross Second Class ribbon. An early political eagle and swastika are pinned on to the ribbon. The reverse is flat with only the negative of the obverse showing. Clearly, this is a specially produced item as an individual die had to be constructed to create this piece. It is not a conversion of any form of standard badge. This clearly shows the early thinking of the designers of incorporating the swastika into the design of the Wound Badge.

The badges were recognised on 30.1.36 when the State Ministry of the Interior decreed that any ex-soldier, who had been wounded in action and not received the award, could now obtain the necessary documentation which would evince the severity and number of wounds he had received. This document would entitle the recipient to receive the award and wear it in public. This meant that the recipient purchased the badge at his own expense. Regulations published on 20.4.39 entitled those wounded, who had served in the Austro-Hungarian military forces allied with Germany and resident in the annexed Austria and occupied Sudetenland and Memel regions, to the bestowal under the same criteria. The inhabitants of the eastern region and the Protectorates of Bohemia and Moravia were given permission to receive the award after 1941. The dates for these regulations are possibly 30.1.42 and 12.3.43. Hitler made a decree on 7.9.43 and this could possibly have made the Deutschen

Plate 186   Reverse Wound Badge 1939 Black Class. Note the badge on the left is struck in copper and has a strange plate annealed into the reverse. That on the right shows the standard stamping with a clear maker's mark, 65.

Plate 187   Reverse Wound Badge 1939 Silver & Gold Classes. Note the variation in pin, hinge and hook assembly.

Plate 188   Obverse Wound Badge '20 July 1944' Black Class First Type. This actual example was awarded to Generaloberst Alfred Jodl.

Volksgruppen in the southeast eligible for the award.

SPANISH WOUND BADGE: BLACK CLASS**

SPANISH WOUND BADGE: SILVER CLASS**

SPANISH WOUND BADGE: GOLD CLASS***

Known Makers: Unmarked
This badge was introduced on 22.5.39 to reward military personnel who were wounded in the Spanish civil war. It took the form of its WW1 counterpart but had a swastika stamped into the helmet. At this point it is important to dispel some of the misconceptions surrounding the award of this badge. The actual number of badges awarded for participation in the Spanish civil war were: Black 182, Silver one, Gold nil.

This design of badge continued to be awarded until at least 1942. It is also possible that the original recipients of the badges awarded for the civil war could, for subsequent wounds sustained in WW2, receive the higher grade in this form. This theory has been denied in other reference books but, due to the limited number of awards, it is highly possible that this practice was applied. One such story has been encountered, where a Panzer man (Heinrich Schell) had received the badge in black for being wounded in Spain. Subsequently, he fought in WW2 receiving a further wound in the Polish campaign. He then fought on the western front in 1940 where he lost his lower leg. For this wound he received the Wound Badge 1939 Gold Class. However, while convalescing in hospital, his commanding officer visited him and upon seeing his Gold 1939 Wound Badge commented that he should have the Spanish Type and subsequently gave him such an example. This was purchased from the recipient and is now in my collection. The quality of the badge is very poor and does not give the impression of the quality that the presentation warranted. This bestowal I believe to be nothing more than a one-off piece of camaraderie that could have been shown in the first months of WW2.

The badge consists of a wreath of laurel leaves with a bow at its base and five berries, or dots, at its apex. The central device of the badge comprises of a WW1 steel helmet surmounting crossed swords, with a swastika stamped into the helmet from the reverse. The field is pebbled but some examples of the badge have this field cut out, leaving the swords and helmet in silhouette.

The reverse of the badge follows the design of the obverse, as the badge is stamped out. How-

ever, one example I have examined of the silver grade, is stamped out as previously described and is then attached to a backing plate. This gives the impression of the badge being formed in a solid manner. This badge is constructed in real silver. A further example has been encountered in gold that is similarly constructed but with a broad blade pin and having two small blow holes situated beneath it. This badge is very lightweight, finely struck and superbly made. The pin to all the badges encountered is usually of a needle pin

The criteria for the award were:
● Up to two wounds: Black award
● Three or four wounds: Silver award
● Five or more wounds: Gold award

The badge came in a black box with a cream flock lining.

WOUND BADGE 1939: BLACK CLASS*

WOUND BADGE 1939: SILVER CLASS*

WOUND BADGE 1939: GOLD CLASS**

Known Makers: 3, 4, 13, 16, 26, 30, 32, 65, 81, 92, 100,107, (in a raised oblong box with rounded ends), 124, L/14, L/22, L/53 (in raised oblong box), L/57, L11, L14, L54
Due to his experiences in WW1, Hitler's concern for the combat wounded prompted him to reintroduce yet another badge to reward those honourably wounded. It came into being on 1.9.39.

It varies from the Spanish form in that the laurel leaf wreath is smooth round the outer rim. The swords have broader blades and the helmet above them is of the new design used by the German armed forces, again with the swastika surmounting it. This is more prominent than in the Spanish type. The dots in the field are in horizontal lines, giving the effect by which newspaper pictures are produced. There is a bow at the base of the wreath with three dots or laurel berries at the apex.

The Black Class is usually found hollow, while the Silver and Gold Classes are usually solid. There are numerous makers and pin constructions. The material is also very varied to even include Bakelite ranging through to genuine silver. Another interesting construction method is a badge pressed from copper which has a copper plate placed into the reverse and peened in. The pin is similar to that found on a Day Badge. The overall quality of the badge is very good.

As the air war progressed, numerous civilian forces became injured and it was considered fitting by Dr Göbbels that they should be rewarded so, from March 1943 at his suggestion, all civilians became eligible for the award. One interesting award was to Sgt Thomas Hellor Cooper in the British Free Corps who was awarded the Black Wound Badge while serving with the SS unit 'Das Reich'. This is the only known British recipient of a German combat award.

The criteria for the Award were:
- One or two wounds: Black award.
- Three to five wounds: Silver award.
- One wound resulting in the loss of hand, foot, eye or deafness: Silver award.
- Five or more wounds: Gold award.
- One wound resulting in total disability, permanent blindness or loss of manhood: Gold award.

Frostbite was the only illness or disease for which the badge could be awarded.

The black badge was awarded in a paper packet. The silver and gold badges were usually awarded in black or burgundy boxes, with respective black or burgundy flock bases. However, as the war progressed, they were also issued in paper packets. There was a cloth version in both black and gold, printed on green cotton. It is therefore possible that there was an example of this badge in silver.

WOUND BADGE '20 JULY 1944': BLACK CLASS: FIRST TYPE*****

WOUND BADGE '20 JULY 1944': SILVER CLASS: FIRST TYPE*****

WOUND BADGE '20 JULY 1944': GOLD CLASS: FIRST TYPE*****

Known Makers: L12

On 20.7.44, an unsuccessful attempt was made to assassinate Hitler by Col Count Claus Schenk von Stauffenberg at the Wolf's lair at Rastenburg, Hitler's HQ in the east. Hitler and the other 24 occupants of the room suffered varying degrees of injury, the most serious being the deaths of Col Brant and Herr Berger, who died immediately and Generalleutnant Schmundt and Gen Korten dying subsequently from wounds they received. The remaining 20 suffered superficial wounds and shock, save for Gen Buhle and Generalmajor Scherff, who were more seriously injured.

To commemorate this attempt on his life and his escape, Hitler introduced a special Wound Badge which he awarded to the 24 occupants, or dependants in the case of the dead. He declined to award himself one of these medals. The first awards of this medal were made on 20.8.44.

The recipients were:
- **Black Award:** KEITEL, Wilhelm Generalfeldmarschall; JODL, Alfred Generaloberst; WARLIMONT, Walter Gen der Artillerie; von PUTTKAMER, Jesko Konteradmiral; ASSMANN, Heinz Kapitän Z

See; von BELOW, Nicolaus Oberst; VOSS, Hans-Erich Konteradmiral; GüNSCHE, Otto SS-Hauptsturmführer.
- **Silver Award:** FEGELEIN Hermann SS-Gruppenführer; HEUSINGER, Adolf Generalleutnant; BORGMAN, G. Oberstleutnant.
- **Gold Award:** BODENSCHATZ, Karl Gen der Flieger; BUHLE, Walter Gen der Infanterie, SCHERFF, Walter Generalmajor; KORTEN, Gunter Gen der Flieger (Post); BRANT, Heinz Oberst (Post); BERGER, civilian (Post); SCHMUNDT Rudolf Generalleutnant (Post).
- **Not known (presumed Black):** von JOHN, Oberstleutnant; BüCHS G. Maj; HAGAN; WEIZENEGGER, Oberstleutnant; HEWELL, Walter civilian; von SCHIMANSKI, Hauptmann.

The firms of C. E. Juncker and Godet were asked to produce designs for this award. That produced by Godet followed very closely that of its competitor but the colour of the grade was applied all over the surface of the badge. There are many other minor variations but the most striking is in the pin which has a broad belly with a semi-circular profile. On the reverse of the body of the badge, under the pin, is stamped, '21' and the silver content, '.800'. An example of each grade was produced and then presented to Hitler who made the final judgement. This resulted in the contract being awarded to C. E. Juncker of Berlin. The trial Godet pieces were kept by Konteradmiral Jesko von Puttkamer who retained them as a memento until his death. His son then made them available to an Austrian collector.

The quality of this badge is very high and each example was hand-finished. This is illustrated by very fine file marks round the edges of the badge. It is estimated that Juncker produced 100 badges. It took the form of the ordinary wound badge with a very finely formed wreath with a bow at the base and three laurel berries or dots at the apex. The helmet is nearer the apex and the swords' hilts are positioned at the second bunch of laurel leaves on either side of the wreath. The upper edge of the hilt of each sword touches the front and back of the helmet respectively. Beneath the helmet are the date and Hitler's signature, both being raised and polished. The field is hand pebbled and matt finished. The reverse is flat and bears minute scratches, which epitomise hand finishing.

The hinge is of the 'on its edge' barrel type with a hook at the bottom. The pin is hand-drawn and slightly curled up at the bottom where it fastens into the hook. On the reverse, beneath the pin, is the maker's mark 'L/12' and the silver content '.800'. It is interesting to note that each recipient received two badges, the award one as described and a Dress Copy which had '.800' and a small '2' to denote that this was the wear copy or second version. No other difference exists between the two types save for this small number.

The wreath, helmet and swords of the black version were artificially blackened. The swastika was less darkened while the date and signature were highly polished and the field was matt silver. The reverse was also artificially blackened including the pin, hook and hinge. The silver version is silver all over, the signature and date being highly polished as before, while the field is again a matt silver. The gold version has a gold or gilt wreath, helmet and swords, with the swastika again being slightly lightened. The date and signature are highly polished silver, while the reverse and pin etc are matt gold.

The criteria for the award were the same as those employed for the Wound Badge 1939. It is assumed that when the recipient was wounded again he received the higher grade of the badge in this form.

The badge came in a black box with black velvet base and silk lid lining.

WOUND BADGE '20 JULY 1944': BLACK CLASS: SECOND TYPE*****

WOUND BADGE '20 JULY 1944': SILVER CLASS: SECOND TYPE*****

WOUND BADGE '20 JULY 1944': GOLD CLASS: SECOND TYPE*****

Known Makers: Unmarked

This badge is the only one of its type known to the author and is in the gold grade but it is expected to exist in black and silver also. It consists, as in the former badge, of a wreath of laurel leaves but this example has a rough edge following the line of the laurel bunches. The ribbon tie at the base is tied tighter and formed of a thicker ribbon. The apex has five berries or dots as in the Spanish Wound Badge type. The date fills the gap between the hilts of the swords. It is also interesting to note that the binding on the hilt on the right-hand sword runs in opposite directions on each of these types and there is a ferrule on this badge adjacent to the top of the hilt and no ferrule on the former kind. The centre of the hilt on this medal is square, with a plain box, whereas the former badge has a square box in the hilt with a bar in it. The signature is larger and is exercised in a flowing hand. It is possible that this badge was intended for further awards when the recipient was further wounded and was produced by a different maker but this is pure conjecture. The reverse was stamped with the silver grade '.935'.

The original collector who owned this badge, B. A. Beyerstedt, contacted Dr K. G. Klietmann of Berlin whose observations were recorded in a letter dated 10.9.64. I quote him verbatim:
'Many thanks for your letter of 3 this month and for sending the wound badge of the 20 July on to me which I received yesterday and will return it today by air-mail registered.

The personal inspection of a badge: I must emphasise it again: is the most important point for telling what it is. This inspection shows me that
a) It is doubtless made in 1944.
b) And made in Germany
c) This item was made by hand from a jeweller
d) It is put together of the following parts:
1. Wreath
2. The grained ground
3. The steel helmet
4. The swords
5. Inscription
All these parts are hollow made and were cut off from other badges except the inscription which was made in addition by hand and then all parts were put together and the silver gilt back was finally put on it. Until now I was not able to identify the hallmark. After this inspection I do not at all doubt that it is a genuine pattern for that time. But after the photographs I could never have told this. From the photographs alone it was not to recognise that it is a genuine item. The later on awarded items looked different and were made of solid silver.'

The good doctor gives two very important lessons in this text. Firstly that personal inspection is all important when deciding if an item is genuine or not and secondly, that for even the rarest of badges there can be many variations due to the innovation of varying manufacturers.

189

Plate 189 Obverse Wound Badge '20 July 1944' Gold Class Second Type.

9. Arm Shields Common to All Services

NARVIK SHIELD: SILVER CLASS**

NARVIK SHIELD: GOLD CLASS**

Known Makers

This shield was instituted on 19.8.40 and comprises a metal shield, pointed at the bottom, surmounted at the top by three lines. The first protrudes the shield's edges, the second is in line with the edges and the third is short of the outline of the badge. On this rests an eagle, head to the viewer's left, with exaggerated downswept wings. In its claws it is clutching a wreath surrounding a swastika. The body of the shield has a box with the word, 'NARVIK' and beneath this is the date, '1940'. The main design of the badge is a crossed single-bladed propeller and anchor, surmounted by an edelweiss. These were the symbols of the three arms of the German fighting forces employed in the capture of Norway. The awards were designed by Prof Richard Klein of München.

This shield was unique in the fact that it was produced in two forms. The silver grade was given to the army and air force, with a backing cloth denoting the service to which the recipient belonged. The gold one was awarded solely to the navy and therefore should only be found with a navy-blue backing. However, gilt examples are occasionally encountered on field-grey cloth worn by Narvik veterans who served in the marine artillery and wore field-grey army style uniforms. One specific example which is known of a Narvik naval veteran, Karl Wilhelm Krause, who had been Hitler's personal orderly and bodyguard from 1934 to 1939. In 1931 he joined the navy and three years later Hitler had chosen him from a line up of other naval prospects. In September 1939, after a petty squabble over some 'spring' water that he had represented to Hitler as bottled mineral water which, incidentally, was Hitler's favourite drink, the Führer sacked him. During the war, Krause served briefly in the navy, then as an ordnance aid in the Reich Chancellery and finally as a captain in an SS Panzer Flak unit, credited with shooting down 45 allied aircraft. Krause was personally awarded the German Cross in Gold by Hitler. From photographic evidence he wore the gilt Narvik Shield on both field-grey and black Panzer jacket.

The total number awarded was 8,577: 2,755 (army); 2,161 (Luftwaffe); and 3,661 (navy). These can be further broken down to the component units

Army: 2.Gebirgs-Division 206, 3.Gebirgs-Division 2,338, others 59, posthumous 152.

Luftwaffe: Flying Crew 1,309, Paratroopers 756, posthumous 96.

Navy: Destroyers 2,672, others 115, posthumous 410.

Merchant Navy: 442, posthumous 22.

The naval form had its prescribed method of wear laid down by an order dated 12.9.40, MV 40, No 674 as, on the left upper sleeve of the greatcoat, frockcoat, reefer and pea jackets, blue shirt of the blue uniform and of the greatcoat and field blouse of the field-grey uniform. Wear on the mess and dress jackets and white shirts of junior NCOs and privates was not permitted until after the end of the war. An additional order, dated 30.1.41, MV 41, No 60, regulated the wear above the sleeve rank insignia of junior NCOs and privates. When a second shield was authorised to a recipient it was to be worn 0.5cm below the first.

Each recipient was issued with three examples of the shield and could purchase additional examples through retail outlets by producing his proof of entitlement.

CHOLM SHIELD****

Known Makers

This shield was introduced on 1.7.42 and consists of a white metal shield with flat top and pointed bottom. The central design is an open winged eagle, clutching an Iron Cross in its talons, the centre of which has a disproportionately large swastika relative to the size of the Iron Cross. Beneath this is the word, 'CHOLM' and then the date of award, '1942'. Polizei Rottwachtmeister Schlimmer, of the Police Reserve Battalion who had been encouraged by Generalmajor Scherer, drew up a design for this arm shield which consisted of a shield slightly longer than the adopted form, with the eagle's head facing to the right. This design was submitted for approval and only after minor changes by Prof Klein of München, was approved by Hitler for production. This measured 65mm high by 40mm wide. There are two forms of this shield, the design of which only varies slightly, in the lettering of 'CHOLM' and the date. The edge rim is also slightly more pronounced on the second type. The general differences lie in the cloth backing. The first type extends above and below the shield equally with a semi-circular profile. The cloth is coarse and a field-grey colour. The reverse has three pins, two at the top and one below, in the middle. The backing paper is usually dark-grey to black. The second type has a cloth backing that follows the outline of the shield. The cloth is of an open felt type and a more green hue. The reverse has four pins, positioned two at the top and two directly underneath at the bottom. The paper backing is normally a light brown-red and often has the number '2,40' in pencil.

It has been stated that the early production pieces were struck in lightweight metallic metal and were backed with the first type large oval cloth patch, while later examples, which would have been sold through LDO outlets, were in non magnetic zinc and mounted on the second type shield shaped backing cloth. The two types that I have used for research were both struck from base metal which then had a silver wash applied. The first type is struck with a slightly convex profile, while the second is flat. The cloth backing measures 102mm by 62mm and 78mm by 54mm, with most of the examples being in these two types and field-blue Luftwaffe backing being rarely encountered. It is possible that examples may exist on navy-blue backing, as naval transport units did operate on the Lovat river near Kholm (as it is usually spelt in English). However, as these troops wore field-grey dress in normal service, such awards were unlikely to have been made on this form of badge. The explanation for the second type would fit most comfortably to these units, for I was most fortunate to obtain from the family of Lt-Cdr Albert McRae part of the Kiel naval headquarters library, which contained some 500 naval insignia and other related material, of which the second type shield was included as the naval example. The colour of the backing also matches that of the naval field-grey dress.

The award was created to reward the garrison that had held a defensive pocket that had been created at Kholm, a small town on the Lovat river in the Kalinin region of Russia. During the winter of 1941-42 a Soviet counter offensive trapped several thousand Germans at this point commanded by Majorgeneral Scherer. Hitler made one of his famous fortress orders, that the pocket be defended to the last man, and the garrison

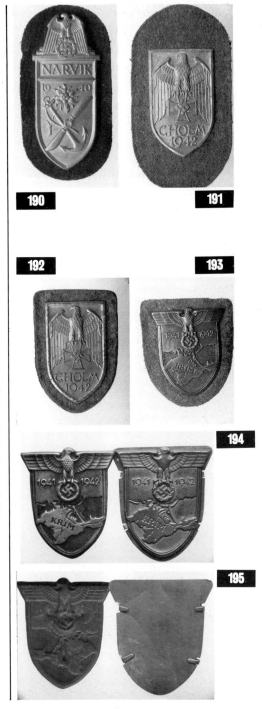

Plate 190   Obverse Narvik Shield Gold Class.

Plate 191   Obverse Cholm Shield.

Plate 192   Obverse Cholm Shield.

Plate 193   Obverse Crimea Shield.

Plate 194   Obverse Crimea Shield. Note the difference in the quality of the stamping between the three. Each shield is in mint condition for its type.

Plate 195   Reverse Crimea Shield. Note the method of attachment to the uniform.

held out against overwhelming odds from 21.1.42 to 5.5.42.

To reward this achievement, the Oak Leaves to the Knight's Cross of the Iron Cross were bestowed upon Scherer and it was he who made the awards to 5,500 assorted men from various units who comprised the defenders of the pocket. Luftwaffe crews were granted the award for landing on the improvised air strip which served the pocket.

The shield was worn on the arm, on a cloth backing piece of the colour of the branch of service.

CRIMEA SHIELD*

Known Makers
This award was introduced on 25.7.42. It comprised a bronze shield that has an army eagle at its top, the wings just breaking the edge of the shield, clutching a wreath surrounding a swastika in its talons. On either side of the wreath are the dates '1941' and '1942' respectively. Beneath this is a map of the Crimean region, with the major rivers and six towns marked on it. The word 'Krim' is impressed on to this map. This shield was produced from a thin ferrous plate stamped with the design. It then has an olive bronze finish applied and artificially patinated. There are three distinct methods of production encountered in both this and the Kuban Shield. The first is a finely detailed badge fixed to a cloth backing corresponding in colour to the service to which the recipient belonged. This cloth backing measures 75mm by 65mm. The reverse has four prongs, two at the top and two directly beneath at the bottom. The whole is covered by a black paper backing. The second form has a less finely defined design with two lugs on the vertical sides of the shield. These are bent over to secure a thin metal back plate. This plate has four notches cut in the edges to secure the clips. In this case there is sometimes no cloth backing provided. When it comes with the cloth backing, the four semi circular lugs are pressed through the cloth and then retained by the back plate, which is then covered by a paper backing. The third form is struck from a slightly thicker plate and has a much less well defined design. The reverse has three pins, two at the top and one directly beneath, in the middle at the bottom.

The shield was promulgated in July 1942 with the following telegram from Hitler to the commander of the forces in the Crimea, Erich von Manstein: 'In thankful appreciation of your particular merit in the victorious battle for the Crimea, with the destruction of Kertsch and the overcoming of the natural and powerful man-made defences of the Sevastopol Fortress, I promote you to Generalfeldmarschall. With your promotion and through the institution of the commemorative shield for all Crimea combatants, I honour, on behalf of the entire German people, the heroic achievements of the troops under your command'.

The badge was to reward the troops engaged in operations in this region in the period from 21.9.41 to 4.7.42. Romanian troops serving with distinction in the Crimea were also eligible for the award. The criteria for the award were:

● To have served in the region for three months.
● To have taken part in at least one major operation against the enemy.
● To have been wounded whilst serving in that region.

It was awarded on a back cloth in the colour of the service to which the recipient belonged. It was authorised for wear on virtually all forms of uniforms, to include white summer dress, tan tropical dress and brown uniform of the Nazi party. The most common was the field-grey of the army. Each soldier was eligible for five examples of the shield. In the case of posthumous awards one shield, accompanied by the possession certificate, was sent to the next of kin. It is estimated that over 100,000 awards were made.

CRIMEA SHIELD: GOLD CLASS*****

Known Makers: J.F.S. 1942
This grade of Crimean Shield was awarded twice and the badge was produced in real gold. The first award was made to Marschal Antonescu of Romania, which he received on 3.7.43 in Bucharest from von Manstein in recognition of the part played by the Romanian divisions deployed in the campaign. The second was to von Manstein himself, which he received from the members of his staff on his birthday, 24.11.43. Manstein also used the design of the gold Crimea Shield as his personal emblem painted on his aircraft and personal vehicles. The exact number of shields produced is not known but it is assumed that more than two examples were made, as photographs show von Manstein wearing the shield both on his tunic and his great coat.

DEMJANSK SHIELD**

Known Makers
This shield was introduced on 25.4.43. It was produced initially in silver-washed zinc then later in plain, grey zinc. It comprises a shield with a pointed bottom and undulating sides. On the top is a box with the name in raised capitals, 'DEMJANSK'. Above the box, at either edge, are two pill boxes with a gun port in each. Between these pill boxes is an eagle with downspread

wings, clutching a swastika surrounded by a wreath in its talons. In the main body of the shield is a single-engined observation aircraft, with a twin-bladed propeller, which is straight across the shield in line with the wings of the aircraft. It is interesting to note that some examples encountered show this propeller as curved. Surmounting the aircraft are large, crossed, double-eged swords, with downswept cross guards. Beneath these is the date '1942'. The badge was placed on a backing cloth of the colour of the service to which the recipient belonged.

This shield was to commemorate the defence of the town of Demjansk by the Second Army Corps who were under the command of Gen Graf Brockdorff-Ahlefeldt and were surrounded by Soviet units. Demjansk is situated some hundred miles north-east of Cholm, between Cholm and Lake Illmen on the northern sector of the Russian front. Amongst the German units were 12, 30, 32, 223 and 290 Infantry Divisions. Also serving with this corps were several non-army units, including personnel of the Reichsarbeitsdienst, organisation Todt, police, Russian auxiliary volunteers and the third SS Panzer division, 'Totenkopf'. They broke out of the encirclement on 21 April but fighting in the area continued until mid October that year. Stiff resistance from the German units, especially Battle Groups Eicke and Simon

Plate 196   Obverse Demjansk Shield.

of the SS Totenkopf Division, committed three entire Soviet armies which the Soviet high command desperately needed elsewhere. SS Obergruppenführer und Gen der Waffen-SS Theodor Eicke was awarded the Oak Leaves to the Knight's Cross of the Iron Cross, becoming the 88th recipient, on 20.4.42 for continued heavy fighting on the Russian front, especially in the area of Demjansk

The defence of Demjansk tied down 18 Russian divisions for over 14 months, for the loss of 3,335 German personnel killed in and in excess of 10,000 being wounded from a garrison strength of 100,000 men. Gen Walter Graf Brockdorff-Ahlefeldt returned from the Demjansk pocket a broken man and died on 9 May 1943. The defenders were supplied by air and the Luftwaffe crews who were engaged in these operations were eligible for the award.

It is interesting to note that the shield is to be worn over the SS arm eagle, in the case of award to those units. Each recipient was entitled to up to five examples of the shield. In the case of posthumous awards, one example of the shield, together with the permission certificate, was sent to the next of kin. Regulations stated that this was the responsibility of the fallen soldier's company commander.

The criteria for the award were:

Ground Forces
- To have served for 60 days in the garrison.
- To have been wounded whilst serving there.
- To have gained a bravery award whilst serving in the garrison.

Luftwaffe Personnel
- To have flown 50 combat missions over the garrison and surrounding area.
- To have flown and landed in the garrison 50 supply missions.

Company commanders were responsible for submitting lists of those in their units who qualified for the award by 31.12.43. Awards ceased on 1.4.44. Approximately 100,000 awards of this shield were made and these were rendered by the garrison commander, Gen der Infanterie Graf Brockdorff-Ahlefeldt.

KUBAN SHIELD**

Known Makers
This shield was instituted on 21.9.43 and is of a similar design to that of the Crimean Shield. It was also produced, like the former, in three distinct manufacturing methods and was produced from both ferrous and non ferrous metal plates which then had a bronze wash applied. The design was stamped into the plate and had the army eagle at the top clutching a wreath surrounding a swastika. On either side of the wreath is the date, '19' and '43' respectively. There is a

band just touching the bottom of the wreath with the word, 'KUBAN' in block capitals. Beneath this is a zig-zag broad line representing the bridgehead for which the badge was introduced to reward the defenders. With the locations KRYMSKAJA, in the middle, LAGUNEN at the top and NOWORO: SSIJSK at the bottom, the badge was then fitted to a back cloth of the colour of the branch of service to which the recipient belonged.

The mighty Soviet counter offensive, following the German defeat at Stalingrad, witnessed the German forces in the south of the Soviet Union pushed helplessly back towards the Crimea Peninsula. A defensive bridgehead was formed between the sea of Azov and the Russian naval harbour at Noworossijsk, with the result that the German units poured into this bottleneck. A determined defence was maintained from 12 February 1943 against the advancing Soviet units along the Kuban River. This successful defence, lasting for several months, allowed many German units to withdraw to comparative safety in the Crimea. The names of the most significant battles fought during the campaign are Lagunen, Krymskaja and Noworossijsk and are commemorated by being placed on the shield.

On 20.9.43 Hitler recognised this defensive achievement with this proclamation: 'To commemorate the heroic battle in the Kuban bridgehead, I institute the Kuban Shield. The Kuban Shield will be worn on the left sleeve of the uniform. The Kuban Shield is awarded as a battle badge to all members of the armed forces and those under the command of the Wehrmacht who, since 1 February 1943 were honourably engaged in the battle for the Kuban bridgehead on land, in the air or at sea. The awards will be made in my name by Generalfeldmarschall von Kleist. The recipient will also receive a certificate of possession. Implementation of the awards is through the high command of the armed forces. Führer Headquarters, 20 September 1943 signed Adolf Hitler'.

However, continuous onslaughts from the Soviet North Caucasian Front Army resulted in the order being given, on 4 September, to evacuate all German and Romanian forces from the area. They withdrew across the Straights of Kerch and the Kuban fell to the Soviet forces on 9.10.43.

The criteria for the award were:
● To have served in the bridgehead for 60 days.
● To have been wounded whilst serving at the bridgehead.
● To have been engaged in one major operation at the bridgehead.

Luftwaffe and navy personnel were also entitled to the award with a complicated points system being employed to qualify their personnel. In the case of the navy, for example, a U-Boat attack on a convoy of ships in the Kuban area represented six points, while being on a boat sunk by enemy action represented 60 points. One day's service represented one point. Each recipient received five examples of the shield free of charge. Posthumous awards were granted with one shield and the award citation.

WARSAW SHIELD*****

Known Makers
This shield was introduced on 10.12.44 and was intended to reward and commemorate those members of the armed forces under the command of SS-Obergruppenführer und Gen der Polizei Erich von dem Bach-Zelewski. Some of the troops that were employed were among the most notorious, with their excesses being repugnant even to the German high command. Some examples of special note are Brig-Gen der SS Kaminiski, a Russian deserter, who formed an anti-partisan brigade named after himself. It was reported by Bach-Zelewski that he had been executed in September 1944 for his excesses in quelling the uprising. There was also Majorgeneral der SS Oskar Dirlewanger who also raised and commanded a brigade named after him. This brigade was made up of ex convicts and poachers. It was for these troops who were employed between 1.8.44 and 2.10.44 that this shield was produced.

It consists of a bronze, pointed bottomed, flat topped shield, with a large eagle filling the field. On the eagle's neck is a swastika and across its chest a scroll with the legend 'WARSCHAU 1944'. Its legs are astride a snake which has its mouth open, a hump in its back that rises between the eagle's spread legs and the tail is at the point of the shield is formed in a circle. The eagle's talons clutch the snake on either side of the hump in its back.

The criteria for the award were:
● To have been on active service at Warsaw between 1.8.44 and 2.10.44.
● To have participated in a minimum of seven days combat.
● To have been wounded in the fighting.
● To have performed an act of bravery during that fighting.
● To have served for a period of 28 days in the combat zone, not necessarily involved in combat, but in a support capacity.
Luftwaffe personnel:
● They were awarded the badge after 20 combat missions over the area.
● After 10 days service in support of the operation.

The badge was designed by Benno von Arent and his design was put into production. However, the

108

factory responsible for the manufacturing of this shield was destroyed in an allied air-raid. The matrix or dies and the on-hand stock of prepared shields were destroyed. It is however possible that some examples escaped destruction.

LORIENT SHIELD: FIRST TYPE*****

Known Makers
The Lorient pocket that encompassed the submarine base was heavily defended against allied attack. A garrison of 26,000 men was gathered from all branches of the Wehrmacht, brought together to prevent the Allies taking possession of Lorient in August 1944. The direct defence of the base was accomplished by a series of buried constructions or fortifications, some of medium importance, others very big and heavily armed, which ensured the protection of the base in the direction of Lorient. The system was completed by anti-tank mines placed at the intersections of roads as well as behind the signal station. Anti-aircraft defence was provided by five rapid´fire Vierling 20mm guns and by balloons moored to the ex-cruiser Strasbourg, which served the purpose of avoiding the premature silting up of the channel. The bunker B2 had protected windows for automatic weapons and there was also a 47mm and a 105 SKC 32 UBTS to defend the entrance of the floating cavities. The garrison of Lorient survived as a pocket of resistance until the end of the war, after being cut off by advancing allied troops subsequent to the drive after the break out from the Normandy beachhead in 1944.

At this point it is worth enlarging upon the construction and general history of the base to give an insight into the need for an award, as well as the complexity of the base. Thousands of workers had been employed to build an enormous submarine base situated on the edge of the Atlantic. This monumental undertaking had no other equivalent in the world. The Lorient submarine base and its outbuildings sheltered the 10th and 2nd Flotillas of U-Boats, (Saltzwedel) as well as the 14th Unterseeboote-Jäger-Flotilla, (submarine hunters). All three were dependent on the 3rd Sicherungedivision, the HQ of which was at Nostang on the Etel. Keroman, the base where these three flotillas were posted, was under the command of Vice-Admiral Matthiae, comprising three parts corresponding respectively to the fortified buildings or bunkers, B1, B2 and B3.

Bunker B1 came into service on 2.9.42 and was a shelter for submarines, consisting of six dry docks among which was a mobile slipway. It was 192 m long and 20 m high, with a roof formed by a flagstone of 7.5 m concrete finished with a steel plate of 40cm. A power station was built on to it, housing six groups of diesel alternators giving an independent source of power in case of an electricity shortage. The thickness of the roof was reduced at this spot to about 4m due to the position of the various diesel rooms and the general design.

Bunker B2 came into service on 8.1.42 and had eight berths, seven of which were dry docks for submarines. Built on to it was a transformer producing 60000/6000 volts to feed the factory in B1, in addition to which the Germans undertook the construction of reinforced stores, which however were never finished. B1 and B2, serving as shelter for submarines, were linked for this purpose by a slipway which ensured the movement of them to dry land for repairs and their re-launching.

Bunker B3, the last to be constructed, came into service on 12.9.42. It was a floating bunker with direct access to the sea and which, with its seven docks, two of which were dry docks, could take ships 85m long. Its dimensions were 170m long and 20m high. The construction of Keroman 1, 2 and 3 was completely finished on 20.3.43. To complement the complex, Vice-Adm Matthiae undertook construction of two 'cathedral' bunkers designed to protect U-Boats under repair and to serve as a food reserve. Between the various constructions was a gallery containing electric cables, the aim of which was to protect the communications between the three buildings and to be completely secure. It should be mentioned that situated on the banks of the Scorff were floating bunkers with two cavities, together with six mooring posts for submarines on the channel.

Among the vulnerable parts of the whole of the 'fortress' were the exterior walls, relatively exposed to direct fire of the enemy naval artillery. The destruction or flooding of the gallery containing the electric cables would have seriously compromised the defence of the three blocks and for that of the slipway, as this would have prevented the exit of any submarines still in B2. In the 'pens' however the submarines were protected from attack. The exit to the slipway was protected by huge, heavily armoured doors but their obliteration or camouflage device was relatively vulnerable and could be jammed by the blast of heavy bombs. The allies planned air attacks using three bombs of 12,000lb nicknamed 'Tallboys', dropped by Lancasters to destroy the Keroman base, the heart of the complex. The first bomb fell on the town, due to an error in calculation, causing numerous civilian victims, the second exploded in the channel but the third fell directly on the constructions of future stores, destroying the buildings already built and bringing communications between buildings to a standstill, through the destruction of the gallery of electric cables.

With regards to the surrender conditions pertaining to the five German fortresses on the Bay of Biscay, St Nazaire, La Rochelle, La Palisse, Lorient and the channel fortress Dunkirk, the following are quotations from orders and signals sent between 1.5.45 and 6.5.45 to and from Dönitz's headquarters at Murwich Flensburg.

On 1.5.45 Dönitz issued the following declaration to all members of the German armed forces: 'I expect discipline and obedience. Chaos and ruin can be prevented only by the swift and unreserved execution of my orders. Anyone who, at this juncture, fails in his duty and condemns German women and children to slavery and death, is a traitor and a coward. The oath of allegiance which you took to the führer now binds each and every one of you to me, whom he himself appointed as his successor.'

On 4.5.45 Adm Friedeburg was authorised by Dönitz to negotiate a separate but partial surrender of all German forces in Northern Germany to take effect from 08.00 on the morning of 5.5.45. This partial surrender included all German forces in Holland, northwest Germany and in Denmark. This was also to include all naval ships in these areas. These forces were to lay down their arms and surrender unconditionally.

On 5.5.45 Friedeburg and Jodl were instructed by Dönitz to fly to Eisenhower's HQ at Rheims to negotiate the surrender of all remaining German armed forces in southern Germany and France.

Following the negotiations, Keitel sent the following radio message to Friedeburg and Jodl: 'Grandadmiral prepared to include garrisons in the channel and on the Channel Islands in truce'.

All five garrisons in the fortress ports were required to surrender unconditionally on 9.5.45. This order was complied with in three cases. The Channel Islands did not officially surrender until 10.5.45 and Lorient also capitulated on the same day. The garrison at Lorient produced a newspaper during the nine-month siege entitled *Kurznachrichten*. An issue of this was published on 10.5.45 and carried details of the surrender.

This shield is one about which there exists great disagreement as to its authenticity and to the very existence of the piece. This will probably continue until someone can come up with incontrovertible proof, one way or another, to its introduction and award before the end of hostilities.

It consists of a thin shield with flat top and rounded bottom. The central design is of a naked warrior with a German steel helmet on his head. In his left hand is an oval shield, with an open winged eagle clutching wreath and swastika in its talons, impressed upon it. In his right hand is a double edged sword. He stands astride a U-Boat pen with a submarine in it and in the foreground are stylised waves. From behind the warrior emanate rays. On either side of the helmeted head is, '19' and '44' respectively. Running round the bottom edge of the shield is the word 'LORIENT'. This design was submitted by Marinebaurat Fehrenberg to the garrison commander, Admi-

ral Henneke, who authorised the production of the shield in December 1944. It is interesting to note, however, that when recently approached for information about the shield Admiral Henneke denied any knowledge of it.

Christian von Tettinek stated, 'the first type was submitted and approved and the dies were produced out of cast iron. However, the dies were of inferior quality and they broke after a short while'. This gives rise to the rarity of the first form as only a few hundred were produced as opposed to the originally proposed 24,000, as stated by Dr Klietmann. The badge was produced in a local fish cannery and was purported to have been produced from various materials, the most likely being the tin plate from which the cannery produced its tins. Holes were then pierced to allow the shield to be sewn on to the uniform. It has been stated that large numbers of the shield were produced and this has been used as an argument to prove that the badge did not exist at all because very few examples have turned up. It has been reported that Marinebaurat Fehrenberg was commissioned by General Wilhelm Fahrmbacher to produce a design for the shield, which might seemingly explain why Admiral Henneke claimed to have no knowledge of it. However, it is stated that the shields were distributed to about one man in every two in the garrison on Christmas night 1944. That Henneke knew nothing about this 'ceremony', if it took place as stated, appears very strange. Furthermore, there is a photograph of a shield whose authenticity is in no doubt, since it is said to have been awarded to a French nurse who was present in Lorient during the siege, identified as Jacqueline D. The example used is one obtained from Dr Mathias, who obtained it along with 10 other examples from a French Intelligence officer who picked them up in the fortress immediately at the end of hostilities. Lefèvre and de Lagarde state that Luftwaffe personnel were meant to have received a shield with their own version of the national emblem on it. Whether any of these shields were actually produced is, of course, highly debatable given the situation the Germans were in at that time. My view is that there were only small quantities produced and this gives rise to its rarity, plus the fact that a photograph of the shield being worn so far has not yet been found but, as with the Metz Cuff title, dextrous detective work will uncover one in due course.

LORIENT SHIELD: FIRST TYPE: VARIATION*****

Known Makers
This is a variation which is almost identical to the badge previously described but, in this case, the shield is raised to symbolise the defence from air attacks which the pocket received liberally.

LORIENT SHIELD: SECOND TYPE*****

Known Makers
This is not an arm shield per se but an unused identity disc which has, 'FESTUNG LORIENT 1944', stamped on it in three lines. This has been reported to be an alternative design when it was impossible to reward the troops with the shield. This item leaves the researcher detective with a lot more enquiry and research to be done.

One interesting comment is found in 'Fakes and Frauds of The Third Reich', Second Edition by Freiherr von Mollendorf, and I quote, 'We have a Lorient Shield given to us by a Leutnant Kröh, formerly of the Kriegsmarine and stationed in Lorient until its surrender in May of 1945. This shield is stamped by hand onto a standard blank (unperforated) zinc German identification disc and holes were punched into it (as in the case of the much rarer 'Dunchirchen' Shield) to enable it to be worn on the uniform. Herr Kröh writes us that he personally has seen a number of shields similar to the one he had but not ever seen the nude warrior now so widely depicted. It is not impossible that the two designs existed simultaneously'. He continues with more observations of reproductions and I draw the reader's attention to them.

This form has also been well researched by Richard Mundschenk, who found an example that had been sewn on to the uniform of a German Coastal Artillery officer. This was obtained in May 1945 by Staff Sergeant Ernest Edwards senior, a member of the 66th Infantry Division. His unit had been engaged in the siege of the fortress and with the culmination of the siege they moved into the fortress and occupied the area. The desire for souvenir hunting led him to discover the discarded uniform, which was unceremoniously deposited with his other treasures in a duffel bag and subsequently shipped back to the United States, where it remained stored in his foot locker and was then deposited in the attic of his Maryland home. He confided in Mundschenk that he had encountered a number of Germans wearing this form of emblem. Upon his death, his son gave Mundschenk a quantity of photographs, one of which showed German prisoners going into French captivity and sporting the emblem. Mundschenk goes on to report his in depth researches into the shield and concluded that the first two types only existed on paper and that this battle honour was only rendered in the most readily available form of material, a standard identification 'dog tag'. Existing stocks of the ID. ovals were simply stamped with the designation, 'FESTUNG LORIENT'. The three existing types which he had encountered were of the Army type, oval. He presumed the Kriegsmarine type were too small in size to be utilised. Two were of zinc and the other aluminium forms. The zinc ones were engraved in large capital letters,

while the aluminium type was stamped in slightly smaller sized letters. His findings would concur with those of Christian von Tettinek and, as has been previously stated, the first type was submitted and approved and the dies were produced out of cast iron. However, the dies were of inferior quality and they broke after a short while. This gives rise to two outcomes. Firstly, the rarity of the first form, as only a few hundred were produced as opposed to the originally proposed 24,000, as stated by Dr Klietmann and secondly, the necessity of continuing the award. It was decided that a temporary device was necessary to identify the recipients and thus the dog tags were employed which would have then been exchanged for the formally designed shield at a later time, after hostilities had ceased. This would also give rise to the fact that the entry was not made in the pay book, as in the case of the Dunkirk Shield, this being done when the shield was awarded in the proper form to the recipient.

LAPLAND SHIELD****

Known Makers
This shield was instituted in and around February or March 1945 and is the last official shield to be awarded by the German high command. It comprises a round bottomed shield with a flat top. Just below the top is a bar that runs horizontally across the shield, breaking the edge. Round the edge of the shield is a rim. On the bar is an eagle, which positively looks more like a chicken. It is interesting to note at this point that the eagle does not incorporate the swastika in its design; in fact it is not employed at all on the badge. Another point of great interest is that the eagle looks in different ways on various badges and I have encountered six slight variations in design and production of this badge. I have not included a breakdown of variations at this juncture as a lot more research work is required. Beneath the bar is the word in capitals, 'LAPPLAND' and beneath this is a map of the area. All the examples encountered are crudely cast, stamped or cut out from aluminium, tin or zinc. Some were merely engraved crudely on to a shield-shaped blank. They were issued without a backing cloth. Round the edges of the shield were drilled a number of small holes through which it could be sewn to the uniform. However, some genuine examples of the shield have been encountered with cloth backings attached. Whether this was done by the recipient after award or if, on very few occasions, the awarding unit had the unit's tailor attach the backing, is unclear. It was intended to reward members of the 20th Mountain Army Group which was under the command of General Boehme who, incidentally, was responsible for the award of the shield.

The 20th Gebirgs-Armee included such

111

diverse units as 6. Gebirgs-Division, 270 Infantry-Division, Panzer Brigade 'Norwegen' and 14 Luftwaffen-Felddivision. Awards on paper were certainly made before the end of the war. Genuine paybook entries for the award are known from April 1945 but it is believed that no actual awards were issued from this time.

Following the end of hostilities, the large German forces in northern Scandinavia were left mainly to their own devices under the control of their own command structures, which answered to the British military authorities. The Germans soon found that their captor, Gen Thorne, contrary to normal British commanders' practice, allowed his prisoners to wear military decorations. During this period it was decided to proceed with the issue of the Lapland Shield. These could, of course, only be produced on what amounted to a cottage industry basis. Obviously the design could not feature the swastika, as the Allies would have taken umbrage at its inclusion. The more liberal view of this large Scandinavia army can possibly be attributed to the fact that the British were seriously considering allowing certain units to defend territory against the onslaught of Soviet forces. This was also considered in the Vienna region of Austria and has led to considerable controversy in British military circles. I have one paybook issued to a Romanian SS volunteer and he categorically states that he was never taken prisoner but was held in reserve, ready to be sent to fight the Soviets.

The criteria for the award were:
● It has been suggested that six months service in the area was required.
● To have been wounded in that theatre of operations.
● To have been engaged in a major offensive or defensive battle in that region.
● To have won a bravery award in that area.

It has been stated 'This shield is of debatable legitimacy as a national award, as it was only authorised on a local level by the army commander and not issued until after the end of hostilities which, technically, makes even genuine pieces postwar'. I would like to amplify the point that the shield was submitted for approval at the beginning of 1945 and received it on 1.5.45. Commanders in the field became the legitimate instigating force and the Third Reich did not cease until 27.4.45, therefore awards during this period have to be considered as legitimate Third Reich pieces, albeit they may not have been given official recognition by the German Federal government.

STALINGRAD SHIELD: FIRST TYPE PROTOTYPE*****

Known Makers
On 2.10.42 Hitler ordered that a design should be prepared for a shield for the defenders of Stalingrad. Ernst Eigener, a war artist with Propaganda Company 637, was instructed to produce the art work, Hitler's wishes having been passed to the press relations department who had authorised the design to be prepared.

This design took the form of a shield with pointed bottom and a closed winged eagle on the top, without a swastika. The centre had a silo amidst the ruins of Stalingrad. These silos, which were a landmark in Stalingrad, had been the scene of many bitter encounters. Facing it, in profile, was a dead German infantryman with a crown of barbed wire round his helmet. Across the shield at the top was a box with the word, 'STALINGRAD' in capital letters.

The high command decided that this design was too morbid for consideration and turned it down. Ernst Eigener did not get the opportunity of submitting another design, as he himself was killed the following month at Stalingrad. Perhaps his design was a premonition of his own future fate.

STALINGRAD SHIELD: SECOND TYPE PROTOTYPE*****

Known Makers
Feldmarschall von Paulus designed this shield and, again, it had a pointed bottom. The top was flat with a box in which was the word 'STALINGRAD' in capitals. Surmounting this was a closed winged eagle without a swastika. The central motif of the shield was that of the silo with the ruins of Stalingrad. Beneath this design there was a stylised river, with the word 'WOLGA' on it. The field had a background made up of snow and clouds. The similarity of both these designs gives rise to the possibility that there must have been some collusion or, if not, that von Paulus had redesigned Eigener's work into a more acceptable design. However Stalingrad fell with a humiliating defeat for Germany, von Paulus surrendering on 30.1.43, taking with him more than 94,000 German troops into captivity. At least 147,000 had died within the city and a further 100,000 had died outside it. Also 2 Romanian, 1 Italian and 1 Hungarian armies had been destroyed. Von Paulus' 6th Army was the first German army to surrender in WW2. One final sting in the tail for Hitler, who had viewed Stalingrad as a personnel struggle with its namesake, was that he had promoted von Paulus to Feldmarschall on 29.1.43, only one day before von Paulus had surrendered to the Russians. This

promotion was to have encouraged him in the battle.

BALKAN SHIELD*****

Known Makers
In January 1945 a shield was awarded for the forces who were engaged in holding the Red Army back and fighting the Partisans in the Balkan region. The design for this shield was produced by Benno von Arent and takes the form of a pointed bottomed shield with a flat top. Across the top of the shield, in large capitals is the word 'BALKAN'. Beneath this is an eagle, not unlike the SS type. On either side, below the under edge of the wing is, '1944' and '1945'. This all surmounts a map of the Balkan region. Dr Klietmann has the original artwork for the shield in his collection and it is dated 7.3.45.

It has always been thought that this badge was never produced or issued but an SS Oberscharführer in the Prinz Eugen division, Fredrich Olesh, told me that he had the job as adjutant, a position which he had held for some time, of awarding approximately 250 of these shields. He was, in fact a personal friend of SS Gruppenführer and Generalleutnant der Waffen-SS Arthur Phleps, to whom he was also adjutant. At the same time they received a wristwatch, inscribed on the back, from Hitler. Unfortunately both the shield and watch were removed from him in an internment camp in England, while he retained his collar patch, cuff title officer's quality, Black Wound Badge, Iron Cross ribbon, shoulder straps and rank patch, all of which he presented to me.

MEMEL SHIELD PROTOTYPE*****

Known Makers
Little is known of this award and it is probably an unofficially recognised one, which might have been instituted by the commander of the 7th Panzer Division, Generalleutnant Dr Karl Mause.

It consisted of a pointed bottomed shield, with a square top. Below the top line of the shield is the word, 'MEMEL', in stylised capital lettering. The central motif is a gatehouse with portal and two square windows above it. On each side is a stylised watch tower resting on battlements. Beneath this is a curious boat-shaped gate with 'NJEMENFRONT' under it, again in similar stylised capitals. However, in truth, it is not a gate but rather a stylised boat. For the Memel Shield shows the municipal arms of Stadt Memel derived from the town seal of the sixteenth century. The seal and arms of the town have always shown the gatehouse with two watch towers on each side and a boat underneath.

The shield, if it existed, would have been to reward personnel who had been involved in the fighting by the 7th Panzer Division during the winter of 1944-45, when Memel was under siege by the Soviet forces.

DUNKIRK SHIELD*****

Known Makers: Unmarked (Always)
Konteradmiral Frederich Frisius had introduced, some time in January or February 1945, a small shield produced in thin stamped brass measuring 40mm by 34mm. The bottom of the shield is rounded and the top square. The edge running all the way round is gently rolled under and there is a small hole in each top corner, with one centrally at the bottom. These holes were there to allow the badge to be attached to the hat. I have seen three examples of this shield, two had no back cloth but the other one did. So, whether or not it was to have been awarded with a back cloth is a point of conjecture. The central device is the watchtower of Dunkirk with stylised waves in three lines on either side of it. To each side of the tower, in line with its top, is the date '1944' two numbers on either side. Across the top in small capitals is stamped, 'DUENKIRCHEN', and round the bottom of the shield is a chain of seven unbroken links. It is considered that there were only 50 awards of this very rare shield. There is a citation that clearly indicates that it was known as, 'Stoçtruppabzeichen' and that it was awarded, in this particular case, for participation in two raiding parties. Whether or not a citation was rendered with every award of the shield is unknown but an official entry was made in the pay book of each recipient to allow him the wearing of the shield. This entry and citation tends to make the award a more official decoration than some of the previous unofficial ones. It is possible that this shield was to reward members of the force who were engaged in such adventures as Operation 'Blücher' and would thus give rise to the very small number that were supposedly awarded out of a total garrison of 15,000. One known recipient of the award was Gefreiter Sigfried Rubusch, whose pay book was made up on 30.1.45 and had a piece of paper stuck into the last page stamped with the Dunkirk command stamp on 18.3.45. This gives rise to the possibility that the award was introduced as early as January 1945 and was issued to commemorate the coming to power of Hitler. Thus it could have been given for operations against the Czechs as early as October 1944 and this would account for the date '1944' appearing on the Shield. Another known recipient was Stabogefreiten Wilhelu Tjardes who received the award on 1.5.45.

Dunkirk was surrounded by the allies after the D-Day invasion and held out until 9.5.45. Hitler had decided that it was most important to turn certain ports in the Channel Islands and those situated on the west coast of France into

197

200

198

201

199

202 **203**

2

Plate 197 Obverse Kuban Shield on black cloth backing.

Plate 198 Obverse Warsaw Shield.

Plate 199 Obverse Lorient Shield First Type.

Plate 200 Obverse Lorient Shield Second Type.

Plate 201 Obverse Lapland Shield.

Plate 202 Obverse Stalingrad Shield First Type. This artist's impression gives an idea of the proposed design.

Plate 203 Obverse Stalingrad Shield Second Type. This artist's impression gives an idea of the proposed design.

Plate 204 Obverse Balkan Shield. Note this is a reproduction to give an idea of the design.

Plate 205 Artist's impression of the Memel Shield.

Plate 206 Obverse Dunkirk Shield.

fortresses, and this was made in response to Admiral Krancke's telegram which contained the following paragraph illustrating graphically the thinking of the fortress policy which encompassed La Rochelle, St Nazaire, Lorient and Dunkirk. It has already been discussed that the principle of the production of a shield is in recognition of the defence of that fortress and gives rise to the production of this particular example. It is also therefore possible, but highly improbable, that shields exist for the other two fortresses. Krancke's telegram states 'It is absolutely essential that the most important harbours on the south and west coasts are denied to the enemy for the longest possible time... The navy will support the defence of the fortress and the fortress

areas through the use of all available naval forces, and when these are lost the weapons and the men are to be used in the defence of the landward perimeters'.

Needless to say, many of those supposedly fortress ports fell to the allies quickly. However La Rochelle, St Nazaire, Lorient and Dunkirk remained uncaptured until the end of the hostilities. One of the last to surrender was Dunkirk and the German perimeter around the hinterland was reinforced by the garrisons of Nieuport and Ostend. The British forces surrounding the pocket were made of battle hardened Czechs. When the fighting in North Africa came to an end, the Czech troops in the Middle East returned to England where, in 1943, they formed into the 1st Independent Armoured Brigade Group. Its 4,500 men were organised in the 1st, 2nd and 3rd Czech Armoured Regiments. In June 1944 the Czech Brigade landed in Normandy and on 9 October infiltrated the German positions in and around Dunkirk. The fortress pocket comprised of between 12,000 and 15,000 men which were made up by units of the 226th Infantry Division, navy and Luftwaffe contingents. These were all put together into an ad hoc defensive force by Konteradmiral Frederich Frisius who commanded the overall garrison. The garrison exhibited its fighting capacity when on the dawn of 5 April Rear-Admiral Frisius opened Operation 'Blücher'. This offensive which could be counted as little more than a raid but enacted with such ferocity, panicked the unsuspecting British forces. The strength of the attack so confused the British headquarters that it was driven to issue orders to blow up the bridges that surrounded Dunkirk. Regaining its momentum the British headquarters mounted a counter-attack which was supported by rocket firing typhoons but even with this superior force they were unable to dislodge the determined German units from their newly gained front line positions. Frisius perceived the close proximity to the final collapse of the Third Reich and signalled the navy high command to establish whether his forces were included in the armistice which had been signed at Lüneburg. Montgomery, obviously peaked at the Admiral's pugnacious defence of Dunkirk, had demanded that Frisius should be included in the armistice agreement. The O.K.M. had only one response to Frisius and that was that he would be informed verbally by them when he was to surrender. Reassured by his high command that his garrison was excluded, he was able to reject the terms offered by the allies. His military honour and that of his men was his only concern and if he held out until the general surrender, the allies could not claim to have defeated his gallant force. Frisius signed the surrender document when the war was indeed ended, on 9.5.45, his honour and that of his men being upheld.

10. Campaign Cuff Titles

KRETA COMMEMORATIVE CUFF TITLE***

Known Makers

On 16.10.42 this award was introduced to reward all personnel of the army, navy or Luftwaffe who had participated or helped in the capture of the island of Crete, which had been defended by the British forces.

This cuff band takes the form of a white cotton strip, 33mm wide, with a border of yellow cotton. In between the borders in capital letters, is embroidered the name 'KRETA' in yellow cotton. On either side of the name title is a sprig of Acanthus leaves in a stylised pattern. This can be found in two distinct types. The normal issue band with a seven leaf cone and a superior quality band with the cone being formed from nine individual leaves. It is important to note at this point that in the past reference works have only recognised that the material in which the band was produced was off-white cotton. But there is a variation of this cuff title, of which original examples have been found, produced on an off-white felt strip. These examples are very scarce. Careful scrutiny and great caution must be exercised when deciding the originality, as a number of reproductions of this award have been produced in this material.

The award was to have been worn on all uniforms including the overcoat or greatcoat. In the case of the navy, the method of wearing the cuff title was laid down by an order dated 14.8.42, MV 42, No. 721, stating that the title was to be worn a prescribed distance from the lower edge of the left sleeve:

- with officer's reefer jacket — 4cm.
- with senior NCO's reefer jacket — 8cm.
- with greatcoat and pea jackets — 8cm.
- with tropical and field-grey field blouses — 15cm.
- with the blue shirt — 15cm.

The cuff title was not to be worn on other naval garments. The date of termination for the award of this cuff title was 31.10.44 for all possible recipients.

The criteria for the award were:

- To have been engaged in a glider or parachute landing, between the dates of 20 and 27.5.41 on the island of Crete.
- To have been engaged in air operations over Crete during the period of invasion.

- In the case of the navy, to have been engaged on active service up to 27.5.41, in the Cretan theatre of operations.
- The army personnel who had been engaged with the naval flotilla that had put to sea on 19.5.41 to attempt landings on the island.

AFRIKA COMMEMORATIVE CUFF TITLE**

Known Makers

On 18.7.41 a cuff title 'AFRIKA KORPS' was authorised for wear by members of this unit who were fighting on the continent of Africa, by Generaloberst von Brauchitsch. Orders (HV41A, Nos. 496 and 778), dated 18.7.41 and 4.11.41 permitted the wearing of the cuff title of the army pattern by all units of the navy that were attached to the Afrika Korps, (DAK), or later to the Panzerarmee Afrika. The cuff title is a cotton band 33mm wide with 'AFRIKA KORPS' in silver block lettering on a dark green background, edged at the top and bottom with a band of silver embroidery, 0.3cm wide. These silver bands are themselves edged in a tan coloured material. The whole of this cuff title was in fact produced, or woven, as one integral piece. This title was worn on the right cuff of service, field service, uniform tunic as well as that of the greatcoat. For members of the Luftwaffe, a plain blue band was authorised with 'AFRIKA' embroidered on to it in silver cotton thread for NCOs and below, and aluminium wire for officers. In this case the cuff title did not have a border. There is also a form that was produced on a navy-blue backing and has the title, in capital letters, 'AFRIKA KORPS' embroidered in golden yellow cotton thread with a yellow thread embroidered border on each side. These three bands were never intended to be considered as an award but just purely a unit recognition. The *esprit de corps* of the troops involved in the north African campaigns gave rise to the ex-members of the Afrika Korps on their return from Africa, wearing either cuff titles as an unofficial honour. The cuff title had been officially permitted on the European continent when a DAK member was on leave there.

To formalise this custom, on 15.1.43, an official cuff title was introduced. This took the form of a khaki coloured band, 33mm wide with a border on each edge of silver coloured cotton. In the centre of this band was embroidered, also in silver coloured cotton, the word 'AFRIKA' flanked on each side by a stylised palm tree. In another form, with a Swastika within the trunk of the palm tree, this had been the sign of the Afrika Korps. Another form that has been encountered has a khaki cotton band measuring 44mm that is turned over, with the top and bottom edges are machine stitched with pale green cotton to fix the edge. On to the centre of the band is placed a border of off-white cotton that is stitched directly to the band. The upper and lower borders are separated by a central field 33mm wide and on to this is embroidered, in silver bullion wire, the title 'AFRIKA'. This is flanked on either side by a palm tree, again in bullion wire. Each of the five fronds has a black cotton central line. The purpose of this band is unknown and can only be considered as an officer's private purchase piece. There also exists a version with a blue band, edged in gold, with gold palm trees and title as before described. The purpose of this type of cuff title is unknown but one theory that has been put forward is that this was to reward naval personnel. One such sleeve band was presented to senior NCO, Heinz Ubinger, in May 1943 for service in Tunis while assigned to a Luftwaffe ground unit. Konteradmiral Wilhelm Meendsen-Bohlken, commander of naval forces in Italy, is pictured wearing a hand embroidered Afrika cuff title as described. After 29.8.44, with the exception of prisoners of war, those missing in action and personnel confined to hospital who could possibly return to active service, no more Afrika titles were awarded.

The German Red Cross nurses in North Africa braved aerial bombardment and artillery barrages. Some were killed and a number were wounded in the course of their duty. These actions led some to be decorated for their bravery under fire. Those Red Cross members who met the requirements were also permitted to wear the 'Afrika Korps' cuff title and later the 'Afrika' campaign decoration. Four nurses were awarded the Iron Cross Second Class and thus became eligible for this cuff title under the condition set out in below. The recipients were: SCHULZ Ilse — Schwester des Deutschen Roten Kreuzes; FOCK Grete — Schwester des Deutschen Roten Kreuzes; WEBER Hanny — Schwester des Deutschen Roten Kreuzes; and MüNCHE Geolinde — Schwester des Deutschen Roten Kreuzes.

In the case of the navy, the method of wearing this cuff title was laid down by an order dated 29.12.42, MV 43, No. 18, stating that the title was to be worn in the prescribed distance from the lower edge of the left sleeve:
- with officer's reefer jacket — 4cm.
- with senior NCO's reefer jacket — 8cm.
- with greatcoat and pea jackets — 8cm.
- with tropical and field-grey field blouses — 15cm.
- with the blue shirt — 15cm.

The cuff title was not to be worn on any other naval garment. This same order prohibited further wear of the Afrika cuff title, with the golden-yellow embroidery on a dark blue band that was without the palm trees, for these were not a campaign title but a unit title of all units fighting in north Africa. The dark blue background, as already described, was that employed for the navy.

The criteria for the award were:
- A minimum of six months on north African soil.
- Being wounded in combat in the north African theatre of operations.
- Contraction of an illness while in the north African theatre of operations. This was to include personnel evacuated to the continent of Europe due to that illness but service must have been in excess of three months before contracting the illness to entitle the possible recipient to be considered for an award of the cuff title under those circumstances.
- From 6.5.43, it was decreed by Hitler that the service time required by those who fought in the final phases of the campaign, be reduced to four months.
- The recipients of decorations awarded in this theatre of operations, to include the Iron Cross, German Cross in Gold, Goblet of Honour or Salver of Honour, would automatically be awarded the cuff title regardless of the length of service in Africa.
- Death of a member of the Afrika Korps in the line of duty, again automatically qualified him for an award of the cuff title. In this case the next of kin received the award document.

'METZ 1944' COMMEMORATIVE CUFF TITLE****

Known Makers
The US Third Army's advance through Europe towards Germany was successfully halted for a short period at the Metz Citadel by stiff German resistance. The action that facilitated the hold up of the US army was between 27.7.44 and 25.9.44. This resulted in the Third Army mounting a major offensive operation against the defenders of the citadel. The defenders comprised SS units — members of the KAMPFGRUPPE von SIEGROTH. Gen von Siegroth was the commander of the officer candidate school VI. From 1.7.44 to November 1944 members of this school were also employed in the defence of the citadel. The Third Army's offensive to break the defence of Metz started on 8.11.44 and was virtually concluded by 20.11.44. The citadel was overthrown, although some diehard SS elements continued to hold on in a region known as Fort Gambelleta where they continued their resistance until 7.12.44.

To recognise the heroic battle of the period 27.7.44 to 25.9.44 Hitler ordered the introduction of a cuff title — 'METZ 1944' — on 24.10.44. This cuff title consists of a black silk band similar to those worn by SS personnel as an honour title, with silver threads numbering seven threads per border on each edge of the band. In silver embroidered wire in the centre of the band is the word, 'METZ', in block letters followed by the date, '1944'. Until 1986, the award had not been positively identified as being actually awarded. However, a photograph of Generalmajor Joachim von Siegroth, who commanded much of the defence of Metz, wearing the cuff title while awarding the Knights Cross of the Iron Cross to Willi Schmuckle in March 1945, proves positively that the cuff title had been awarded at the time.

The criteria for the award are unknown.

'KURLAND' COMMEMORATIVE CUFF TITLE****

Known Makers
On 12.3.45 Hitler ordered the introduction of a cuff title to reward the defenders of the besieged Courland region of Latvia, at the request of the general of Army Group Courland. The German forces in Courland had been isolated when the Soviet westward advance reached the Baltic to the south. These forces were not withdrawn but continued to resist in many fierce battles until they eventually surrendered at the time of the main German capitulation in May 1945.

This cuff title was produced locally at Kuldiga, in a weaving mill. The band is of unusual design as the reverse has a form of cross stitch joining the two outer edges together, these outer edges having been turned over. The obverse has a bold black top and bottom edge inside which is a line of black oblong dots and inside these is a fine thin black line. Between these two thin lines, in capitals, is the legend, 'KURLAND'. Before the 'K' is a shield with a black cross as its central motif, not unlike a Balkan Cross. The shield is square topped with a pointed base. This shield is, in fact, the crest of the Grand Master of the Teutonic Knights. The other side has a similar shield but in this case it is black, with a white moose's head looking inwards to the left from the viewer's position, this being the coat of arms of Mitau. The overall colour of the band is off-white and the material is of a rough cotton.

The precise criteria for the award are a little vague but generally take the same form as that for the Afrika cuff band. The award was also to be used as a campaign commemorative title for those who had been engaged in the battles for Courland. The cuff title saw actual distribution by the end of April 1945 with the allocation going firstly to the enlisted personnel, then the NCOs, then the officers. Awards were made right up to and including the day of the German surrender, 8.5.45.

Plate 207   Obverse Kreta Cuff Title.

Plate 208   Obverse Afrika Cuff Title.

Plate 209   Obverse Afrika Cuff Title. Observe that it is embroidered in silver bullion on a light brown cotton band.

Plate 210   Obverse Metz 1944 Commemorative Cuff Title.

Plate 211   Obverse Kurland Commemorative Cuff Title.

Plate 212   Reverse Kurland Commemorative Cuff Title.

11. Commemorative and Campaign Awards

CROSS OF HONOUR 1914-1918 FOR COMBATANTS*

CROSS OF HONOUR 1914-1918 FOR NON-COMBATANTS*

CROSS OF HONOUR 1914-1918 FOR NEXT OF KIN*

Known Makers

I have decided to describe these three classes together as the basic design of the crosses is so similar and the historical background to each is interrelated. The crosses consist of a type that is known as pattée with a virtually central medallion. The whole measures 38mm across. It has a raised edge line that measures 1mm and a recessed field. Within the raised edge line is a 0.5mm raised line.

The Combatants' Type has a wreath of laurel leaves at the centre, tied at the base with a ribbon tie with the ends cascading into the field of the lower arm. On each side of the wreath are five bunches of three leaves, with two laurel berries at each joint. On the central field, in raised numerals, are the two dates of WW1, '1914' and '1918', placed over each other. Through the angles of the cross are placed a pair of double edged swords that measure 41mm.

The reverse is plain with, in some cases, the maker's name on the lower arm. From the upper arm is a 1.5mm to 2mm extrusion, through which runs the ribbon ring. The overall colour of the cross is bronze.

The ribbon can come in a variety of widths ranging from 25 mm, 27mm, 29mm and 30mm. In the last case the ribbon is made up of 3.5mm black, 5mm white, 4mm black, 5mm red central stripe, 4mm black, 5mm white and 3.5mm black stripes.

The Non-Combatants' Type is the same, save that the laurel wreath is exchanged for a wreath of oak leaves of similar design. The swords are omitted but the same ribbon is employed.

The Next of Kin Type is the same as the Non-Combatants' Type, except that the cross is finished in black and the colours of the ribbon are reversed, giving 3.5mm white, 5mm black, 4mm white, 5mm red central stripe, 4mm white, 5mm black and 3.5mm white stripes.

The crosses were the creation of Eugene Godet of Berlin, who received the commission from the Reich Chancellery.

These awards were instituted on 13.7.34 by president Generalfeldmarschall von Hindenburg and were to commemorate war service in WW1 by combatants, non-combatants and to act as a memorial to those who had lost their lives, by honouring their next of kin. These awards were the only official commemorative pieces introduced during the period of the Third Reich. WW1 was calculated as being from 1.8.14 to 31.12.18. Every citizen of the German Reich and also those who had lost their German nationality as a result of the Treaty of Versailles, were eligible, if they had rendered military service to Germany or her allies, including service in the Red Cross.

By 1.2.37 the following numbers of awards had been approved:

- Combatants 6,202,883.
- Non-Combatants 1,120,449.
- Widows 345,132.
- Parents 373,950.

To recognise those eligible in the Saar, Danzig, Austria, Czechoslovakia and the Memel regions, as they were reintegrated into the Reich, orders were made by the Reichsminister of the Interior. The dates of the orders for qualification of people in those areas varied. For the Saar the period was 21.3.35-30.6.35, for Austrians and Sudeten Germans the opening date was 30.10.38 and for Germans in the Memel land 29.5.39. The period for entitlement for all these concluded on 30.6.40. An order of 30.6.42 expanded the award to include German and Austrian allies who had fought with those two countries' forces. It was further expanded by an order of 12.3.43 with eligibility being extended to those people of the Protectorate of Böhmen und Mähren and finally, by Hitler's personal orders on 7.9.44, those members of the Deutschen Volksgruppen in the southeast. The approving authority was vested in the Ministry of the Interior. The cross was worn on either a medal bar or in the form of a ribbon on a ribbon bar. In this case a small pair of crossed swords represented the Combatants. These awards ranked above service and occupation awards but below combat related ones.

They were presented uncased, or in a binder having the award document on one side and the cross on the other, or in a hard hinged case. This could be more commonly with a black outer shell, or with a red Leatherette covering. They have a gold tooled line round the edge with a hinge and a press-stud catch. The upper lid liner is white satin with, in black Gothic print, 'TREUE UM TREUE' and a facsimile of von Hindenburg's signature. The lower tray has a velvet pad recessed to take the cross and a lip at the top to allow the ribbon to run beneath it. This pad is completely detachable from the lower tray that itself is lined with a glazed white paper.

SPANISH CROSS WITH SWORDS: BRONZE**

SPANISH CROSS WITH SWORDS: SILVER**

SPANISH CROSS WITH SWORDS: GOLD***

Known Makers: CEJ, CEJ (in rectangular frame), 4, L/11, L/13, L/15, L/16, L/21, L/52 (in an oblong box)

The basic design was the same for each version and takes the form of a Maltese Cross. This measures 56mm across with the width of the arms, and 23mm across the points. The arms of the cross have a 1.5mm rim. The recessed fields produced by the rim are lightly pebbled. In the centre is a circle on to which is placed a 15.5mm raised circular dish that has a 1mm raised edge line and a further similar line indented by 2mm.

The inner recessed central field has a raised swastika with the arms touching the circle. The high parts of the medal are polished, while the pebbled areas are matt. Between the arms of the cross are flying Luftwaffe eagles clutching swastikas in their talons. The eagle emblems are separately struck and very neatly soldered to the arms of the cross. The area between the arms of the swastika can be voided or solid depending upon the manufacturer. This feature does not always indicate superior quality of manufacture. Beneath the eagles run two crossed swords with their hilts at the bottom of the cross. The swords are double edged, have a central raised spine and a raised edge line on either side. They have a crossguard with oblong box at the centre and quillons tapering from the edge to the central box. The quillons and box have a fine raised edge line and the recessed fields of the quillons have eight raised vertical lines, while the box has a vertical spine. The hilts are barrel shaped, with small round pommels and wound with nine twists of twisted cord. The swords measure 62mm from the tip to the pommel and the crossguard is 10mm across. The swords themselves are part of the stamping that forms the convex body of the cross.

The reverse is plain and has a hinge, massive pin and 'C' form hook that is soldered directly to the lower arm of the cross. The cross is made in either silver, which comes in varying grades and

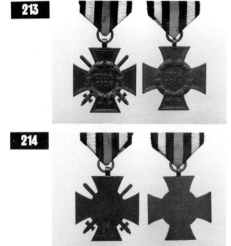

Plate 213 Obverse Cross of Honour 1914-1918 for Combatants & Cross of Honour 1914-1918 for Non-Combatants.

Plate 214 Reverse Cross of Honour 1914-1918 for Combatants & Cross of Honour 1914-1918 for Non-Combatants.

Plate 215 Obverse Spanish Cross with Swords Silver Class.

Plate 216 Reverse Spanish Cross with Swords Silver Class. Note the silver content.

Plate 217 Obverse Spanish Cross in Gold with Diamonds.

Plate 218 Reverse Spanish Cross in Gold with Diamonds.

Plate 219 Obverse Spanish Cross with Diamonds Dress Copy.

Plate 220 Reverse Spanish Cross with Diamonds Dress Copy.

is then bronzed, left silver or gilded, or in bronze, which is then silver-plated or gilded. The crosses produced in silver and then finished in the various colours are believed to be the actual award pieces, while the plated and gilded forms are the second pieces.

Hitler instituted these awards to reward bravery by members of the Condor Legion on 14.4.39. Conditions for the awards were laid down on 10.8.39.

It would appear that there was no prerequisite for having a higher award and the grade of the cross tended to be related to the rank of the person to whom it was to have been awarded. Who received which grade was dependent upon the highest Spanish decoration a German 'volunteer' received.

The grades of the awards were as follows:
- Combatant recipients of the Campaign Medal were awarded the Spanish Cross in Bronze with Swords.
- Combatant recipients of the Red Military Service Cross received the Spanish Cross in Silver with Swords.
- Combatant recipients of the Military Medal of the Breast Star to the War Cross, were awarded the Spanish Cross in Gold with Swords.

The criteria for the award were:
- To have been a 'volunteer' in the Condor Legion and to have fought in Spain.
- To have taken part in certain naval or air actions including:
  a) The air attack on 29.5.37 on the German pocket battleship *Deutschland* in the waters off Ibiza.
  b) The bombing of Almeria on 31.5.39 in reprisal for the attack of the *Deutschland*.
- For serving continuously for three months in Spanish waters.
- For special acts of valour or merit, in a combat situation.

Following the air attack mentioned above the *Deutschland* sailed to Gibraltar where it disembarked 22 dead (later rising to 31) and 83 wounded. They were attended to by British personnel at the British Military Hospital. This led to a number of awards to British medical personnel of the German Red Cross Decoration 1937-39 in varying grades but not the Spanish Cross of any grade. A temporary funeral was conducted in Gibraltar, where the cortege with the coffins draped in the German battle flag was escorted by Royal Marines. The coffins were later disinterred and returned on board the *Deutschland*, which sailed to Kiel where the dead were given a state funeral on 17.6.37.

Known British recipients of the German Red Cross Decoration 1937-39 were one matron, 12 sisters and other medical staff at the military hospital at Gibraltar and these include: Capt John Primrose Douglas RAMC — Cross of Merit 26.7.1937; Sister Catherine McShane — Frauenkreuz 26.7.1937; Mrs M. G. Burton — Frauenkreuz 26.7.1937; Mrs Margaret Paula Lewis — Frauenkreuz 26.7.1937; Miss Cargill Lockhead — Frauenkreuz 26.7.1937; Miss Nora Smyth — Frauenkreuz 26.7.1937; Cdr H.J. Murphy — Cross of Merit 13.1.1938.

Numbers awarded were: Bronze 8,462; Silver 8,304; Gold 1,126.

The Spanish Cross in all its grades, was to be worn on the right breast pocket of the uniform.

The badge was awarded in a green box with a burgundy lining. The lining is sometimes dove grey and the outer case has been encountered in blue, with a blue satin liner and blue velvet base. There are cases which have the LDO emblem or just the letters stencilled on to the lid in silver.

SPANISH CROSS WITHOUT SWORDS: BRONZE**

SPANISH CROSS WITHOUT SWORDS: SILVER****

Known Makers: CEJ, CEJ (in rectangular frame), 4, L/11, L/13, L/15, L/16, L/21, L/52 (in an oblong box)

This badge was introduced on 14.4.39 and comprises a Maltese Cross as described in the previous section but without swords, and in the quadrants are the Luftwaffe eagles each clutching a segmented swastika in its talons. The cross is convex with a massive hinge, pin and hook on the reverse. It was made in either silver that was bronzed or left silver for that grade and these are considered to be the awarded type. Those produced in bronze that were silvered or left in their natural colour, again to represent the relative grades, are considered to be the second or private purchase types. There was no Spanish Cross in Gold without Swords, although there seems to be evidence that an order authorising it to be instituted was issued.

This award was rendered to military personnel for service in Spain or Spanish Morocco. It could also be awarded to civilians and technicians who had taken part in assisting the forces in Spain from July 1936 to March 1939. This was to include members of Lufthansa who ferried materials and aircraft to Spain. The bronze and silver crosses are relatively rare and no gold crosses were awarded. Numbers awarded were: Bronze 7,869; Silver 327.

Who received which grade was dependent upon the highest Spanish decoration received:
- Civilians and non-combatants who received the Campaign Medal were awarded the Spanish Cross in Bronze without Swords.
- Civilians and non combatants who received the Red Military Service Cross were awarded the Spanish Cross in Silver without Swords.

The criteria for the award were:
- Three months service in Spain.
- An act that substantially assisted the war effort but not in a combat field.

The Spanish Crosses in both grades were to be worn on the right breast pocket of the uniform.

The badge was awarded in a green box with burgundy lining, but blue boxes with blue liners and blue velvet bases and green boxes with dove grey liners have been encountered. Examples with the LDO symbol or LDO stencilled in silver on the lid, have been observed.

SPANISH CROSS IN GOLD WITH DIAMONDS*****

Known Makers: J. Godet u. Sohn

This badge was produced in tombac that was gilded and takes the form of the preceding decorations but in this case the cross is more convex. The overall size of the badge is larger than the other pieces described in that the height of the badge measured from point to point of the Maltese cross is 60mm and the length of the swords is 65mm. The width across the points of the arms is 25mm. The swastikas clutched by the Luftwaffe eagles are segmented. The central plate with the diamonds measures 18.5mm.

The arms of the cross are flat with a 2mm edge line that is polished and chamfered to the outer edge. The pebbled parts are matt, these pebbled marks being hand raised. The raised portions of the other parts of the cross are highly polished. The centre, however, is quite different in that it is a separately constructed plate, fixed to the body of the cross independently. The construction of this plate again was by hand and, in this case, the swastika's arms are broader and the circle surrounding also broader. Next to this circle are set 14 rose-cut diamonds. There is no outer circle to the border of the diamonds, so that the actual facets and claw setting of the diamonds form the outer edge of the circle. The setting for these diamonds has been described in other references as silver but I would suggest that it is platinum, as it is in the other awards constructed in this manner to mount this type of diamond. The setting could also be produced in white gold.

The reverse has a large pin and hinge construction. The pin is attached at the upper arm of the cross with a large hook secured to the middle of the bottom arm. The central device is held on to the cross by a disc on the reverse which is slightly convex, which mirrors the front plate and has two open type rivets protruding through it. On this plate is, hand engraved in flowing script, 'J. Godet & Sohn. K,G.' and underneath, 'Unter dem Linden'. Beneath this in the centre, in larger Arabic numerals is '53'.

This badge was instituted on 14.4.39. The precise nature of the criteria for the award is a little obscure but it would seem it was rendered to the commanders and particularly successful pilots of the Kondor Legion. Hitler took it upon himself to award this decoration personally to all the 27 recipients upon their return from Spain.

The recipients of the Military Medal with Diamonds were awarded the Spanish Cross in Gold with Diamonds. The three commanders of the Kondor Legion — Sperrle, Volkmann and von Richthofen — were awarded the special class of the medal with diamonds and thus should have been the only recipients of this class of the Spanish Cross. However, Hitler considered this as his personal award and retained the prerogative of presenting it to those combatants deserving of it in his opinion.

The known recipients were: BALTHESAR Wilhelm Oberleutnant; BERTRAM Otto Oberleutnant; BODDEM Wilhelm Lt; EBERHARD Kraft Oberleutnant; ENSSLEN Wilhelm Oberleutnant; FEHLHABER Paul Lt; GALLAND Adolf Oberleutnant; HARDER Harro Hauptmann; HARLINGHAUSEN Martin Maj; HENRICI Oskar Lt; Graf HOYOS Max Oberleutnant; von KASSEL Hans-Detlef Oberleutnant; LüTZOW Günther Hauptmann; MEHNERT Karl Oberleutnant; MöLDERS Werner Hauptmann; Frhr von MOREAU Rudolf Hauptmann; NEUDöRFFER Wolfgang Hauptmann; OESAU Walter Oberleutnant; Frhr von RICHTHOFEN Wolfram Generalleutnant; RUNZE Heinz Lt; SCHELLMANN Wolfgang Hauptmann; SCHLICHTING Joachim Hauptmann; SEILER Reinhard Oberleutnant; SPERRLE Hugo Gen.d.fl; STÄRCKE Bernhard Oberleutnant; VOLKMANN Helmut Gen.d.fl.; WOLFF Karl-Heinz Maj.

However, David Littlejohn and Dr Klietmann both state in their books that there were 28 recipients. This further recipient is believed to be Oberstleutnant von Thoma who is also accredited with having received the Spanish Military Medal with Diamonds. It has also been stated, but is as yet unsubstantiated, that there were only three recipients of the medal.

This award was to be worn on the right breast pocket of the uniform.

The box for this award has been described as white covered with calf skin, with a gold line round the lid. It is square with rounded corners and was produced with a white flock base and lid liner. It has also been stated by authoritative sources that some boxes were similar to the blue boxes in which the standard crosses were awarded.

SPANISH CROSS IN GOLD WITH DIAMONDS: DRESS COPY*****

Known Makers: L/12, CEJ

As this was a private purchase piece and variations do occur in the construction of the badge, it is difficult to write with finality. I have encountered three distinct forms. The first form I have observed on three occasions, the second on two and the last is unique. It is not known whether every recipient purchased an example of this type for general wear or if these private purchase examples were issued on certain occasions to the original recipient. However, the second type was supposed to have been given in conjunction with the award type of cross and the two examples I have encountered were presented, or owned, by Major Martin Harlinghausen and Hauptmann Gunther Lützow.

The first type of cross is similar to that of the awarded type, save for the central ring which is formed in two parallel circles. The swastika in this version is at the same height as the two circles, with its points touching the inside of the smaller circle. The field produced between the circle's edge and the arms of the swastika is pebbled, as is the field between the two lines. Set directly into this are 12 white sapphires, which are smaller in size and number than the diamonds in the awarded type. They also fit directly between those two lines which gives a completely different appearance to the centre of this award. The plate on to which the swastika and sapphires are set is fixed to the body of the cross by two ball rivets.

The cross and the plate are made of silver and the reverse sometimes has the hallmark applied between the two rivets. It has a large pin with a hinge fixed to the upper arm. The lower one has a large retaining hook. The whole of the badge is gilded and produced in a very high quality.

The second form is produced from a standard cross and measures 57mm in width and 23mm across the tips of the arms. The centre has a diamond setting reminiscent of the award type but, in this case, the claw settings holding the diamonds make an irregular edge while the inner edge of the setting has a 2mm flat line. The width of the total setting is 21mm.

The reverse is similar to the standard piece. It has a massive hinge, pin and 'C' form hook soldered to an oval plate which is fixed to the bottom arm of the cross, just above the point of the V of the lower arm. The central diamond setting is held on to the reverse by a circular plate that mirrors the inner plate of the obverse and measures 13.5mm. This has two protrusions on either side, which are drilled and through which are placed two large rivets that are peened over. In the centre of the plate and struck directly on to the reverse of the cross, is the maker's mark in an oblong box, 'CEJ' or 'L/12'. The whole of the reverse is finely matted giving a dull gold effect.

The third type is also produced from a standard cross and measures 58mm across and 23mm across the tips of the arms. The outer line running round the arms measures 2mm and is gently chamfered to the outer edges. The central diamond setting measures 17.5mm and the claws in this case have only a very finely serrated appearance to the edge. The inner line setting is 1mm and this allows the swastika to be more pronounced.

The reverse is plain and shows no sign of where the central diamond setting is attached to the body of the cross. It has a small barrel hinge and square tapering pin and 'C' form hook that is attached directly to the body of the cross. The pin has a round ball at the point. At the centre of the cross is the silver content, '800' and on the pin is a further '800' intaglio. This badge is purported to have belonged to Generalmajor von Richthofen and was supposedly a personal gift from General Franco.

This badge was contained in a red box with maroon silk lid liner and matching maroon velvet base. The upper lid has an oblong gilded silver plate, that has in hand engraved Gothic script, in two lines, 'Kampfgeschwader Boelcke' which was placed over the arms of the swastika. The inside of the lid has the Luftwaffe flying eagle. The other forms of boxes are unknown but it is assumed that they were just the manufacturer's or jeweller's protective cases.

CROSS OF HONOUR FOR THE RELATIVES OF THE DEAD IN SPAIN****

Known Makers: J.Godet u. Sohn
The cross was constructed of bronze or bronzed metal taking the same form as the breast cross but is smaller. At the top is a ring for the suspension ribbon, which is 30mm wide and consists of the German and Spanish national colours, with thin outer vertical stripes of red, yellow, red, yellow, red, white and a wide central stripe of black to represent mourning. The reverse is concave and plain.

The number of awards of this cross was 315 and the actual recipients were the next of kin in a set order of priority.

This medal was announced on 14.4.39 and was to honour those volunteers who had fallen in combat, or died of wounds, or as a result of illness, disease or accident sustained while serving in Spain or Spanish Morocco. Relatives of those listed as missing in Spain also received the award.

The award was to be worn at all times and in the case of men, it was fixed over the left breast pocket. Usually it is found on a court mounted ribbon, that is to say that the ribbon is furled below the medal and the reverse of the ribbon is padded, the whole item being formed on a metal plate with its own individual pin mounting at the top. The medal is usually found clipped on to a hook which enables the ring of the medal to be easily removed. In the case of women, the ribbon was formed into a bow.

The box to this award is an oblong green case with an off white liner and an embossed representation of the cross on the lid.

GERMAN DEFENCE MEDAL*

Known Makers: 4, Steinhauer & Lück
This award is of an oval medal measuring 40mm high by 33mm wide. The edge of the medal is made up of a wreath of single oak leaves, tip overlapping stalk. At the base and apex is a crossed ribbon tie and on either side, oak leaves. The inside of the wreath is ringed by a fine raised inner edge line. The field is flat and on to it are superimposed three distinct designs. The lower third has a square pillbox superimposed upon it at an angle revealing two gun ports, the one on the left being slightly smaller than that on the right. It has two banks running upwards in a 'V' from the base ribbon tie and these are finished to represent grass. The centre of the field has a crossed double-edged sword and a round bladed spade and the upper segment has the national emblem of the open winged eagle clutching a wreath within which is a swastika. The wings on either side stretch to the outside edge of the oak leaf wreath. The three emblems represent the fortifications of Germany, the co-operation between military and civil engineering, overseen by the Nazi Party.

The reverse has the same outer design as the obverse with the three emblems replaced by a six line inscription in raised capital letters, that reads, 'FüR, ARBEIT, ZUM, SCHUTZE, DEUTSCH-, LANDS.' (For Work to the Defence of Germany).

From the top of the medal, through an integral eyelet, is placed the medal ribbon suspension ring. Early strikings of the medal were made from solid bronze. However, those produced following the 1944 production order were mainly produced from zinc and coloured with a bronze finish. It was worn last, after all other medals, but in front of foreign awards.

The ribbon is 30mm wide with a 1.5mm sand-yellow edge stripe, 4.5mm white stripe and an 18mm sand-yellow central band.

Hitler instituted this medal on 2.8.39 and it was initially awarded to those members of the armed forces, including civilian personnel in the employ of the military, who took part in the planning, construction or defence of German fortifications during the period of 15.6.38 to 31.3.39, which resulted in the construction of the 'Siegfried Line'. The minimum time required to qualify for the award to construction workers was 10 weeks, while military assignment in a fortifications position only required three weeks. Those members of the armed forces who had already received the Commemorative Medal of 1.10.38 or the Commemorative Medal for the Return of the Memel Region, were not authorised to receive the medal. Awards of the medal ceased on 31.1.41 by which time 622,064 had been awarded.

In August and September 1944, following the successful allied invasion of 6.6.44, a force of some 200,000 workers was rushed to the Siegfried Line to strengthen and renovate its defences in anticipation of the allied advance towards Germany and, in an attempt to encourage the labour force to complete their assigned task, Hitler reinstituted the award on 10.10.44.

The following translation of an SS order provides the relevant requirements and procedures:

'Because of the Führer's proclamation of the presentation of the German Defence War Honour Award, the following has been announced for the Wehrmacht and Waffen-SS inclusive, the German Defence War Honour Award can be presented to members of the Wehrmacht and others not belonging to but in the service of the Wehrmacht, who have been working for the establishment of the fixed defensive positions since 6.6.44, which were to prevent danger from coming to the German people.

'People who have sworn allegiance to the Führer as members of free foreign volunteers in the Wehrmacht, also are authorised. Those who have received the German Defence War Honour Award at an earlier date, will receive for the time since 6.6.44 a bar to recognise additional duties.

'In accordance with this regulation, members of the Waffen-SS scheduled to receive the German Defence War Honour Award from their respective groups, must be submitted in a list, without reason for the award, providing family name, first name, rank, service, birthday and place of birth, submitted in one copy to the SS - Führungshauptampt Adjutant.'

This award procedure was a little slap happy at times. I have an example from a recipient who was a foreign volunteer in the Waffen-SS of Soviet origin. He received the medal complete in packet, with ribbon unattached and small citation made out with the award date, 10.10.44, but with the personal details left blank. Along with his colleagues, his instructions were to fill them in himself in ink as per the instructions. He decided, in his wisdom, to maintain the award and citation as presented in his pocket. He would not, therefore, incriminate himself if he should fall into enemy hands, which was his eventual fate. On the other hand, he was able to plead ignorance of German preventing him from filling out the form correctly.

The medal was presented in various forms of container. The award case for the medal was probably restricted to very special awards and then only to the first series production. It was in a two-piece hinge construction, fastened by a press-stud catch. The outer finish is a dark purple without any lid derivation. Inside the lid is purple-brown satin while the lower portion is purple-red velvet. The example awarded to Viktor Lutze has rounded corners to the box, with a white lid interior. The lower half being lined with a white card edge liner. The more common method of presentation was in a paper packet that was either tan or mouse-grey with the medal's title printed in black Gothic lettering on the front, 'DEUTSCHE, SCHUTZWALL = , EHRENZEICHEN'.

GERMAN DEFENCE MEDAL BAR*****

Known Makers: No Known Maker

This award is highly suspect as it was approved in theory for award to those who had received the original medal. What the design of this 'bar' was is unknown and it may never have been manufactured or issued.

It has been reported that the bar was approximately the same size as the Prague Bar, and had the date '1944' upon it with the original colour being bronze to match the medal. Dr Klietmann records that in 1945 the Ordenskanzalei had instructed a medal manufacturer in Berlin to produce 5,000 bars with 1944 upon them. The firm was bombed out and it is unclear as to whether the bars were produced and then destroyed by enemy action or never put into production due to the bombing. However a sanguine note to collectors is that copies of the bar are known to have been made in Germany since about 1957 and collectors are advised that any now offered may well be post war reproductions and possibly inaccurate.

MEDAL FOR THE WINTER CAMPAIGN IN RUSSIA 1941-42*

Known Makers: 4, 10, 13, 19, 20, 65, 73, 107, 110

On 26.5.42, Hitler introduced this medal for the campaign in Russia. It comprises of a round medal measuring 36mm across with, at its top, a stick grenade surmounted by a German steel helmet. The height of the medal from the base to the top of the eyelet on the helmet is 44.5mm. Round the edge of the medal is a recessed rim of approximately 1.5mm and inside it a 1mm lip, as a border for the central motif. The helmet and rim are silvered on both the reverse and obverse. The obverse is concave from the lip on the rim and on this field is a closed winged eagle standing on a square swastika. This surmounts a branch of leaves. The whole of the design is blackened.

The reverse from the rim is convex, again blackened with, in capital letters, 'WINTERSCHLACHT' and in larger ones, 'IM OSTEN' and finally the date, '1941/42'. At the base is a broad bladed sword, crossed with a branch of leaves similar to that found on the obverse.

This design had been created by SS Unterscharführer Ernst Kraus and I consider it to be one of the best designs of the whole series of combat awards. The period of qualification for this award was from 15.11.41 to 15.4.42 and by order of the OKW consideration for rendering the award ceased on 4.9.44. It was to be worn on the medal bar when uniform regulations prescribed, but even though it was a campaign medal it took precedence over the War Merit Medal. The usual manner of wear was either by the ribbon being worn diagonally through the second buttonhole of the tunic or in conjunction with the Iron Cross Second Class and/or the Decoration for Bravery and Merit of the Eastern People Second Class or as a ribbon bar worn over the left breast pocket.

The region that this campaign medal was to represent stretched eastwards of the Ukraine and Ostland or east of the Finnish-Russian border of 1940, known as the operational area 'Finnland'.

Those entitled to the award were:

● Military personnel and civilians, to include female personnel who were in the service of the armed forces.
● Administration personnel.
● Personnel killed or listed as missing in action.
● Foreign volunteers serving in the Wehrmacht provided that the award was recommended by a divisional commander or more senior officer.
● Civilians working in factories in the aforementioned region.

The criteria for the award were:

● To have been engaged in combat in the theatre of operations for two weeks.
● 60 days to have been spent continuously in the combat theatre of operations.

● To have been wounded in that combat zone.
● For being frostbitten (for which a wound badge was also awarded).

For Luftwaffe Personnel the criterion was 30 days to be spent over enemy territory.

It was presented in a paper packet which was either brick red, blue or buff, with the name printed on the front.

BRAVERY AND COMMEMORATIVE MEDAL OF THE SPANISH 'BLUE DIVISION'**

Known Makers: Deschler und Sohn
The medal has a 32mm diameter and a 1mm raised edge line. The resultant field is flat and on to this is superimposed the design that is proud of the raised edge line. At the base of the

Plate 221 Obverse Spanish Cross with Diamonds Dress Copy. Note the settings of the diamonds. This actual award belonged to Hauptmann Gunther Lutzow.

Plate 222 Reverse Spanish Cross with Diamonds Dress Copy. Note the method of attachment of the diamond setting to the body of the cross and the maker's mark, CEJ, in a box.

Plate 223 Obverse Cross of Honour for the Relatives of the Dead in Spain.

Plate 224   Obverse German Defence Medal.

Plate 225   Reverse German Defence Medal.

Plate 226   Obverse Medal for the Winter Campaign in Russia 1941-1942.

Plate 227   Reverse Medal for the Winter Campaign in Russia 1941-1942.

Plate 228   Obverse Bravery and Commemorative Medal of the Spanish 'Blue Division'.

Plate 229   Reverse Bravery and Commemorative Medal of the Spanish 'Blue Division'.

Plate 230   Obverse Bravery and Commemorative Medal of the Spanish 'Blue Division' Spanish made.

obverse is a swastika with a spray of laurel leaves emanating from either end of the horizontal arm. The spray consists of four leaves in each and these are arranged differently in each bunch. Across the centre of the field of the medal is a double-handed, double-edged sword that runs from just inside the raised edge line horizontally, to just inside the line on the other side with the pommel on the viewer's left. Superimposed on to this are two identical shields with flat tops and pointed bottoms. On the one on the viewer's left is superimposed the Wehrmacht eagle with the Falangists' crushed arrows on the other. Superimposed directly above the shields and on to the medal's field is a German steel helmet, facing to the viewer's left, with the faint outline of a raised decal with the Wehrmacht eagle upon it.

The reverse has, at the bottom, an Iron Cross with the ribbon in a broad 'V'. From either side is a spray of leaves, on the left laurel and on the right, oak. On to the central field, in raised capital letters, is the six line inscription 'DIVISION, ESPAÑOLA, DIE, VOLUNTARIOS, EN, RUSIA.' (Spanish Volunteer Division in Russia). At the top of the medal is an integral ribbon ring suspender, through which is placed the ribbon ring, which is normally marked with a number '1'. This is the touch mark for the manufacturer. The medal was constructed of fine zinc that was gilded. This, with age, often takes on a bronze appearance.

The ribbon is a 30mm band, similar to that of the Iron Cross Second Class, with the addition of a central yellow stripe. It has a 4mm black edge stripe, an inner 2mm white stripe, an 18mm central band of red with a 3mm yellow central stripe.

This medal was introduced on 3.1.44 to reward the services of the Spanish volunteers who fought on the Russian front between 1941 and October 1943.

Although Franco resisted Hitler's advances to join the Axis powers, he did allow Spaniards to serve as volunteers in the 'Crusade Against Bolshevism'. Within hours of the German invasion of Russia, von Ribbentrop received a Spanish offer of aid and on 24.6.41 he secured Hitler's approval for the participation of a Spanish volunteer legion in the campaign. In Spain, there was no lack of volunteers although, initially, only 4,000 volunteers were called for. However, 10 times that number, most of them veterans of the civil war, presented themselves for consideration by the legion. It was quite apparent to the authorities that they could do much better than a mere token legion and that they would have no difficulty in raising a full division which, in Spanish terms, meant in the region of 19,000 men. Possibly Franco saw this as tangible evidence of his good faith and support for Hitler's aims, without being drawn into the Axis proper. Volunteer regiments were raised in Madrid, Barcelona, Seville

and other main cities. With the legion thus formed, it was announced on 27.6.41 that the commander would be Gen Augustin Munoz Grandes. Since Spain was not at war with any nation, let alone the Soviet Union, there was a problem of how the volunteers should be dressed. It was not possible for them to adopt the uniform of the Spanish forces. This gave Franco the opportunity to produce what was to be a symbolic Spanish uniform. It consisted of the red beret of the Carlist movement, the blue shirt of the Falangist movement and the khaki trousers of the Spanish Foreign Legion, while officers wore a khaki tunic with a blue collar and blue cuffs. Before being sent to the front they were obliged to dress in the field grey German Army uniform with, on the right upper arm, a shield in the Spanish national colours surmounted by the word, 'España'.

On 13.7.41 the first batch of volunteers left Madrid for Grafenwöhr in Bavaria, where they became officially the 250 Infantry Division of the German Army, with a strength of 17,924 officers and men in four infantry regiments. Normal Spanish practice was to have four regiments to a division but German custom demanded only three. This resulted in one of the Spanish regiments being disbanded and its personnel reallocated among the three remaining regiments. The three resultant regiments were numbered Infantry Regiment 262, (mainly recruited from Barcelona), Infantry Regiment 263 (Valencia) and Infantry Regiment 269 (Seville). Each regiment had three battalions of four companies. An artillery regiment — numbered 250, like its parent division — was also added. This consisted of three batteries of 105mm guns and one of 150mm heavy guns.

On 20.8.41 the division was considered adequately trained after its five weeks at Grafenwöhr and was taken by train to the German-Soviet border. The front line was, at this time, over 1,000km away and to reach it, the division had to proceed on foot. Upon arriving at Smolensk where it had expected to join Army Group Centre in its offensive against Moscow, it found itself redirected north to Leningrad where it formed part of the German 16th Army. The Spaniards saw their first action on 12.10.41 when they were put into the line in the sector between Lake Ilmen and the West Bank of the Volkhov River. A major German offensive against Leningrad opened four days later. Both that action and the bitter cold took their toll. Death, wounds and frostbite so seriously depleted the Spanish ranks that there was alarm in Madrid that the Blue Division was about to disintegrate. Since the honour of Spain, rather than just the fate of one division, was at stake, replacements were rapidly rushed to the front. The division was to remain as part of the force besieging Leningrad for the rest of its time in Russia.

However, as the war situation deteriorated for the Axis powers, Britain put increasing pressure on Franco to declare Spain's absolute neutrality and to remove his forces from Russia. By the spring of 1943, the Spaniards had begun negotiations with the Germans for withdrawal of the Division. The order to withdraw was finally given to Gen Emilio Esteban-Infantes on 14.10.43. He had, incidentally, replaced Munoz Grandes as commander in December 1942. To reduce the resentment of the Germans, and indeed of many of the volunteers themselves, it was announced that a 'Spanish Legion' consisting of some 1,500 men would be allowed to stay on and continue the battle. It was commanded by Col Navaho and known as the Legion Española die Voluntarios, (L.E.V.), and was assigned to the 121st Division of the German Army. However, even this token force was ordered by the Spanish government to return home in March. Although the nominal strength of the Blue Division was 18,000 men, by a system of regular rotation of troops (and casualties) as many as 45,000 may have seen service with the 250th Infantry Division between June 1941 and October 1943. Of these, some 4,500 fell in action and around 16,000 more were wounded or taken prisoner. The term 'Blue Division', although widely used, was derived from the wearing of their blue shirts and was not the official designation which was the Division Española die Voluntarios, (D.E.V.). Latterly, by no means, not all its members were voluntarios! Conscription had to be applied to keep up the numbers. Genuine volunteers, however, continued to remain in the German forces even after Spain had declared her neutrality. These were, in part, members of the L.E.V. who refused to return home after the official withdrawal of the Legion and partly made up of fresh volunteers smuggled across the Pyrenees to Lourdes in France, where Sonderstab F, a special Army unit, collected these illicit warriors and passed them on to the Waffen SS. A Spanish volunteer battalion served with the Waffen SS to the bitter end, taking part in the final defence of Berlin in April and May 1945. This unit was commanded by Hauptsturmführer Miguel E. Sanchez. Volunteers were allowed to wear any Spanish decorations that they might hold, as well as any Falangist insignia or badges.

The Blue Division's seriously sick and wounded were treated at hospitals in Mestelevo, Riga, Vilna, Königsberg, Berlin and Hof (Saale), which were operated principally by Spanish Medical Staff. These included many volunteer nurses from the Spanish Army and the Falange's women's section and were known as the Sanidad Militar.

In 1937 Franco had appointed Mercedes Milá Nolla, as Inspector Gen of women auxiliaries of the Sanidad Militar. Lt-Col Pellicer was appointed Inspector of Hospitals. The Spanish army nurses of the Sanidad Militar in Germany wore a uniform that comprised of a Khaki blouse which had unusual pocket design, dark brown leather buttons and white collar and cuffs. Displayed at the throat was the emblem of the Spanish Red Cross and nursing badges and decorations could be worn on the pocket. They also wore a black belt with a silver-grey Sanidad Militar buckle-plate, a pleated Khaki skirt, light brown stockings and dark brown shoes. They also wore a headdress of Khaki wimple and white coif, upon which was pinned a silver-grey metal badge of the Spanish army's medical branch Sanidad Militar.

The medal was presented in an oblong maroon box with a paper hinge. The inside showed the card colour of the box. The medal was ignominiously wrapped in off-white tissue paper. The more common container was a medal envelope which was beige with the complete title of the medal printed in black Gothic letters in five lines 'ERINNERUNGSMEDAILLE, FüR DIE, SPANISCHEN FREIWILLIGEN, IM KAMPF GEGEN DEM, BOLSCHEWISMUS.' The medal was wrapped, as before, in tissue and separate from the ribbon.

BRAVERY AND COMMEMORATIVE MEDAL OF THE SPANISH 'BLUE DIVISION'**

(Spanish Manufacture)
Known Makers
This medal is identical to its German-made counterpart, except that the die is slightly modified, so that the shields on the obverse are more pointed and the German eagle and swastika have a slightly different appearance. The outer edge line is thicker with that on the reverse being approximately twice as thick. The lettering on the inscription also varies in that it is more pronounced. The medal ring suspender is also more pronounced and in the form of a barrel or ball.

This version is the form that has been produced officially since the war in Spain. There is good reason to believe that it was produced before the end of the war and is a legitimate Third Reich piece. Franco permitted the wearing of German awards in their original form and their manufacture has to be considered legitimate, as the Spanish authorities could justifiably produce the award for their nationals. The award officially produced in this form is quite scarce but this should not reflect an inflated collector's value.

12. Military Civil and Political Long Service Awards

ARMY, NAVY AND AIR FORCE LONG SERVICE MEDAL 4 YEARS SERVICE*

Known Makers: L/13, L/15

The design forms a round medal measuring 30mm across. It has a raised edge line and on to the flat field produced is placed the inscription, in raised Gothic capitals that run from 7 to 4 o'clock, 'TREUE DIENSTE IN DER WEHRMA-CHT' (True Service in the Armed Forces). The Wehrmacht eagle is placed on to the field at the centre. The eagle's wings are partially opened, with its head looking to the viewer's right and a swastika clutched in its claws. At the top of the medal is placed an eyelet, through which runs the ribbon ring. The medal is 2.5mm thick and the overall colour is of matt, patinated silver. The medal is produced in varying types of base metal.

The reverse has a similar raised edge line and on to the flat field produced, inset by 1mm, is a circle of oak leaves in the form of a wreath. The circle has a solid inner and outer edge line with a tie, at 12 and 6 o'clock respectively. The ties are formed by lines, giving the effect of ribbons that are wound round the wreath. There are a number of variations in the designs of these ties. From the lower one, on either side, run five oak leaves with raised veins. On to the flat field at the centre is placed a large, raised, Arabic 4. The medal was designed by Prof Richard Klein of Munich.

The ribbon is a cornflower blue, which can come in different shades and measure 27-35mm in width. To denote the recipient's service, a silver eagle was added to the ribbon. In the case of the Army and Navy, this was the straight eagle with outstretched wings. It measured 25mm across by 10.5mm high. However, the eagles employed on the ribbon bar were sometimes used incorrectly on the medal ribbon. These measure 15mm by 9mm and 15mm by 8mm, while the Luftwaffe employed a flying eagle that measures 18mm by 13mm. Again, smaller ones are encountered measuring 14mm by 10mm and 11mm by 8mm. It must be stressed that there is a wide variation in the sizes of these emblems and readers may have variations not listed. This is not to be considered unusual.

The medal was worn either on a furled, court mounted ribbon or with the others on a medal ribbon bar. It was authorised for wear on the parade or walking out dress uniform. It took precedence below decorations. At other times a ribbon bar was worn above the left breast pocket and on it was worn the relevant emblem denoting branch of service, as well as the grade of the award.

The medal was awarded for the completion of four years service and during the early years of its institution was bestowed in a special ceremony by the commanding officer. With the outbreak of war and as it progressed, actual issue of the service award ceased. The 4 Year Medal could be worn on its own or in conjunction with the 12 Year Medal, and in conjunction with the 18 Year Cross. It was decreed that only two long service awards could be worn at the same time.

The medal was presented in a green paper packet with the title of the medal upon it 'Dienstauszeichnung mit Hoheitsabzeichen u. Band IV'. The packet was, in some cases, just a clear cellophane protective wrapper.

Plate 231 Obverse Army Long Service 4 & 12 Year Medals.

Plate 232 Reverse Army Long Service 4 & 12 Year Medals.

Plate 233 Obverse Long Service 18 Year Cross. Note the Luftwaffe eagle.

Plate 234 Reverse and obverse Long Service 18 Year Cross. Note the simple change in the design.

Plate 235 Obverse Long Service 25 Year Cross. Note the simple change in the design.

Plate 236 Reverse Long Service 25 Year Cross.

Plate 237 Obverse Long Service 25 Year Cross with 40 Year Service Emblem.

Plate 238 Obverse SS Long Service Medal 4 Years Service.

Plate 239 Reverse SS Long Service Medal 4 Years Service.

131

240

241

242

243

Plate 240   Obverse SS Long Service Medal 8 Years Service.

Plate 241   Reverse SS Long Service Medal 8 Years Service.

Plate 242   Obverse SS Long Service Cross 25 Years Service.

Plate 243 · Reverse SS Long Service Cross 12 Years Service.

ARMY, NAVY AND AIR FORCE LONG SERVICE MEDAL 12 YEARS SERVICE*

Known Makers: L/13, L/15

The obverse design of this medal is identical to the 4 Year Medal while the reverse is also the same, save that the '4' is replaced by an Arabic 12. The ribbon is also the same, with the same form of eagles applied to denote branch of service. However, the whole of the medal and the eagles are finished in gold.

There is, however, an interesting obverse design that has no outer edge line and the Gothic lettering is slightly larger. The eagle is also slightly different in that it has a more pronounced head. The reverse is identical to the standard form and the medal is 3mm thick and made of a heavier high grade metal alloy.

The medal was awarded for the completion of 12 years service and awarded under the same conditions as the 4 Year Medal. The 12 Year Medal was worn in conjunction with the 4 Year Medal, and in conjunction with the 25 Year Cross, and the 40 Year Cross.

The medal was presented in a green paper packet with the title of the medal printed upon it, 'Dienstauszeichnung mit Hoheitsabzeichen u. Band III'. The packet was sometimes just a clear cellophane protective wrapper.

ARMY, NAVY AND AIR FORCE LONG SERVICE CROSS 18 YEARS SERVICE**

Known Makers: L/13, L/15

This award consists of a Finnish Cross or a Greek Cross with slightly widening arms. It is also known as a St George's Cross. It measures 36mm across and has a 15mm central medallion. Round the arms of the cross is a raised edge line. Indented by .5mm is a further one, and this is followed by a similar line indented again by .5mm. The central field of the arms of the cross are raised, gently bevelled and slope down towards the outer edge line of the arms of the cross. The central medallion has a similar raised outer edge line and a similar one indented by .5 mm. The central field is finely pebbled and is slightly convex. On to this is superimposed a raised Wehrmacht eagle.

132

The reverse of the cross is identical to the obverse, save that the eagle is replaced by an Arabic 18. The cross, like the medals, was designed by Prof Klein. The overall colour of the cross and the relevant ribbon eagle is silver. From the upper arm of the cross is an eyelet through which is placed the ribbon suspension ring. The ribbon is identical to that described in the 4 Year Medal.

The cross was awarded for the completion of 18 years service and awarded under the same conditions as the 4 Year Medal. The 18 Year Cross was worn with the 4 Year Medal.

The cross was presented in a green carton which was compartmentalised and finished inside with a mouse-grey flocking, with the Arabic 18 surrounded by an oak leaf wreath stencilled on to the lid in silver.

ARMY, NAVY AND AIR FORCE LONG SERVICE CROSS 25 YEARS SERVICE**

Known Makers: L/13, L/15
This award is similar in design to the 18 Year Cross. It measures 40mm across and also has an 18mm central medallion. Round the arms of the cross runs a 1.5mm raised border. The field of the arms of the cross has a fine, raised pebbling. The central medallion has a fine, raised edge line and a similar one indented by 0.5 mm. The field of the tramline produced is plain, while the central field has a similar fine, raised pebbled finish. On to this is superimposed the Wehrmacht eagle. From the upper arm is an eyelet, through which passes the ribbon ring.

The reverse of the cross is identical to the obverse, save that the Wehrmacht eagle is replaced by an Arabic 25. The overall colour of the cross and the relevant ribbon eagle, is gold. The ribbon is identical to that described in the 4 Year Medal.

The cross was awarded for the completion of 25 years service and awarded under the same conditions as the 4 Year Medal. The 25 Year Cross was worn in conjunction with the 8 Year Medal.

The cross was awarded in a green box with a press-stud catch. The outer green covering is simulated leather, while the inside lid liner is white silk and the base is compartmentalised and finished in mouse-grey velvet. On to the lid is stencilled the Arabic 25 in a oak leaf wreath, finished in gold.

ARMY, NAVY AND AIR FORCE LONG SERVICE CROSS 40 YEARS SERVICE***

Known Makers: Unmarked
This award comprised of an oak leaf spray which was added to the ribbon of the 25 Year Cross. The spray measures 34mm across the tips and

17mm high. The base has a ribbon curling downwards from a knot at the centre. From the knot, in a 'V' form, are two oak leaves. From each side is a larger leaf overlapping two smaller ones. The area between the ribbons and the leaves is usually solid; however this, in some cases, can be found voided. This latter version is not as desirable as the former. The emblem is attached to the ribbon by two flat pins that are put through the ribbon. The reverse of the emblem is plain and flat. The overall colour of the emblem is matt gold.

The emblem was awarded for the completion of 40 years service and awarded under the same conditions as the 4 Year Medal. The 40 Year Cross was worn with the 8 Year Medal.

The emblem was presented in a small green box. In some cases, it was possible to encounter the cross with the emblem attached in a red hard case with gilt Arabic 40 within a wreath of oak leaves. The case had a press-stud catch and the inner lid liner was of white silk, while the lower portion was segmented and finished in a maroon velvet liner. This is similar to that employed for the Faithful Service Decoration for 40 Years Service.

SS LONG SERVICE MEDAL: 4 YEARS SERVICE**

Known Makers: Unmarked
The award comprises a round medal measuring 38mm in diameter with a raised 1mm edge line. The central field slopes gently from the edge and the whole of the field is finely stippled. Inset from the edge line by 2.5mm is an open topped wreath with a wrapped ribbon base. From this, on either side, are four oak leaves with stamped veins. At the base of each wreath is a pair of acorns, one on either side. The Sigrunen, the runic symbol of the SS, is superimposed in the field of the wreath.

The reverse has a similar raised edge line and the field has a similar stippled effect. At the centre is a 29mm high, stylised Arabic 4. Superimposed across this in four lines is the inscription 'FüR, TREUE DIENSTE, IN DER, SS.' (For Loyal Service in the SS). At the top of the medal is placed an eyelet. This is of a specific design and requires the collector to take special note. It has its edges chamfered to a central, raised spine and the whole is also slightly counter-sunk. Through this is placed an unusual ribbon ring which is known as a closed teardrop suspender. That is to say, it is not round but elongated, measuring 17mm long and 9mm wide at its widest point. The medal is finely struck from bronze, which is patinated with a matt black finish. When the medal has been handled, it often shows signs of the base metal through the patination which, when aged, gives an attractive tonal contrast. The medal was designed by Prof Karl Diebitsch of Munich. It was suspended from a plain cornflower blue ribbon measuring 35mm wide. When only the ribbon was worn on the uniform it had a small facsimile of the obverse of the medal attached to it.

The award was introduced by Hitler on 30.1.38 and the regulations initially decreed that the SS Long Service Decoration Fourth Class was to be a round medal, made of bronzed iron. On the obverse is a swastika with raised Sigrunen. On the reverse is circumscribed 'Für Treue Dienste in der SS' and in the middle a large Arabic 4. However, on 21.10.38 Hitler changed the regulations for this award to that described above. The reason for the changed design and colour of the medal can only be assumed since the 8 Year Medal and 4 Year Medal would have been indistinguishable in wear and would have necessitated the addition of a medal definer in the form of an emblem being attached to the ribbon. This would have added confusion to the award criteria. However, as yet no examples of the proposed first design have been encountered and it is safe to presume that none were produced or, if they were, they were melted down.

This medal was awarded to those members of the SS who were in the SS-Verfügungstruppen, SS-Totenkopfverbände and the SS-Junkerschulen who were on active service and had served honourably. This award was made for four years service and could only be conferred on NCOs and below. The accumulation of service time could be accrued from the re-founding of the NSDAP in 1925 and through the 'Time of Struggle' (the 'Kampfzeit', which was interpreted as being from 1925 to 1933). Service in the latter counted as double time as did active military service.

Recommendations for award came from the Reichsführer-SS and the final approval vested with the Chancellery. It is believed that the bestowal of the medals ceased by the end of 1941.

It came in a presentation case formed of a black cardboard box with a mouse-grey flocking interior that is compartmentalised in the lower tray. On to the lid is impressed in silver, the SS Sigrunen.

SS LONG SERVICE MEDAL: 8 YEARS SERVICE**

Known Makers: Unmarked

The award comprises a round medal measuring 38mm in diameter with a raised 1mm edge line. The central field is deeply recessed and dips sharply from the raised edge line. On to the central field is placed a square swastika. The tip of each arm just touches the raised edge line. It measures 26mm across. The swastika has a raised 1mm edge line running round its arms. The line does not extend across the top of the arms and the fields produced at the centre of the arms of the swastika and that of the medal, are finely stippled. On to the centre of the swastika is superimposed a round 17mm wreath. This has a ribbon tie at the base comprising five bands and from either side emanate five single oak leaves with recessed central veins. They meet tip to tip at the apex of the wreath. On to the vertical arms of the swastika that are visible through the centre of the wreath, are superimposed the Sigrunen. The raised portions of the obverse of the medal are finely polished.

The reverse has a raised edge line and a less recessed field. This is also lightly stippled and on to the centre is superimposed, in low relief, a 29mm high Arabic 8. Superimposed across this, in four lines, in capital letters, is the inscription 'FüR, TREUE DIENSTE, IN DER, SS'. At the top of the medal is placed an eyelet. This eyelet is identical to that described above for the 4 Year Service Medal. The medal is finely struck from bronze that has a light chocolate matt patination, with the highlights polished to give an attractive contrast. The medal was also designed by Prof Diebitsch. There is a variation that has been encountered, which employs an identical design to that described but it has been increased in size from 38mm to 42mm in diameter, with a pro rata increase in the medal's other dimensions. Two theories can be offered for the production of this medal. Firstly, that this was a manufacturer's design test strike. This theory requires a different die to be produced to create the medal and from this a reduction to the approved design. Considering the cost of producing a die, this tends to be a rather flawed theory. German manufacturers, renowned for their position and pedantic handling of business costs, would have balked at this wasteful practice. The other theory is that this is the original size of the medal proposed and was to distinguish the 4 (original design) and 8 Year medals apart in wear, before the change on 21.10.38 to the design of the 4 Year Medal described above.

The granting of the medal followed the same criteria as those employed for the 4 Year Medal. It is also believed that bestowal of this award ceased in late 1941.

The medal was suspended from a plain cornflower blue ribbon that measured 35mm. When only the ribbon was worn on the uniform, it had a small facsimile of the obverse of the medal attached to its centre.

It came in a presentation case that formed a black simulated leather case with button catch. The inside of the lid is white satin while the lower compartment, which is sectioned, is burgundy coloured flocking. Impressed on to the simulated leather on the lid are the Sigrunen.

SS LONG SERVICE CROSS: 12 YEARS SERVICE***

SS LONG SERVICE CROSS: 25 YEARS SERVICE*****

Known Makers: Unmarked

The design of these two medals is identical, the only exception being the colour employed to denote the grade: silver for 12 and gold for 25 years. They both were the creation of Prof Diebitsch who was the head of the Hauptamt Persönlicher Stab Reichsführer-SS, Chef amt Munich. It was his job to deal with 'all artistic and architectural questions which interested the Reichsführer'. Some of his other creations were the police and SS swords, as well as the much sought after 1936 SS chained dagger. He was also responsible for the touch mark commonly referred to as the 'SS proof mark' which, in reality, was the logo denoting Diebitsch's work. The famous Allach SS porcelain factory came under his control in 1939, when he was named director and he used a similar touch mark as its logo, which is to be found on the base of all its creations. His mark has also been observed on some of the ceramic works decorating the walls of the SS Junkerschule in Bad Tölz. His sense of artistic and architectural excellence are summed up in a statement delivered by him where he stated 'We know that all we may produce will be critically examined by those who come after us and we do not want these later generations to give a poor verdict on our work'. His perception of stylistic lines and runic forms intricately laced together, have left a legacy of some of the finest collectables for the Third Reich enthusiast. He was finally promoted to Oberführer on 20.4.44.

The crosses comprise a square swastika that measures 38mm across with the arms voided. Each arm measures 9mm wide. Round the arms runs a raised 1mm edge line, indented by 1mm. This stops at the ends of each arm. The field produced is finely stippled. On to the centre of the swastika is positioned a wreath. This has, at its base, a ribbon tie that is furled round it in six twists. From this, on either side, runs the wreath former which has five small protrusions on both its edges. On to the former is superimposed an oak leaf that has a raised spine and no veins. The tip of each leaf overlaps the stalk of the next at the point where the protrusions are positioned. The leaves meet tip to tip at the apex of the wreath. It measures 22mm across and the former and oak leaves are 4mm wide. On to the vertical arms of the swastika is superimposed the SS Sigrunen. These, the wreath and the raised edge line are burnished, while the field of the arms of the cross is matt silver or gold.

The reverse design of the swastika is the same as the obverse, save that the wreath is omitted.

However, the former and one oak leaf is visible in each quarter of the void of the swastika. The inscription, in raised capital letters, is superimposed in three lines on to the arms of the cross 'FüR, TREUE DIENSTE IN DER, SS'. The inscription and raised edge line are burnished, while the field is either matt silver or gold, depending on grade.

At the top of the medal is placed an eyelet. This eyelet is also of the teardrop form encountered with the 4 and 8 Year medals. This form of ribbon ring is the one normally met on these awards and can be considered a good rule of thumb by which to identify reproductions, which invariably employ normal, round rings. However, there were instances where the second and first class awards were produced with a circular ring. This is proven by the illustration on pp34-35 of the 1939 edition of Dr Heinrich Doehle's book *Orden und Ehrenzeichen im Dritten Reich*, published in Berlin in January 1940. In this case, the eyelet has been changed for a thick ball suspension connecting the round suspension ring. It is possible that this design was changed to that employed on the 4 and 8 Year medals with the change of the former design on 21.10.38.

The crosses were suspended from a plain 50mm cornflower blue ribbon on to which either a silver or gold SS Sigrunen was embroidered. The original order stating that they were to be woven into the ribbon seems not to have been implemented. There are original examples of smaller width ribbon being employed, especially in conjunction with the medal ribbon bar. Reichsführer-SS Heinrich Himmler's medal bar sports a Second Class Cross, with much enlarged SS Sigrunen embroidered into it. This is the type shown in Doehle's book on the cross with the round ring. There is another unexplained variation which occurs when the ribbon only was worn on the uniform. It had a small SS Sigrunen embroidered on to it in the relevant colour representing the grade.

The granting of the medal followed the same criteria as those employed for the 4 Year Medal. It is also believed that bestowal of this award ceased in late 1941.

The medals came in a presentation case comprising a black simulated leather hard case with button catch. The inside of the lid is white satin, while the lower compartmented section is burgundy coloured. The ribbon, in these cases, was folded and placed in the upper ribbon compartment horizontally. Impressed in the lid are the silver SS Sigrunen for the second class and gold for the first class.

Plate 244 Obverse NSDAP Long Service Cross in Bronze 10 Years Service.

Plate 245 Obverse NSDAP Long Service in Bronze 10 Years Service Variation.

Plate 246 Reverse NSDAP Long Service Cross in Bronze 10 Years Service Variation. Note the left-hand cross has 6 oak leaves and the other has 5 forming the wreath.

Plate 247 Obverse NSDAP Long Service Cross in Silver 15 Years Service & Gold 25 Years Service.

Plate 248 Reverse NSDAP Long Service Cross in Silver 15 Years Service & Gold 25 Years Service.

136

Plate 249 Obverse Faithful Service Decoration for 40 Years Service.

Plate 250 Reverse Faithful Service Decoration for 40 Years Service.

Plate 251 Obverse Fatihful Service Decoration for 50 Years Service.

Plate 252 Reverse Faithful Service Decoration for 50 Years Service.

NSDAP LONG SERVICE CROSS IN BRONZE 10 YEARS SERVICE**

Known Makers: 1, 10, 19, 20, 100, RZM M1/52

This cross consists of a type that is known as pattée or formy — one that has arms curving outwards with straight ends, eg the Iron Cross Second Class. The measurement across the arms is 43mm and across the ends 23mm. In the quarters of the arms of the cross are three rays flanked on either side by a part of one. These rays have central spines and pointed tips, the central one being longer than the outer ones. At the centre of the cross is a wreath of single oak leaves laid tip on stalk, with a cross tie at the base and meeting tip to tip at the apex. There are six leaves on either side of the wreath which measure 2.5mm and the wreath is 22mm across. The central field of the wreath is slightly convex and lightly stippled. On to this is superimposed the eagle and swastika in an oak leaf wreath. The eagle's wings measure 27mm across and their ends, which are cut straight and diagonally, break the wreath and rest on the fields of the horizontal arms of the cross. The upper line of the wing has a 'C' curl from the eagle's body and then runs horizontally outwards with three distinct breaks. Beneath the 'C' curl are two lines of individual fletching running from the body to underneath the upper line of fletch. The upper has seven distinct feathers and the lower nine. The outstretched portion of the wing on either side is formed of five straight lines. The oak leaf wreath clutched in the eagle's claws measures 7mm across. The arms of the cross have a flat 1.5mm edge which then has a slight rise. Just inset and superimposed on to this is a 2mm raised, ribbed line similar to that found on the Iron Cross. The central fields of the arms of the cross are slightly raised and lightly stippled giving the impression of being infilled with enamel. The thickness of the arms at the beaded edge is 4mm and across the centre, 6mm. From the top of the upper arm is an integral protrusion that is drilled to take the ribbon suspension ring. In this case it is usually small, measuring 8mm and it is possible to find the RZM number on the ring, but it is not necessarily so in this size.

The reverse design is the same as the obverse, save that the eagle and swastika are omitted. On to the central field of the wreath is the inscription in Gothic script, in four lines, 'TREUE, FüR FüHRER, UND, VOLK.' (Loyalty to Leader and People). The cross was produced as a one piece stamping and was usually manufactured from a lightweight alloy artificially coloured a light bronze and normally with a silk-like finish.

The ribbon is a 30mm band of mid-brown with a 2mm white stripe indented by 1mm, with a 0.5mm gap separating it from a further 2mm white stripe. In the case of men, the award was worn on the medal bar above the left breast pocket and ranked behind the military service awards. However, in the case of SS personnel, they wore the award in front of their military decorations. When this was worn by a female recipient, the ribbon was replaced by a similar one of 15mm worn round the neck. It has also been reported that the upper arm of the cross is converted to accommodate a metal ribbon suspender, through which the ribbon passes and is fastened in a bow. When the ribbon only was worn, a small bronze emblem of an oak leaf wreath with the eagle and swastika surmounted upon it, was worn on the ribbon, on the ribbon bar. This emblem could be worn on the 30mm or 15mm widths of ribbon.

On 2.4.39 Hitler ordered the institution of the Long Service Awards for the NSDAP to represent 10, 15 and 25 years service and these were to be awarded to qualified party members of both sexes. Service in any of the following organisations as an officer or other ranks counted: Nazi Party, the so-called 'Political Leaders', SA, SS, NSKK, NSFK, and as officers only in the HJ, DJ, BDM and JM. In the case of the NSBO, in any rank prior to 1933 or after this date, as an official in the DAF. Service time in two of the aforementioned organisations running concurrently did not count as double time. The first date from which service could be counted was the refounding of the Nazi organisation in February 1925. Service between February 1925 and 30.1.33 was counted as double in recognition of the 'Kampfzeit' by members of the Old Guard. Service had to be unbroken but an exception was made for:

● Compulsory military service provided it did not exceed two years duration.
● Service in the Spanish Civil War during the period 1936-39.
● Military service in WW2.

Awards were made annually on 30 January with the last date for eligibility being 31 October the previous year. The first awards were made on 30.1.40 with a further award on 20.4.40. The awards were then given out on 30 January thereafter. Party members who lost their lives in the cause of the party were awarded the relevant grade of the cross. These special awards were made on 20.4.42, 20.4.43 and 20.4.44.

The cross was presented in a brown oblong box, with a gold national emblem embossed on the top of the lid. The lower interior of the box is off-white flocking and compartmented. However, in many cases, the inside of the box was just the unfinished plain, white card in which the box was produced. The RZM code can often be found stamped on the base of the box.

NSDAP LONG SERVICE CROSS IN BRONZE 10 YEARS SERVICE (VARIATION)**

Known Makers: No Known Maker

This cross is superficially the same as that described above but it has a number of slight differences that sets it apart from the other and warrants it being given its own categorisation. The arms of the cross measure 42mm across and 23mm across the ends. At the centre the wreath of oak leaves measures 21mm across and is made up of five leaves on each side which measure 2mm across. The whole of the wreath and the central field, as well as the eagle and swastika, is a separate piece that is fixed to the body of the cross. The eagle has a wingspan measuring 26mm and the upper line of fletch that runs from the 'C' curl is continuous. The two rows of individual feathers beneath the 'C' curl number seven in the top line and 10 in the lower. The oak leaf wreath in the eagle's claws measures 6mm across. The arms of the cross have a flat 1mm edge that has a slight rise with a 1.5mm raised rib line just inset and superimposed on to it. However, this has a flat inside edge. The lightly stippled field is deeply recessed at this point and rises from it to the centre. The thickness of the arms of the cross at the beaded edge, is 3.5mm and across the centre of the cross is 8.5mm.

The reverse is the same as the obverse and as described previously, with the noticeable difference in the number of leaves. The wreath is also pronounced but part of the body of the cross and is approximately 1mm proud of it. It is produced from a heavy alloy that is artificially bronzed with a matt finish. This takes on a rather dull and lifeless appearance. The ribbon suspension ring in this type is usually 12mm and the RZM code of the manufacturer is often found stamped upon it.

All the other criteria for the cross and its award are identical. This is just a variation in the manufacturing technique and bears no significance in the award structure.

NSDAP LONG SERVICE CROSS IN SILVER 15 YEARS SERVICE**

Known Makers: 1, 10, 19, 20, 100, RZM M1/52

This cross is identical to the 10 Year Service Cross and can be found in two manufacturing forms but, as these are both identical, they do not warrant being categorised as two distinct types. They are referred to, for obvious reasons, as the thick and thin type. Both have all the exposed metal parts silver-plated while the fields are infilled with translucent blue enamel. The wreath portion on the obverse and reverse are separate parts that are attached to the body of the cross, thus making it a three part construction. The measurements should be interpreted loosely

in the case of both the thick and thin types. For the thin type the thickness across the beaded edge is 2.25mm and across the centre of the cross 6mm. In the case of the thick type the measurements are 3.5mm and 10mm respectively. The other dimensions of the cross are as previously described.

It was suspended from a 30mm blue band with a 2mm silver wire embroidered strip indented by 1mm from the edge with a similar one inset by 0.5mm. The cross was worn in the same manner as the 10 Year Cross and could be worn in conjunction with it. When the ribbon only was worn, a small silver metal emblem as described for the 10 Year Cross was attached to the 30mm or 15mm ribbon.

The award was instituted on 2.4.39 by Hitler to reward 15 years service in the relevant organisations. The box was finished in blue instead of brown and was to compliment the colour of the cross and had a silver national emblem stencilled on to the top of the lid.

NSDAP LONG SERVICE CROSS IN GOLD 25 YEARS SERVICE****

Known Makers: 1, 10, 19, 20, 100, RZM M1/52

This cross is identical to that described before and can be found in two distinct manufacturing forms. Because the design of both is identical, it does not warrant a separate categorisation but they are referred to by collectors, for obvious reasons, as the thick and thin type. Both have all their exposed metal parts gilded while the fields are infilled with opaque white enamel. The wreath portion on the obverse and reverse are separate parts which are attached to the body of the cross, thus making this a three-part construction. The measurements of the two types of cross must be given a little latitude and in the case of the thin type, the thickness across the beaded edge is 2.25mm and across the centre of the cross 6mm. The thick type has measurements in the same areas of 3.5mm and 10mm. The other dimensions of the cross are the same as already described.

It was suspended from a 30mm red band with a 1mm white stripe, a 2mm gold wire stripe and a 1mm white stripe, all indented by 1mm from the edge. There is another form of ribbon measuring 30mm which is of red watered silk and has indented, by 0.5mm, a woven 2mm silver wire stripe with a 1mm gap and a similar 2mm silver wire woven stripe. The purpose of this second form of ribbon is unknown but it has been suggested that it was for members of the SA who objected to the former ribbon and its association with the 'Golden Pheasants' as the officials of the NSDAP were nicknamed.

The cross was worn in the same manner as the 10 Year Cross and could be worn in conjunction with it and the 15 Year Cross. When the ribbon only was worn, a small gold metal emblem as previously described was attached to the 30mm or 15mm ribbon.

The award was instituted on 2.4.39 by Adolf Hitler to reward 25 years service in the relevant organisations.

The presentation box has an exterior in dark red leatherette, with a gold embossed eagle on the lid. The upper lid interior is white satin and the lower compartmented section is recessed to take the ribbon separately, laid horizontally across the box, while the cross in its own compartment. The whole of the base is covered in beige velvet.

FAITHFUL SERVICE DECORATION FOR 25 YEARS SERVICE*

FAITHFUL SERVICE DECORATION FOR 40 YEARS SERVICE*

Known Makers: 1

The design of these two crosses is identical save for the colour which was intended to denote grade. The design was created by Prof Richard Klein of Munich and comprised of a cross pattée or formy. The measurements across the arms of the cross are given as 42mm but a wide variation exists ranging from 40.5mm to 42mm. As a result there can be a wide variation of the following measurements. Round the arms of the cross runs a raised 1mm edge line, another of similar size runs round the arms of the cross adjacent, but slightly recessed. At the centre is a 14mm square medallion slightly higher than the outer edge line. On to the central square medallion is superimposed a raised swastika with the legs following the outer lines of the medallion. There is a fine edge line around the arms of the swastika and the central field produced is filled with black opaque enamel. The fields of the arms of the cross are finely stippled. In the quarters of the arms of the cross are placed part of a wreath of oak leaves. The gap between the inner edge of the wreath, the arms of the cross and the central square medallion, are voided. Each segment of the wreath comprises of two bunches of two oak leaves overlapping one another tip over stalk. The outer edge of the leaves takes the line of the wreath, which measures 6mm.

The reverse of the cross follows the same design as that of the obverse save that the swastika is omitted and the square medallion now has a matching outer raised edge line and an adjacent recessed one, similar to the arms of the cross. The central field is recessed and stippled and on to this is superimposed, in raised Gothic capital letters, the three line inscription, 'FüR, TREUE, DIENSTE' (For Loyal Service). The recessed parts of the cross are finished in matt

silver or gold, while the raised portions are burnished. This includes the leading edges of the ends of the cross. From the upper arm is positioned an eyelet, through which is placed the ribbon suspension ring.

The ribbon comprises a 35mm cornflower blue band. When worn on the ribbon bar, a miniature of the cross corresponding to the grade was attached to the centre of the ribbon. The decoration ranked with the other service awards but military service awards took precedence over them. Only the highest class could be worn at any one time.

An interesting question is how was it possible that an award of the 25 Years Service Cross citation could be made in 1938 and then the 40 Years Service Cross could be awarded in 1941? This seems to be a paradox. The explanation is that the award of the 25 Years Service Cross was bestowed on the institution of the award and did not technically represent 25 years service but could took into account 37 years service and, as there was no intermediate award between the two, the 40 Years Service Cross was bestowed when appropriate.

On Hitler's accession to power he perceived the necessity of drawing all the long service awards of the states and industry under one umbrella. This Nazi concept was to draw these awards into direct governmental control and was contrary to that employed by the Weimar government which, after WW1, had devolved government into the states (Länder). These awards were first mooted in a Führer decree of 14.11.35 where, as well as the 50 Years Service Cross, a fourth grade for 10 years service had also been envisaged but this was never issued. Early in 1936 the Reichsminister of the Interior initiated steps to establish such awards and on 30.1.38 these awards were instituted to recognise loyal service to the German people. Consideration of service time began when the prospective recipient reached the age of 18. Any break in service for duty with the military in the capacity of an administrator or on active duty, was allowed to count towards the total time for loyal civil service, as did service in the civil organisations of the police and labour service. The recommendations for the awards had to be forwarded through the Reich Minister of the Interior for interim approval and to the President of the Reichschancellery for final approval.

The crosses were contained in presentation cases that, in the case of the 25 Years Service Cross, is a cardboard box in red simulated leather. The interior is compartmentalised and finished in dark red flocking. On the lid is embossed the numeral 25, surrounded by a silver spiked circle. In the case of the 40 Years Service Cross, it came in a presentation case that comprised a hard case of hinged construction with press-stud catch and an exterior of red simulated leather. The base is compartmentalised and finished in dark red velvet, while the upper inside of the lid is finished in padded white satin. Sometimes there is the manufacturer's trade mark stencilled in small letters in the lower right-hand corner. Embossed on top of the lid is an oak leaf wreath, surrounding an Arabic 40.

FAITHFUL SERVICE DECORATION FOR 40 YEARS SERVICE WITH 50 YEARS OAK LEAF CLUSTER*****

Known Makers: No Known Maker
The enabling order for this cluster was made on 12.8.44 by Hitler and in this he decreed 'No 1 (1) Als Anerkennung für 50 Jährige Tätigkeit im öffentlichen Dienst stifte ich zum Treudienst-Ehrenzeichen ein Eichenlaub. Das Eichenlaub wird in Gold am Bande der 1. Stufe getragen' (As recognition for 50 years activity in public service I donate for this faithful service an oak leaf decoration. The award will be worn with a gold ribbon of the first grade). This order was introduced at the same time as the Police Long Service 25 Years Service Cross with 40 Years Cluster and the Fire Brigade Decoration First Class with 40 Years Cluster. The design of the award is presumed to be an oak leaf spray which was added to the ribbon of the Faithful Service Decoration for 40 Years Service. The base has a ribbon curling downwards from a knot at the centre. From the knot, in a 'V' form, are two oak leaves, from each side is a larger leaf overlapping two small ones. The area between the ribbon and the leaves is usually solid, however this, in some cases, can be voided. This is because this emblem was used to denote 40 years long service in the Army, Navy and Air Force. The emblem is attached to the ribbon by two flat pins that are put through the ribbon. The reverse of the emblem is plain and flat. The overall colour of it is gold. It is unclear if the Arabic numerals '50' were placed above the emblem to denote the number of years of service. If this was the case, as with the Police Long Service Cross 25 Years Service with 40 Year Cluster and the Fire Brigade Decoration Second Class with 40 Year Oak Leaf Cluster, it is logical to suppose that similar provision would have been embodied — if not explicitly but implicitly — for this award. The numerals would then have comprised two individually pressed figures measuring 23mm high in the case of the '5' and 22mm for the '0'. The edges would have been gently sloped upwards and produced a fine edge line. The field produced would have been crossed horizontally by small rounded lines and both the pressed figures would have been gilded.

However, there is only one known example of this medal and it is very unlikely that the award was ever presented. The grade was introduced by decree of Hitler on 12.8.44 and it was to recognise 50 years of loyal service. There is serious question as to whether or not the device was awarded in conjunction with the 40 Years Long Service Cross.

FAITHFUL SERVICE DECORATION FOR 50 YEARS SERVICE**

Known Makers: 1
This award takes the form of the crosses described in the Faithful Service Decorations for 25 and 40 Years Service, with the exception that the field of the upper arm of the cross has a raised Arabic '50' superimposed upon it. The body of the cross is silver-plated while the wreath and the 50 are gilded.

The reverse is again identical to that described in the Faithful Service Decorations for 25 and 40 Years Service, with the exception that the inscription has been changed to 'Für, Treue, Arbeit' (For Loyal Work). The wreath on the reverse is also gilded. From the upper arm is positioned an eyelet through which is placed the ribbon suspension ring. This very often has a small number '1' punched into it, which is the manufacturer's touch mark and relates to Deschler und Sohn of Munich.

The ribbon is a 35mm cornflower blue band. When worn on the ribbon bar a miniature of the cross was affixed to the centre of the ribbon. The decoration ranked with other service awards, but military service awards took precedence over it.

This special grade was introduced on 30.1.38 to recognise employees of private firms who had completed 50 years of continuous service with one firm that operated in the free market economy. However, the recognised breaks in service as prescribed to take into account military call up or other like service, was counted towards the award.

Recommendation for the award were forwarded from the firm employing the recipient to the Reichsminister of the Interior for interim approval, who then forwarded it to the President of the Reichschancellery for final approval. Great importance was attached to the award of the cross and each award focused a great deal of publicity upon the recipient when it was presented.

The cross was contained in a presentation case that comprised a hard case of hinged construction, with press-stud catch and an exterior of red simulated leather. The bottom part of the box is compartmentalised and finished in dark red velvet, while the upper inside lid is padded and finished in white satin sometimes bearing the manufacturer's trade mark that, in this case, is often Deschler und Sohn: München. Embossed on the lid top in gold, is an oak leaf wreath surrounding an Arabic 50.

13. Political Awards

GERMAN MOTHERS' CROSS BRONZE CLASS 1ST PATTERN*****

GERMAN MOTHERS' CROSS SILVER CLASS 1ST PATTERN*****

GERMAN MOTHERS' CROSS GOLD CLASS 1ST PATTERN*****

Known Makers: Unmarked

This decoration comprises a cross with the three upper arms being the same length and the lower one being slightly longer measuring 35mm by 42mm. The individual arms slope outwards to the ends which, in turn, are gently scalloped. The arms of the cross have a fine raised outer line and a similar one inset by 1mm. This tram line is infilled with white opaque enamel. The central fields of the arms of the cross are lightly stippled and infilled with semi-translucent blue enamel which, upon close inspection, gives the impression of watered silk. In the quarters of the arms is a sunburst made up of a central pointed ray, with two similar ones on either side that decline in height. Between each ray is a raised spine. The measurement across the longest point is 28.5mm. At the centre of the arms is a superimposed button measuring 14mm across. This has a raised outer edge line and a similar one indented by 1.5 mm. The resultant field is lightly stippled with the inscription, in raised letters, 'DER DEUTSCHEN MUTTER' (The German Mother). The button is convex and the central field has a swastika with fine raised edge lines. The fields produced are filled with opaque black enamel and the raised field infilled with opaque white enamel.

The reverse has the four line inscription in flowing hand engraving, 'DAS, KIND ADELT, DIE MUTTER, ADOLF HITLER.' (The Child Ennobles the Mother). From the top of the upper arm of the cross is an integral square ribbon suspender. The design was the creation of architect Franz Berberich. The only differences between the crosses is the colour and the silver or gold finish was applied to the basic bronze cross, after it had been hand engraved.

The cross was worn round the neck suspended from a long ribbon. This measures 10mm and has a 1mm white edge stripe, 1mm blue, 1.5mm white and a 4mm blue central band. In addition to being worn about the neck, the cross was also worn in its full size suspended from a bow and attached to the lapel. There is another form of ribbon measuring 12mm wide with a 0.5mm blue edge stripe, 1.5mm white stripe, 1.5mm blue stripe and a central 5mm red stripe, 1.5mm blue stripe, 1.5mm white stripe and a 0.5mm blue edge stripe. The reasons for this second ribbon are unclear, but may well be the result of the manufacturer producing an alternative prototype for consideration.

A miniature, either suspended from a bow or made into a brooch, was also authorised. The miniature is encountered with the first type inscription. There is also a full size version of all grades of the cross fitted with pin backs, to allow them to be worn as brooches.

This form of reverse was in existence for only a short period of time and therefore genuine examples of these crosses are very rare. It is unknown whether this cross was a special form with the inscription awarded to particularly important women and therefore the second pattern ran in tandem with this type. As each example has been engraved from the bronze grade and then finished in the relevant colour, it was necessary to have only bronze examples with a plain reverse awaiting the hand engraving, however there are examples of all three grades of this type. Thus, the conclusion can be drawn that there were two types. This form for special award and the second type for general award, or the whole of the production was going to be awarded in this manner and the hand engraving was too expensive to facilitate the viability of the project. This theory is somewhat nullified by the fact that the third form had the date and Hitler's signature stamped into the reverse as an integral step in production. This could have been achieved from the inception of the decoration. The most likely format of the award was that there were two forms of the cross, engraved and not engraved. This did not please the recipient or the local NSDAP hierarchy and the third form was introduced to bring unanimity into the decoration. I have an example of the third type in bronze which has the date and signature hand engraved and this gives further weight to the theory. However, I must stress that these are only theories based on fact, but the second form is undoubtedly not a mistake in the manufacturing process.

The background to this award was that 2,000,000 German males had been killed during WW1. The result was that Germany had a reduced male population which, in turn, meant that more women had to work and reduced the number of men of fighting age. In France, the loss of virtually a generation was to dramatically affect the military strategy of the post-Versailles era and lead to the construction of the Maginot Line — huge fortifications in place of the missing soldiers. Hitler, however, perceived an alternative solution to the problem. There were more marriageable women available than men and thus a large number of women of child bearing age remained 'unproductive'. The solution was to advocate the virtues of motherhood, remove the stigma of illegitimacy and exalt the virtues of large families. This was achieved by making illegitimate children wards of the state, giving cash incentives for each child born and make an award that the community at large could recognise and admire — the fundamental principle of Nazi propaganda. This was achieved by the creation of the German Mothers' Cross on 16.12.38.

The award was introduced to reward women who produced large families and the criteria was based on:

- Having 4 and 5 children: Bronze;
- Having 6 and 7 children: Silver;
- Having 8 or more children: Gold.

All of these children had to reach the age of six months for their mothers to be eligible for the award and the women had to be of German origin. When Austria, the Sudetenland, the Protectorate of Bohemia and Moravia, Memel District and Danzig were all incorporated into the Greater Reich, then females of German origins in these districts were also made eligible on the same grounds as their German counterparts.

The awards were made on Mothering Sunday, which is the second Sunday in May. The first awards were presented on 21.5.39. There was a special presentation on 1.10.39 and a further award ceremony on 24.12.39. From then on the awards were given on 18.5.40, 24.12.40, 18.5.41, 24.5.41, 17.5.42, 24.12.42, 16.5.43, 24.12.43, with the last reported bestowal on 14.5.44. However, I have an original document made out for 20.5.45 in Reichenbach. Whether this is a piece of local initiative or the last official awarding ceremony is unclear.

To illustrate the scale of this award, I have included some figures. When the award was first instituted approximately 3,000,000 women qualified for one of these awards and from 25.12.39 to 18.5.40, 620,697 crosses were authorised: 346,350 Bronze, 152,494 Silver and 121,853 Gold.

In the two lower grades the crosses came in a large blue paper packet with, in Gothic script, the derivation and name of the cross. The Gold Class Cross came in a hard hinged and compartmentalised box. The exterior is dark blue leatherette with a facsimile of the award embossed in gold on the lid. The interior has white padded satin in the lid that often has the name of the maker stencilled on to it at the base. The lower tray is off white velvet. In some cases, the Silver Class was awarded in a hard hinged case as described for the Gold Class, but with a silver facsimile of the award embossed on the lid. This form of case is scarce.

GERMAN MOTHERS' CROSS BRONZE CLASS 2ND PATTERN****

GERMAN MOTHERS' CROSS SILVER CLASS 2ND PATTERN*****

GERMAN MOTHERS' CROSS GOLD CLASS 2ND PATTERN*****

Known Makers: Unmarked

The obverse design of these crosses is identical to that described above. The reverse is plain, ie without inscription, and flat. The main point to note is that this form did not miss the stamping process as has been previously believed, as the hand engraving had to be put on to a blank reverse and from studying the three grades, it can be deduced that the engraving was done on the bronze grade and the colour was added after this part of the process. This is shown by the fact that the bronze inscription is in different shades, conducive to the marks produced by the engraver and their subsequent variation in oxidisation. On the other hand, the silver and gold grades have a universal finish to the engraving.

The criteria for the award of the varying grades is the same as described in the First Pattern Crosses, as are the citations and presentation packets and box.

GERMAN MOTHERS' CROSS BRONZE CLASS 3RD PATTERN*

GERMAN MOTHERS' CROSS SILVER CLASS 3RD PATTERN*

GERMAN MOTHERS' CROSS GOLD CLASS 3RD PATTERN*

Known Makers: Unmarked

The obverse design of these crosses is identical to that described in the First Pattern Crosses. However, the white enamel running round the cross is sometimes a little wider in some examples than others. This must not be considered unusual considering that some 80 different manufacturers were involved in producing them by the end of the war. There are also examples produced in the closing stages of the war which were not enamelled but had been filled with paint to give the impression of enamelling. These examples are considered quite scarce although not expensive for the collector.

The reverse is the same save for the change in inscription which comes in four lines '16., DEZEMBER, 1938, ADOLF HITLER'. The Führer's signature is quite different in this case to that in the aforementioned crosses. This inscription is impressed into the reverse of the cross as an integral part of the production process. However, an example known to the author has been hand engraved. This may be a transitional piece, fitting somewhere between these three models. The maker's LDO number can sometimes be encountered on the lower arm of the cross. The reverse of the miniature has the same inscription as that found on the large cross.

The award criteria is the same as described in the First Pattern Crosses as are the citations, the presentation packets and box.

GERMAN MOTHERS' CROSS GOLD CLASS WITH DIAMONDS*****

Known Makers: No Known Maker
This cross is identical to that described in the First Pattern Crosses, with the exception that the arms of the swastika have been drilled out to accommodate 17 small rose-cut diamonds. The purpose of this award is unknown but at least two examples exist. The first was to recognise a mother of 16 children from Dresden. A second example was auctioned in Manion's International Auction House, where it was stated that 'The following lots were recently obtained directly from the veteran who took them as war booty from Schloss Klisshein'. It has also been reported that two other examples have come to light in the former DDR, both with their documents and in the hands of the original recipients. The information obtained alludes to the fact that these awards were also bestowed on the recipient for families in excess of 15 children. It must be stressed that these last two finds are unsubstantiated and are, at present, awaiting official verification.

The criteria for the award of this grade are unknown as is the citation that accompanied the award. However, it can be concluded from the sketchy information available to the collector that the bestowal of this award was rendered for the production of 15 children or more. The box was as described in the First Pattern Crosses.

COBURG BADGE*****

Known Makers: Unmarked
This award consists of an oval, slightly convex, badge that was originally produced in bronze. It has a narrow wreath of laurel leaves round its edge measuring 2mm across. These have three leaves in each bunch, with two berries at their tips. At the base they meet stalk to stalk, without a tie. There are 10 bunches on either side and the top two bunches on either side do not have the laurel berries. The top leaves meet at a model of Coburg Castle. The Castle has two spires on the viewer's left with a large roofed building and a small adjacent pinnacle on the right. At the base there are two little, poorly defined huts set on to a curved ground. Inside the wreath is a flat field that measures 4mm, with a raised 0.5mm line.

The central oval void has a large swastika measuring 16mm across and the width of the individual arms is 4mm. From the top of the badge, superimposed over the castle and swastika, with its tip resting at the joint of the laurel leaf wreath at the base, is a double-edged sword with straight quillons, twisted grip handle and a pronounced ball pommel. From the top of the pommel to the edge of the lower wreath at the base of the badge, measures 54mm and the width across the badge measures 39mm. The field of the wreath has the inscription, in raised capital letters, starting at the left of the sword's tip, '1922 . MIT HITLER' broken by the quillon and repeated on the right side, 'IN COBURG . 1932' (1922 With Hitler in Coburg 1932). The field round the lettering is stippled with slightly raised lines.

The reverse is plain with a thin hinge and a pin that has a circular retainer and a 'C' type hook at the bottom. The pin is not always as described in all cases. It has also been noted that an example has the numeral '1' stamped on to it. The thickness of the badge is 4mm across the thickest part and at the wreath, 2mm.

There is a second version of the badge which is thinner and has the mark on the reverse. These badges are of later manufacture as the RZM code did not come into being until 1935 and as this award was introduced in 1932, it was impossible for the mark to be applied on the original badges. It was worn on the left breast of the party uniform above other party awards and badges.

The award was instituted on 14.10.32, to recognise the 10th anniversary of the Nazi triumph over the Communists in Coburg. The badge was declared an official party and national decoration in a decree signed by Hitler on 6.11.36, who had taken a personal interest in the design. It had been the highest party award since its inception in 1932 and was held in greater esteem than the Blood Order itself. This is a rare award as only 436 names were entered on the official party roll of recipients who were entitled to the badge.

The background to the award dated back to the early years of the NSDAP when it was struggling to develop in the chaos of post-Versailles Germany. On 10-11.10.22 some 700 members of the fledgling party had come into conflict with local Marxists during a rally in the communist-controlled city of Coburg. Politicians of both extremes used the event — which had been instigated by the city fathers to promote cultural awareness — for their own ends and it was to prove, with the humiliation of the Marxists, one of Hitler's earliest successes in extending the influence of the party outside its Bavarian heartland.

Whether or not the badge was presented in a box of any type is unknown to the author.

Plate 256 Obverse Coburg Badge.

Plate 257 Reverse Coburg Badge.

Plate 253 Obverse German Mothers Cross-Gold Class First Pattern.

Plate 254 Reverse German Mothers Cross-Gold Class First Pattern.

Plate 255 Obverse German Mothers Cross Gold Class with Diamonds.

Plate 255A The German Mothers Cross on a bow – as worn by a female in uniform.

Plate 258 Obverse Gau Thuringen Commemorative Badge-Silver Class.

Plate 259 Reverse Gau Thuringen Commemorative Badge-Silver Class.

NÜRNBERG PARTY DAY BADGE OF 1933**

Known Makers: C. Balmberger
This badge is finely struck in bronze that is artificially patinated. It is 52mm high by 34mm wide and the design comprises of a closed winged eagle holding a wreath continuous small bunches of oak leaves. There are three oak leaves in each bunch and 10 bunches running visibly between the eagles talons. These bunches measure 1mm across. The central field has a raised swastika. The eagle and swastika surmount a view of the city of Nürnberg and its castle. This design is placed just above a raised panel that has diagonal cuts at the bottom, which is squared off. The panel has a three-line inscription in raised capital letters of varying size, 'N.S.D.A.P, REICHSPARTEITAG, NüRNBERG 1933.'.

The reverse of the badge is flat with a vertical groove, into which a pin is inserted and then soldered in.

A rally, the first since 1929 at Nürnberg, was held on 31.8.-3.9.33. It was known as Parteitag des Sieger (Victory Party Rally) and marked the Nazi accession of power on 31.1.33. At this rally, Hitler formally recognised the Adolf Hitler SS Standart and the dedication of the SS Standarten took place. This was formed from SS-Sonderkommando Zossen and SS Sonderkommando Jüterbog. A total of 785 men from these two units were present and, on the last day, a salutary round was fired by a Reichswehr battery. Gruppenführer Sepp Dietrich received the banner with the name 'Adolf Hitler' on the box. The two Sonderkommandos were granted the right to wear the name Adolf Hitler on an arm band on the left arm. From this day forward the unit bore the designation 'Adolf Hitler Standart'. Hitler, at this time, was reviewing the necessity of the rowdy SA and its leader, Ernst Rohm. The formation of this unit was a very important deviation from the important position normally ascribed to the SA and reflected the decline in the fortunes of Rohm's force. Although an important event, historians have tended to undervalue the Day Badge, for it was given official recognition as a decoration of the party under regulations governing the awards of the party and its form of dress on 16.3.35. This order deals with the implementation of the laws as regards the insidious attacks on the state and the party and with the protection of the party uniforms. It continues 'find enclosed all the articles listed under this order which belong to the party officially, flags and badges of the German National Socialist Workers Party and its affiliated associations', and lists these awards particularly, 'SA — Sportsabzeichen, Coburger Abzeichen, Abzeichen der Parteitag 1929 und 1933, Abzeichen des SA: Treffens Braunschweig'. These are then followed by a second list of civil permitted badges of the party and its associates. This order reinforces that of 20.12.34.

There is a further order on 14.11.35 which does not specifically include the 1933 badge, but relates to 'Traditionsabzeichen' and the other awards of the party.

On 6.11.36 Hitler introduced a further order that formalised the awards of the party and forbade the wearing on party uniforms badges that had, by tradition, become considered genuine party commemorative or honorary awards:

'They may be worn on the civilian overcoat or jacket by all party members on the left lapel. All party members who were permitted to wear their party badge or the national emblem badges which were issued at the party gatherings may now not be worn at all, except that issued in the year 1929 but the ones which will be issued in future at such gatherings may only be worn for the duration of the gathering. The wearing of club medals on duty or party uniform is herewith forbidden or any of the party's associated branches.'

The badge is seen being worn with other awards on period photographs from 1933 through to at least 1942. This poses the problem of why is the 1933 party badge so worn? Also in the Organisationsbuch der NSDAP, 1943 edition, there are three black and white illustrations of The Golden Party Badge, set centrally on a single page, The 1933 Party Day Badge, also set centrally on a single page and the Nürnberg 1929 Party Day Badge, with just a short paragraph above it, being used as the end of the introduction. This could be purely and simply because it represents 10 years of Nazism, which I feel is unlikely, or that the badge had a greater signification in Nazi history. The order of 6.11.36 clearly states that 'Ehrenzeichen der Partei' were permitted and this badge could have acquired the status of a 'Traditionsabzeichen'.

THE COMMON GAU COMMEMORATIVE BADGE: 1923***

THE COMMON GAU COMMEMORATIVE BADGE: 1925***

Known Makers: R. Wächtler & Lange, Mittweida
Both these awards are identical except for the date and I will describe them as one. The badge consists of a circular 45mm wreath of oak leaves measuring approximately 9mm at its widest part. It is produced from pressed silver that is formed in an irregular manner, so that the leaves and acorns are arranged more naturally. On to this is fixed a swastika that measures 46mm across the tips of the arms and 33mm across the flat edges

of the arms. They have a lip and then a raised edge line. At the centre is the date, 1923 or 1925, in raised numerals. The field is then painted a silk black.

The reverse shows the hollow form of the wreath and two doughnut rivets at 9 and 3 o'clock respectively. At the top is a hinge that is a piece of silver which has been bent over to return upon itself. Through this is placed a piece of silver wire that has one end through the left-hand part of the hinge. It is then bent at a 90° angle and runs for 35mm. This is then bent in a 360° angle and returns to the adjacent 90° angle, where it is similarly turned in the opposite direction. This pin construction produces a line down the centre of the pin that is indicative of the maker. The whole of the wreath on the obverse is artificially patinated in a smoke effect, while the reverse is a dark green-grey. The stamping of the swastika can be seen and at the centre, in small raised capital letters, is the maker's name and address in four lines, 'R. WÄCHTLER, & LANGE, MITTWEIDA, 800', the last being the silver content of the badge. This is the only known manufacturer of the award that has so far been authenticated.

These awards were introduced in 1933 and the right to award the Common Gau Commemorative Badges was vested in the local Gauleiter of the eight Gaus that used the same design for their individual Gaus — Sachsen, Bayerische, Ostmark, Halle-Merseburg, Hessen-Nassau, Magdeburg-Anhalt, Mecklenburg and Lübeck — who presented them in recognition of loyal, outstanding service to the party by its members in the Gau during the period of the 'Kampfzeit'. One has the date 1923 and the other 1925. The missing year in Nazi party history is 1924, when Hitler was in prison as a result of the failure of the 9.11.23 Putsch, to which the first date obviously refers. The second refers to the date when the party was reformed. These were recognised party awards but were not designated as national awards. They were to be worn on the left breast pocket. A miniature was also produced that was to be worn on the civilian clothing. This, although official, was not as in the Golden Party Badge. Restrictions were levelled on the wearing of the Gau Badge in that only one could be worn at any given time, even if the recipient had received a second from another Gau, and none was supposed to be worn when the Golden Party Badge was worn. However, this was not always strictly adhered to and high party officials can often be seen in photographs wearing the Gau Badge in conjunction with the Golden Party Badge.

Whether or not the badges were presented in a box is unknown to the author.

GAU THÜRINGEN COMMEMORATIVE BADGE BRONZE CLASS*****

GAU THÜRINGEN COMMEMORATIVE BADGE SILVER CLASS*****

GAU THÜRINGEN COMMEMORATIVE BADGE GOLD CLASS*****

Known Makers: Unmarked

These three badges are of all the same design, originating from the Gau Thüringen Rally Badge of 4.6.33, that commemorated Gau Treffen, Erfurt. The badge comprised a stylised eagle that looks to the viewer's right. The wings are formed as in a corner of a square and the upper one has a large leading edge that runs from the eagle's body with a 'C' shape and has two small breaks on the first portion. From the 'C' shape emanate a further six lines of fletch with two breaks that mirror the upper two. The left wing points downwards and is of similar design, with three further lines of fletch. The eagle's body curves to the viewer's right and has a distinctive head with pronounced eye and strong beak. From this are five lines of fletch with four, five, six, six and three feathers. Superimposed across the chest at this point is a large swastika that is held in the eagle's claws, as if held by fingers. The upper arm has, in raised capital letters, 'N.S.D.A.P.' and across the centre, 'FüR TREUE', and on the lower arm, 'THüRING.' (NSDAP For Loyalty Thüringia).

The reverse of the badge shows the negative of the obverse and has a horizontal pin which is the same as that employed to attach the ribbon of a medal on to a tunic. This is soldered directly on to the body of the badge. At the position of the stamping of the right claw, is the issue number of the badge. This is found in impressed numerals. The interesting thing about these, is that the numbers seem to have no significance to the grade of the badge, thus one encounters silver badges with numbers 402, 909 and 946, and bronze badges with numbers 826 and 982. The pin is normally found in a round needle pin form but it can also be found with a flat broad blade pin. The badges are formed in pressed brass, which is then artificially patinated a chocolate brown. The reverse of these badges shows a light, nearly gold appearance and the obverse has this light colour showing through the darker colour on the leading edges of the badge. The same brass badge is used for the gold class. It is then gilded and then similarly treated to form the patinated effect. The silver badge is produced in solid silver that is stamped at the bottom of the badge with a small 800 silver grade. Some badges have been encountered that are the bronze badge which has a light silver wash applied and this seems to bubble with age. Whether these are genuine silver badges or if they are bronze badges silver dipped is unknown to this author.

These badges were introduced on 17.6.33 by Gauleiter Fritz Sauckel as an award to the thousand most senior fellow fighters of Gau Thüringia. It was to be worn on the left breast of the party uniform. A miniature was produced for wear on the civilian dress. This has been encountered in a large size and a small 9mm size. Restrictions were levelled on the wearing of Gau badges generally, in that only one could be worn at any given time if the recipient held two, a second from another Gau, and none was supposed to be worn when the Golden Party Badge was worn.

The badge was awarded in a hard-hinged case with a dark red, pebbled leather finish with no inscription or emblem on the lid. The upper interior of the lid is lined in medium blue satin and the lower section is in dark blue velvet.

GAU SUDETENLAND COMMEMORATIVE BADGE*****

Known Makers: Unmarked
This badge consists of an oval wreath measuring 55mm high by 44mm wide with the breadth of the oak leaves constituting the wreath being 7mm. The wreath is finely struck from nickel silver and has a ribbon tie at the base that measures 7mm at its mid point. This is split into three equal sections that are enamelled in the colours of the Sudetenland, black, red, black. On the left, in raised numerals, '19' and on the right, '38' — the date of the founding of the Gau. From these, on either side, are six bunches of two oak leaves that meet at the apex tip to tip. The definition on the wreath is excellent and superimposed on to it is an eagle clutching a swastika in its claws. The eagle is three dimensional with pronounced chest and elegant head, with an extended neck. From the body extend its legs that are fully fletched. The wings are downswept with an angular appearance. The upper box portion of the furled wings has three lines of individual feathers: two, two and three. The two lower lines have five in each. From the lower line emanate five lines of vertical feathers. The eagle measures 40mm from the bottom of the swastika to the top of the head and 28mm across the wings. The wreath is 3.5mm thick and 7mm across the eagle's chest. The eagle is produced from tombac that is gilded.

The reverse is flat with two protrusions, through which is riveted the eagle with round headed rivets. At the top is a hinge that takes a flat bladed pin and at the base is a 'C' type hook. Some examples were produced with the manufacturer's logo and the silver content mark. This badge also had a finely made miniature for civilian wear. This Gau Badge is one of the most finely produced of the political series and also one of the rarest. It was worn on the left breast, below the Iron Cross First Class.

It was instituted at Christmas 1943 by the Gauleiter of the Sudetenland, Konrad Henlein, thus making it the last officially recognised Gau Badge to be introduced. The badge was to recognise the fifth anniversary of the founding of the Gau. The exact details of the criteria for the award of this extremely rare badge are unknown to the author, as are details of the presentation box that accompanied it.

HONOUR BADGE FOR MEMBERS OF THE NATIONAL SENATE OF CULTURE *****

Makers: Deschler
This award consists of an oval measuring 56mm by 44mm wide with 16 small points round its edge. Each of these has three small lines. Indented by 4mm is a raised oval line that is surmounted by a separate plate which has a twisted wire outer line. The central field has an eagle with downswept wings. The upper and lower line of fletch have five individual feathers on each wing. The downswept parts have four segments, while the inner edges of wings and legs are separate, as is the gap between the legs. The eagle surmounts an Ionic column that, in turn, sits on a swastika. Round the field in capital letters is, 'REICHS KULTURSENAT.' The field is infilled with cream coloured opaque enamel and the metal parts of the badge are gilded. The markings on the eagle and column are outlined in dark oxidisation and the other metal parts are lightly toned.

The reverse of the badge is plain and shows a recessed oval. This has a raised outer edge line and the field has two open rivets at the top and bottom. Above the lower rivet is impressed the issue number of the badge and below in small stamped capital letters 'GES. GESCH. SILBER. DESCHLER MüNCHEN 900.' There is a horizontal barrel hinge, needle pin and 'C' form hook. The badge was designed by Prof Richard Klein of München and worn on the left breast of the uniform. It was also permitted to wear the badge on civilian clothes.

The badge was introduced on 28.11.36 by the governing body of the National Senate of Culture to be awarded to its entire membership to recognise the members' contribution to the cultural heritage of Nazi Germany and it was on this occasion that the 125 members of the Senate were invested with the award.

The tightening of control on the arts began on 22.9.33 with a law that established a National Chamber of Culture, or Reichskulturkammer, which was a nationwide organisation embracing all those whose professional remuneration came from art, music, the theatre, press, radio, literature or the cinema. Its purpose was to act as a co-ordinating point for the various arts, with the

148

ultimate control of the chamber vesting in the Minister of Propaganda, Dr Joseph Göbbels. This power was delegated nominally to the National Senate of Culture, which was established on 15.11.35. Göbbels had long controlled the communications media and the establishment of the chamber offered him the opportunity to extend his control still further and utilise those various art forms to convey his propaganda themes to a wider audience. The chamber was composed of individuals connected with the various arts or those who had assisted in the advancement of German culture and it was from these members that the Senate was formed. It is doubtful that the membership of the Senate underwent very many changes, which would have limited the demand for badges and gave rise to probably less than 300 being awarded. This assumption is purely speculative and for the reader to gauge the comparative rarity of the award. The citation that accompanied the award is unknown to the author. The badge was awarded in a hard-hinged case with a press-stud catch. The exterior of the case is red, the inside of the lid is lined with white satin while the lower section is black velvet and recessed to accept the badge, with the outer edge finished with white, twisted satin cord. There is no upper or inner lid inscription or provision for the inclusion of the miniature badge. The award came with a small card that was carried at all times giving proof of entitlement to wear the badge.

MEMBERSHIP BADGE OF THE GERMAN ACADEMY FOR AERONAUTICAL RESEARCH

HONORARY, ORDINARY AND ASSOCIATE MEMBERS BADGE IN GOLD*****

MEMBERSHIP BADGE OF THE GERMAN ACADEMY FOR AERONAUTICAL RESEARCH

SUPPORTING MEMBERS BADGE IN SILVER*****

MEMBERSHIP BADGE OF THE GERMAN ACADEMY FOR AERONAUTICAL RESEARCH

CORRESPONDING MEMBERS BADGE IN BRONZE*****

Known Makers: Laurer
These badges are not, strictly speaking, a decoration or badge of honour but are on a par with that of the National Senate of Culture. However, so prestigious were both these organisations that their awards gained the unofficial status of honour awards during the time of their existence.

The German Academy for Aeronautical Research was founded by Göring on 24.7.36 by an order made at Bayreuth, with the principal idea of giving the leaders of German aviation a platform for the exchange of information. At the Ministry of Aviation, in its hall of honour, the president, Hermann Göring, emphatically stated that, 'the spirit of solidarity was an essential precondition for the reaching of the Academy's ambitious goals'. Further in his comments, he made it abundantly clear that what he referred to as 'the spirit of solidarity', were in fact Nazi ethics and values. The formation and infrastructure of the Academy perfectly suited the Nazis, as it enhanced a small élite core of scientists. The ideal of 'leadership', or more properly translated 'domination', could not be fully imposed as this depended upon the scientists considering that this policy was advantageous. According to the foundation decree, its role was to be of a purely scientific nature, results of research papers written on the field of aviation were to be presented to the Academy by its members. These papers were then to be translated into practical applications by others. The scientific faculty for this purpose was the Lilienthal-Society for Aviation. This, in organisational and infrastructure terms, represented the second tier at the apex of German aviation research.

In the early days of the academy, Göring and his Ministry of Aviation actively sponsored the academy in all its undertakings, holding flamboyant and extravagant functions which overshadowed the aims and activities of the academy. Over the ensuing years, the Ministry lessened its grip and, with the outbreak of war, the academy's work was discontinued. In 1940, however, their work was recognised as being of the utmost importance and the research programme restarted with a fervent intensity but stripped of all the former social glamour. Their researches were extended with exploration into the fields of rockets and nuclear power where the members broke new ground. They also furthered development in piston, as well as jet propulsion, engines. The Germans led the world with their work on high-altitude flying and aviation-related medicine.

At the general meeting of the Lilienthal-Society held in München on 12-14.10.37, the new national emblem of the Aviation Research Institute was announced. It comprised a large stylised eagle with its head facing to the viewer's right, with outstretched wings and a swastika grasped in both claws. The eagle and swastika were then enclosed within a wreath comprising of 24 oak leaves. The similarity between this and the Luftwaffe eagle symbolised the close association

149

between the two organisations. The academy was to be composed of 60 regular members and a total of 100 associate, honorary, sponsoring and outstanding scientific members. During the period between 1937 and 1942 the statutes governing membership were always complied with. Göring, in 1936, proposed an important restriction to the number of nominations. He reasoned that aviation research, then in the elementary stages, was soon to place new and outstanding scientists in the forefront of technology. These worthy scientists could then be nominated for membership prior to completion of the first five years existence of the academy. Göring's proposal meant that a large number of positions were to be kept vacant in anticipation of the large number of research scientists who were to be nominated to the academy. However, the expected technical scientists possessing 'great leadership potential' failed to materialise and earn their way into the academy with the result that, despite the great potential, the academy never had more than 45 regular members. The other category of membership including the 'group of one hundred' also stagnated. There were only 86 members, including the foreign scientists. It was not until an additional 58 associate members of German nationality were nominated on 1.3.42, that the academy achieved its statutory goal. During WW2, the names of foreign members did not appear on the membership roll, therefore new nominations were required to fill the gap between the actual and statutory number of members. The academy had a total of 218 members during its existence and all were awarded badges consecutively numbered. Each member received a full size and miniature badge bearing the same number. These were first introduced at the beginning of January 1938 and were confirmed by an order outlining their design, dated 2.11.38. It also defined the three classes of membership and the colour of the award. Honorary, ordinary and associate members received the badge in gold, supporting members in silver and corresponding members in bronze. The large badge was, according to dress regulations, to be worn on the left lapel of the formal dress coat. The miniature could be worn at any social gathering which was in accordance with 'the dignity of the academy'. On formal occasions members of the presidium, ie the president Hermann Göring (1937-45), the vice-president Erhard Milch, (1937-45), Willi Messerschmitt (1939-44), Kurt Tank (1944-45) and the chancellor Adolf Baeumker (1937-45), were permitted to wear a chain of office signifying their position within the academy, in place of their gold badges. The president's chain varied in design to that of the vice-president's, having a solid lower portion to which the insignia of the academy was appended, while that of the vice-president was an open worked scroll. The chain was designed by Paul Casberg, the Berlin artist,

who had his logo stamped on the reverse of the insignia suspension.

The membership badges were all identical in design. This comprised a large stylised eagle with its head facing to the viewer's right, with outstretched wings and a swastika grasped in both claws. The eagle and swastika are enclosed within an irregular thin wreath, which is composed of 16 single oak leaves, eight on each side in bunches of two, that met tip to tip. At these points in the lower portion of the wreath, they meet with single acorns and two bands. The badge is 47.5mm high and 37mm across the widest point of the wreath. The oak leaves making up the wreath measure 4mm across. The wingspan of the eagle is 51mm while from the tip of the swastika to the top of the eagle's head is 22mm. The oak leaf cluster is 11mm high and 13.5mm wide. These measurements are taken from the bronze award, while the silver gilded

Plate 260 Obverse Gau Sudetenland Commemorative Badge.

Plate 261 Reverse Gau Sudetenland Commemorative Badge.

badges are slightly larger in the dimensions of the wreath and thickness of the badge. The silver and gold class badges were produced in silver, the latter being gold plated, while the bronze class badges were cast in bronze. The manufacturer, Laurer of Berlin and Nürnberg, went to great lengths to be extremely accurate in the production of these badges. The large size badge has a finely chiselled pattern that is matted. The overall finishes of all the grades of the award is artificial patination, with the leading edge of the wing and swastika being burnished. In the bronze class badge this shows as gold. The reverse is also burnished to a mirror-like finish, with the membership number and the logo of the company stamped into it. The silver and gold badges have a small silver content number stamped on to the wreath at the lower right-hand position. Again, in the case of the bronze class badge, the back is gold. The badge is attached to a small oak leaf cluster by an oval ring, allowing the badge to swing freely. To the back of the cluster is attached a needle pin. Besides this form of badge, Laurer also produced another form of badge which was soldered directly to the oak leaf cluster, thus eliminating the swinging effect. This was possibly because some of the recipients found it annoying to have to be constantly aware of the badge whenever they leant forwards.

262   **263**

Plate 262   Obverse Honour Badge for Members of the National Senate of Culture.

Plate 263   Reverse Honour Badge for Members of the National Senate of Culture.

MEMBERSHIP BADGE OF THE GERMAN ACADEMY FOR AERONAUTICAL RESEARCH: HONORARY, ORDINARY AND ASSOCIATE MEMBERS MINIATURE BADGE IN GOLD*****

MEMBERSHIP BADGE OF THE GERMAN ACADEMY FOR AERONAUTICAL RESEARCH: SUPPORTING MEMBERS MINIATURE BADGE IN SILVER*****

MEMBERSHIP BADGE OF THE GERMAN ACADEMY FOR AERONAUTICAL RESEARCH: CORRESPONDING MEMBERS MINIATURE BADGE IN BRONZE*****

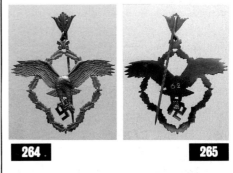

264 .   **265**

Plate 264   Obverse Membership Badge of the German Academy for Aeronautical Research in Gold.

Plate 265   Reverse Membership Badge of the German Academy for Aeronautical Research in Gold.

Known Makers: Laurer

The miniature pin for each grade is identical, save for the finish. It comprises a smaller version of the eagle that is employed as the central design on the large sized badge. The wingspan is 30mm and the height of the badge from the bottom of the swastika to the top of the eagle's wings is 28mm.

The reverse is plain save for the maker's mark and logo that is stamped into the reverse of the swastika and the issue number that is stamped into the right-hand wing. Another form has been met where the reverse has been engraved with the date, '21.1' on the left-hand wing and '1938' on the right. A long needle pin is attached to the badge at the top of the wing joint. This is twisted from just below the level of the tip of the swastika.

The badge was to be worn on the lapel of the civilian dress on any formal occasion at which the large badge was not to be worn, according to regulations.

14. Citations, Presentation Cases, Packets, Ribbons, Miniatures & Denazification

CITATIONS

It is impossible to describe the subject of citations in detail in this book since the whole topic is a subject in its own right. The main thing to look for is — as usual — quality. The multiplicity of each type of citation makes this a fascinating study. Do not be afraid to have many citations all the same as every one is unique. Groups of documents are much more interesting than single items. So if you have the opportunity of an unusual document or just one that you do not have, do not break up the group merely to get rid of the others accompanying it because you already have others in your collection.

PRESENTATION CASES AND PACKETS

Just as with citations, these have become a subject in their own right and, in the case of packets, make an inexpensive and spectacular collection. They have been greatly underestimated in importance and rarity and often discarded. In the case of boxes, a medal or award badge is greatly enhanced by being in its original case. They also become very important as in the case of the Eagle Order, which have the grade and specific title that were relevant to a given period of their history. The design of the case subtly changed with the redefinition of the award as did the embossed eagle on its lid. One cautionary note must be struck at this point. Reproduction cases and boxes are being produced and these can make excellent displays, if the materials are right, with the correct medals. It must always be remembered, however, that the reproductions are designed to deceive the unwary and caution must be exercised.

RIBBONS AND MINIATURES

In the Nazi field, there is a great variation in widths of ribbons and in the style employed to support the emblem. One way of collecting on a budget is to try and obtain a sample of every type of ribbon produced. The method I would suggest is to identify every medal with a ribbon. Then, with the clear stamp mounts, place a sample of the ribbon inside a loose-leaf stamp album, mount it on the page and title it with Letraset (or similar). Title the page with the medal's nomenclature and date of institution and then put the various widths on the page, with the measurements beneath in similar lettering.

The other method is to try and get the single medal clasp with the relevant emblem attached. This can be expanded by trying to get multiple clasps to show the inter-relationship of the medals as well as their position on the bar. This can be seen as a similar exercise that can be achieved in conjunction with your ribbon album.

Miniatures are a vast subject and can be found in many sizes. Personally I only collect miniature medals on ribbons to accompany the full size awards. This is purely a personal decision which helps to limit my own collection and I would not advise you to take this path necessarily.

DENAZIFICATION

With the ending of the war in Europe, it became Allied policy to actively remove the swastika and other Nazi emblems from Germany. There became a need to rebuild the shattered nation and its civil and military authorities. A new constitution was granted and, eventually, the Federal Republic of West Germany was born. The Soviets replicated this situation with a Communist state in East Germany. In 1957 the German Federal Parliament debated the need to consider the awards that had been introduced during the Nazi regime. After much deliberation, it came to the decision that a number of awards would be permitted and, if they did not have the swastika in the original design, then they could be worn in their old form or be manufactured anew in their previous design. This leads to a problem for the collector when ascertaining the date of production of a certain piece. These unaltered pieces include the Ostvolk awards, Afrika, Kreta, Kurland and Metz Cuff Titles and the Red Cross Decorations that returned to their original 1934 style. Both the Silesian eagle and the Baltic Cross are produced in their pre-Nazi form albeit Nazi approved Free Corps awards. This particularly causes concern as the same manufacturers who produced the Red Cross awards from the same dies and the 'birthday' of an individual piece is very hard to ascertain for the inexperienced collector.

15. Cataloguing, Appraising, Valuing & Housing Your Collection

AVAILABILITY AND VALUES

The one thing to be said is that all items are available — at a price. But the chance of falling on the great rarity is like winning the jackpot in any lottery. It is the dream we all hold and one, I am sure, that spurs on all true collectors. It must be remembered that a great rarity at the time of award, such as a Kultur Medaille, will be equally rare today. On the other hand, a Knight's Cross of the Iron Cross was sparingly awarded but the production was far greater than its award figures. The Oak Leaves and Oak Leaves and Swords were produced on a mass production run as it was cheaper to run the machinery and produce a greater quantity than desired, sort out the best examples and store the rest for possible future use. The silver could be melted down from this form as easily as from any other. Silver, in itself, is an inexpensive metal, malleable and easy to work. So, because a badge is produced in silver does not necessarily make it more valuable. Moreover, it is often easier to work in silver when producing reproductions.

I am also worried about placing values on medals in this context. I have given an estimated 'rarity value' for each medal which will give an approximate idea as to its commercial value. However, this should be seen in conjunction with the other important part of the valuing equation — 'Collector's Desirability'. This is really the most important part of the equation and is very susceptible to change — from fashion, from a new source increasing the supply or whatever — and thus, like all antiques or other investments, the values can go down as well as up. It is also important to remember that, with such an international market affecting the price, that currency fluctuations can also have a dramatic effect. For example, the effect of a fall in the value of the Pound is to reduce the price to an overseas buyer whilst, possibly, *increasing* the Sterling price to the seller.

As I discussed in the beginning of the book, the hobby has come of age. What is available now depends on those reputable dealers who will part exchange or obtain for you the piece that you require to complete your set. Their importance and knowledge cannot be underestimated.

To sum up then, decide what medals you are going to collect, plan the extent of the collection and, if possible, get a book or make a list of all the medals you want and mark them off as you acquire them. This is really an essential for you to feel that you are 'getting somewhere' and will keep your interest all the time. Over a period of time and with new information appearing regularly it will prove possible to produce a catalogue of all German WW2 medals — indeed this book and the author's earlier works are stages in this process — but even then new variations will appear. After all, that is part of the fascination of collecting.

HOUSING YOUR MEDALS

There are many ways of keeping a collection but care must be taken when selecting materials for use in the storage of medals, as corrosive gases can be emitted by a variety of substances. These gases are present in the atmosphere but generally at low concentrations. However, materials such as wood, fabric and adhesives used in a storage system may emit these substances, producing higher concentrations which can cause deterioration of objects in the storage area.

Silver is tarnished by reducible sulphides, commonly hydrogen sulphide and carbonyl sulphide, which can be emitted by fabrics, especially those made of wool and by some adhesives.

Copper and its alloys are corroded by chlorides, sulphides and organic acids. The source of these may again be fabrics but also certain plastics. For example, polyvinyl chloride (PVC) can give off gases containing chlorine.

Acidic papers and boards, wood, wood composites and some adhesives can release organic acids. The corrosion of lead is initiated by acetic acid and basic lead carbonate is formed. Formaldehyde, which is emitted by wood composites, can also corrode lead by the formation of lead formate.

As an extra precaution, an absorbent material may be incorporated into the storage system should an artefact be particularly prone to corrosion. Charcoal cloth, a fabric made from activated carbon may be used to absorb all types of gases. Zinc oxide pellets, which react with hydrogen sulphide and hence reduce the rate at which silver tarnishes, can also be used.

The usual form of display worldwide is a medal cabinet containing a number of flat trays and sooner or later the serious collector will have to consider the possibility of buying or making one. The price you will have to pay for a cabinet will depend largely on the quality of the workmanship and the number of trays it contains. Try to avoid buying a cabinet if the trays have been cut to take several shapes of medals on each tray. These have usually been made to meet the requirements of a particular collector and can be extremely inconvenient and space-wasting to anyone else. There are very few new cabinets being made at the present time.

● **Wood**

Always remember when buying or making a cabinet to select mahogany, walnut or rose wood as other woods, such as oak or cedar, contain a resin which is liable to tarnish your medals, which may prove difficult to remove without damage. Those specified woods are usually suitable for the storage of silver artefacts. However, in tests, lead almost always corroded and copper occasionally corroded in the presence of wood, especially oak. In general, when any wood is to be used, it should be well seasoned and dried. Tropical hardwood like mahogany are the least harmful. However, due to ecological factors, it is preferable that such woods are not used.

Adhesives are an important consideration. Cascamite (a powdered urea formaldehyde adhesive) is a general woodwork glue which may be used for construction of cabinets and inserts. Glues based on polyvinyl acetate emulsions should be avoided.

Wood-composites such as plywood, fibreboard and blockboard, are generally unsuitable for use with lead and often unsuitable for use with copper. This is due to harmful, volatile materials emitted by both the wood and the adhesive. Manufacturers are becoming aware of problems associated with volatile gases and some types of fibreboard, eg Medite, are designed to have low-level emissions of formaldehyde. These low emission fibreboards are often suitable for use, though testing of each type is recommended.

● **Plastic cabinets and trays**

Plastic cabinets and trays are an alternative to using wood. At present, of those tested, only one type of plastic tray has been found to be suitable for use with all metals. Further information can be obtained from the British Museum. Plastic cabinets are also available for housing these trays. The cabinets have not been tested but presumably are made from the same plastic as the trays and are thus suitable for use.

● **Metal cabinets**

Stove-enamelled metal cabinets may be used for storage of all types of materials.

● **Lining materials**

Drawers or trays within the cabinets are often lined. Plastozote, a polythene foam available in a variety of colours, may be used as an insert with suitably sized profiles cut out to accommodate the medals. The foam will afford protection to the medals, as it will prevent them moving around and suffering damage when the drawers are opened and closed.

Textiles may be used to line drawers and trays. Felt or woollen felt discs should not be used in proximity with silver, as they emit sulphide gases which will cause rapid tarnishing. Other fabrics can also cause problems. A looped nylon fabric may be a suitable alternative, as it has smaller quantities of felt. It will not fray when cut, acts as a 'cushion' and is available in a variety of colours.

● **Paper envelopes**

Another convenient method of keeping medals is in envelopes made from white paper, which may be kept in storage boxes long enough to contain between 150 and 200 medals. A description of each medal can be written on the outside of the white envelopes. Many envelopes are made of poor quality paper, which will become acidic and unsuitable for use in storage. Envelopes should, therefore, be made from archival quality paper or board.

● **Plastic envelopes and boxes**

The most popular way of keeping medals in North America is in medal folders which may be kept in a bookcase. These have a number of pouches forming the page. Information such as name, date and numbers awarded, may be printed on sticky labels placed on the reverse of the pouch. Although this is certainly a compact and convenient way of keeping medals, it does not compare with the more conventional and handsome mahogany medal cabinet in which the medals may be arranged and ticketed as desired. Some plastics may degrade and produce harmful vapour or droplets of plasticiser. Therefore, archival quality plastic envelopes should be used. These are made of polyester or high quality polythene. The medals can be stored individually in plastic boxes such as clear, /colourless polystyrene boxes. These may be lined with Plastozote foam to avoid mechanical damage.

TICKETING AND CATALOGUING

It it usual to place medals on white circular tickets on which may be written a short description of the medal, its catalogue number and perhaps your own reference number. Most medal dealers supply their own tickets when selling medals and you may wish to keep these, while writing any additional facts on a second ticket of your own. It is also a good idea to make a separate list of your medals, either on a card index or on loose leaves. Better still, in this computer age, is a data base that stores the information. Paper discs should be made of archival quality paper or board.

INKS

Inks used for annotating paper discs should have a permanent colour and be tested for acidity prior to use. Several pens have been tested by scientists in Glasgow. The following were found to be suitable for archival purposes — Artline Calligraphy Pen black EK 243, Edding Profipen 0.1 1800, Pentel Document pens permanent MR 205 (black and blue), GPO standard ballpoint pen PO SP15.

LIGHT

On occasions, whilst on display, silver medals have acquired a white 'bloom'. This has been shown to be a result of photochemical degradation of the original silver chloride patina, forming powdery metallic silver. It is unlikely that medals would be continually exposed to bright light whilst in storage but this potential hazard should be borne in mind.

CLEANING MEDALS

Generally speaking, **DO NOT** attempt to clean medals. I have seen more good medals ruined by cleaning than from any other cause and unless you have obtained expert advice or practised on medals of little value, it is better to leave them alone. There is a difference between the tone or bloom of a medal and ordinary dirt. A beautiful tone in which many colours of the rainbow can be seen is caused by natural oxidation of the surface with the atmosphere and can take years to form. Although it may make a silver medal look much darker than when it was new, a tone can enhance the look of a medal and to clean it off reduces the medal's value. This is particularly true of bronze medals which are often found with a hard smooth green coating. This is known as 'patina' and on no account should this be removed. Dirt on the other hand can be removed from gold and silver medals by first soaking them in warm soapy water and then brushing with an old toothbrush.

Medals made of pure gold never corrode and should not require more than washing and brushing. Sometimes silver medals become tarnished almost black from the sulphur acids in the air. This will not normally be noticed in country districts but in London or near any large industrial area a medal may become tarnished in a very short time. The best way to remove this is by gently dabbing the surface with a piece of cotton wool soaked in 'Silver Dip' which can be obtained from most stores. The polishing cloth sold with 'Silver Dip' should not be used as it will shine the surface and spoil the look of the medal. A 10% solution of ammonia will also remove tarnish and improve silver medals which

contain copper as an alloy. When 'Silver Dip' is used the medals need only be dried with cotton wool but it is advisable to thoroughly wash any medal cleaned with ammonia.

Medals made of copper, or copper with other alloys, are the most likely to require attention at one time or another. Verdigris is the usual enemy and appears as green spots. If the area of corrosion is not great or very deep, a bone needle may be used to loosen and remove the verdigris. Badly contaminated medals should be alternately soaked in a 20% solution of sodium sesquicarbonate and worked with the bone needle.

Zinc will be frequently found and should it become necessary to improve such medals, they are best treated by immersing in a 5% solution of caustic soda containing some zinc or aluminium filings, after which they must be thoroughly washed. It is advisable to varnish the medals in order to prevent any further oxidation of the surface. This should only be done if actual damage has occurred, for sealing the medal can seal in the source of the deterioration.

Lead, tin and iron were rarely, if ever, used on original medals and are normally found in conjunction with fake items.

An excellent method of removing grease from any medal is to wipe with cotton wool soaked in petrol or lighter fuel. Should a stronger action be needed, trichlorethylene may be used but only in a well ventilated room as this substance is used as an anaesthetic.

The surface of silver and copper medals can be improved by using a brush on which a spot of linseed oil has been placed.

TERMINOLOGY

This final chapter it is hoped will endeavour to explain some of the terminology used in the text of the book, to describe the method of production and manufacture and the subsequent markings that those medals and badges have applied to them in various ways.

The method of marking medals and badges underwent a number of changes during the period of the Third Reich and is quite a complex study in itself. The types of mark that can be encountered on medals and badges I have codified down for simplicity into seven types:

- Maker's name and address.
- Maker's logo.
- RZM code.
- Mint mark.
- Serial number.
- Silver mark.
- LDO number.

● Maker's Name and Address
This was found on the best quality badges and could be either cast or struck into the design of

the reverse of the badge. On some examples where the address has been actually stamped into the badge, it is found either on the pin or the body of the applied insignia. It is interesting to note that not all the badges of one manufacturer at the same time of production carried the name and address, indicating that they possibly sold the item wholesale to a third party for finishing or that they only selected superior quality items to bear their name. However, this is pure conjecture.

● **Maker's logo**
This fell into the same category as that of the name which has been fully described above and was often used in conjunction with it, as this was used as the trade mark of that firm or organisation.

● **RZM code**
This was the authority which authorised the production of the awards that were produced for the party and allowed, on instruction from the party through this controlling organisation which was situated at the Brown House in Munich and party headquarters in Berlin, the relevant manufacturers to produce those awards. The Reichszeugmeisterei, or RZM for short, would award a number which was accompanied by a logo formed by the letters RZM which was contained in a circle with the M at the bottom. Depending on the type of award that the company was producing, the relevant form of coding would be applied as follows but prefixed by M1/.

NUMBER	FIRM	LOCATION
1	Meyer & Franke	Luckenwalde
2	Richard Conrad	Weimar
3	Max Kremhelmer	München
4	Karl Gutenkunst	Oranienburg
5	Walter Simon	Dresden
6	Karl Hensler	Pforzheim
7	Herman Schanzlin	Pforzheim
8	Ferdinand Wagner	Pforzheim
9	Robert Hauschild	Pforzheim
10	Robert Schenkel	Pforzheim
11	C. Balmberger	Nürnberg
12	Gebr. Hähne	Lüdenscheid
13	L. Christian Lauer	Nürnberg
14	Matth. Oechsler & Sohn	Ansbach
15	Ferdinand Hoffstätter	Bonn a. Rhein
16	Dr Franke & Co KG	Lüdenscheid
17	F. W. Assmann & Söhn	Lüdenscheid
18	Gold und Silber Scheide Anstalt	Oberstein ad Nahe
19		
20	Gustav Emil Ficker	Beierfeld
21	Paul Meybauer	Berlin-Waidmannslust
22	Johann Dittrich	Chemnitz
23	Wilhelm Borgas	Eutingen
24	Overhoff & Cie	Lüdenscheid
25	Rudolf Reiling	Pforzheim
26		
27	E. L. Müller	Pforzheim
28	Gebr. Trautz	Pforzheim-Dillweissenstein
29	Otto Riedel	Zwickau
30	Robert Metzger GmbH	Pforzheim
31	Karl Pfohl	Pforzheim
32	Gustav Ramminger Inh. Hans Kuhnle	Pforzheim
33		
34	Karl Wurster	Markneukirchen
35	Wächtler & Lange	Mittweida
36	Berg & Nolte AG	Lüdenscheid
37	Julius Bauer Söhn	Zella-Mehlis
38	Carl Wächtler	Weimar
39	Robert Beck	Pforzheim
40	O. C. Meinel & W. Scholer	Klingenthal
41	H.A. Köhlers Söhn GmbH	Altenburg
42	Kerbach & Israel	Dresden
43	Julius Maurer GmbH	Oberstein ad Nahe
44	C. Dinsel	Berlin-Waidmannslust
45	Friedrich Linden	Lüdenscheid
46	Alfred Stübbe	Berlin
47	C. Th. Dicke	Lüdenscheid
48	Alexander Wollram	Dessau
49	Adolf Baumeister	Lüdenscheid
50	Richard Sieper & Söhn	Lüdenscheid
51	Noelle & Hueck GmbH	Lüdenscheid
52	Deschler & Sohn	München
53	Gebr. Wegerhoff	Lüdenscheid
54	Fa. A. Fries, Beuster & Schild	Berlin-Hohenschönhausen
55	August Enders AG	Oberrahmede
56	Erfurter Knopffabrik GmbH	Erfurt
57	M. Winter	München
58	M. Kutsch	Attendorn
59	Paul Cramer	Lüdenscheid
60	Gebr. Cosack	Neheim
61	Ossenberg-Engels	Iserlohn
62	Gustav Hähl	Pforzheim
63	Steinhauer & Lück	Lüdenscheid
64	Albert Winges	Trusen
65	E.F. Wiedmann	Frankfurt/Main
66	Fritz Kohm	Pforzheim
67	Karl Schenker Schwab.	Gmünd
68	Gustav Maier	Pforzheim
69		
70	Franz Otto	Wuppertal-Elberfeld
71	Gesell & Co	Pforzheim
72	Fritz Zimmermann	Stuttgart

73	Karl Erbacher	Pforzheim		127	Alfred Stübbe, Inh	Berlin-
74	Boerger & Co	Berlin			Herbert Tegge	Waldmannslust
75	Otto Schickle	Pforzheim		128	Eugen	Pforzheim
76	Hillenbrand & Bröer	Lüdenscheid			Schmidhäussler	
77	Foerster & Barth	Pforzheim		129		
78	Paulmann & Crone	Lüdenscheid		130		
79	Walter Amlauf	Leipzig		131		
80	R. Dürr & Fr. Seiter	Pforzheim		132		
81	Rütting & Mertz	Lüdenscheid		133		
82	Leistner & Co	Leipzig		134		
83	Willy Annetsberger	München		135		
84	Ernst Schneider	Lüdenscheid		136		
85	Alois Rettenmaier Schwab.	Gmünd		137		
				138		
86	Ernst Schneider	Lüdenscheid		139		
87	Karoline Gahr	München		140		
88	Josef Schulte-Ufer	Sundern		141		
89	Gustav Bühnert	Döbeln		142		
90	Apreck & Vrage	Leipzig		143		
91				144		
92	Karl Wild	Hamburg		145		
93	Gottlieb Friedrich Keck & Sohn	Pforzheim		146		
				147	Eduard Gösel	Wien
94	Friedr. Keck	Pforzheim		148	Heinr. Ulbricht's Wwe.	Wien
95	Josef Fuess	München				
96	F.O. Naupert	Rosswein		149	Lentwerk Brüder Schneider AG	Wien
97	M. Nett	Gravier u Prägeanstalt Fürth		150	Franke & Sohn	Heidenreich-stein
98	G. Danner	Mühlhausen		151	Rudolf Schanes	Wien
99	Peter Wilhelm Heb	Lüdenscheid		152	Franz Jungwirth	Wien
100	Werner Redo	Saarlautern		153	Friedrich Orth	Wien
101	Gustav Brehmer	Markneukir-chen		154		
				155	Schwertner & Cie Eggenberg	Graz
102	Frank & Reif	Stuttgart				
103	Carl Poellath	Schroben-hausen		156	Argentor-Werke	Wien
				157	Phil. Turks Wwe	Wien
104	Otto Fechler	Bernsbach		158	Karl Pichl	Innsbruck
105	Hermann Aurich	Dresden		159	Hans Doppler	Wels
106	Funcke & Brüning-haus	Lüdenscheid		160	E. Reihl	Linz
107	Emil Juttner	Lüdenscheid				
108	Schröder & Co	Lüdenscheid				
109	Glaser & Sohn	Dresden				
110	Tweer & Turck	Lüdenscheid				
111	Gebr Gloerfeld Metallwarenfabr. KG	Lüdenscheid				
112	Robert Deitenbeck	Lüdenscheid				
113	Gebrüder Dornbach	Lüdenscheid				
114	Paul Cramer & Co	Lüdenscheid				
115	E. Schmidhaussler	Pforzheim				
116	Hermann Wernstein	Jena-Löbstedt				
117	K.F. Vogelsang & Co	Lüdenscheid				
118	Erich Gutenkunst	Berlin				
119	Georg Bonitz	Schwarzenberg				
120	Wilhelm Deumer	Lüdenscheid				
121	Walter Demmer	Lüdenscheid				
122	I. Deutschbein GmbH	Euskirchen				
123						
124	Gebrüder Lange	Lüdenscheid				
125	Cramer & Dornbach	Lüdenscheid				
126	Karl Fr. Schenkel	Pforzheim				

Plate 266 Obverse Wound Badge 1939 Silver Class in the denazified or 1957 form.

● **Mint Mark**
This form of mark was found on the badges and medals produced in the state mints of Prussia, Berlin, Munich and Vienna. It is unusual to encounter these marks on medals.

● **Serial number**
Serial numbers, or individual naming of medals, were used on very few awards in Germany as the award document was the important part of the medal and it was possible to purchase extra examples of nearly all awarded medals. These numbers are encountered on such examples as the Golden Party Badge, Blood Order and TeNo Honour Badge.

● **Silver marks**
These give the percentage of silver per 1,000 parts of pure metal. That is to say '.950' contains 950 parts of silver to 1,000 parts and these marks can be in any combination. As a guide, the British standard of silver was set down in 1238AD as 92.5% pure which is represented by '.925' (known as Sterling Silver).

● **LDO number**
This was introduced in 1941 to try and control the production of medals and orders. During the early years local dignitaries were able to produce all kinds of awards which, in some instances, became elevated to official awards. Officially introduced awards, however, were strictly controlled from the Führer's chancellery and rigidly upheld by the Leistungs Gemeinschaft Deutscher Ordenshersteller (LDO). It published information booklets about the profession to keep the producers aware of new developments and production methods and can be considered very much a trade guild.

Licences were issued for the manufacture of these officially recognised orders, decorations and badges which were to be accompanied by a code designation or, as it was known, Herstellellungszeichen. From March 1941, it was required by the organisation that the producers would stamp their 'L' number to their products. The chancellery laid down the regulations and the LDO supervised their implementation as a self-regulating organisation. This seems somewhat confused, considering the 'L' designation changed nearly annually from its introduction. Some firms entered the system being awarded an 'L' number and then were either dropped or withdrew from the organisation, subsequently to be reinstated with a different 'L' number. For some inexplicable reason, some manufacturers were awarded multiple 'L' numbers.

LDO NUMBER	FIRM MAKER'S MARK	LOCATION
1	Deschler & Sohn	München
2	C. E. Juncker CEJ	Berlin
3	Wilhelm Deumer WD	Lüdenscheid
4	Steinhauer & Lück S & L	Lüdenscheid
5	Hermann Wernstein HW	Jena-Lobstedt
6	Fritz Zimmermann FZS	Stuttgart
7	Paul Meybauer PM	Berlin
8	Ferdinand Hoffstädter	Bonn a Rhein
9	Leifergsmeinschaft Schmuckhandwerker Pforzheim	Pforzheimer Pforzheim
10	Foerster & Barth	Pforzhiem
11	Grossmann & Co.	Wien
12	Frank & Reif	Stuttgart-Zuffenhausen
13	Gustav Brehmer GB	Markneukirchen/Sa
14	L. Chr. Lauer LL	Nürnberg-W
15	Friedrich Orth FO	Wien
16	Alois Rettenmaier	Schwabisch-Gmund
17		
18	Karl Wurster KG	Markneukirchen/Sa
19	E. Ferd Weidmann	Frankfurt/Main
20	C.F. Zimmermann	Pforzheim
21	Gebr. Godet & Co	Berlin
22	Boerger & Co	Berlin
23	Arbeitsgemeinschaft fur Heresbedarf in der Graveur-u Ziseleurinnung	Berlin
24	Arbeitsgemeinschaft der Hanauer Plaketten-Hersteller	Hanau/M
25	Arbeitsgemeinschaft der Graveur-Gold- und Silber- chmeide-Innungen	Hanau/M
26	B. H. Mayer's Kunstpragaenstalt	Pforzheim
27	Anton Schenkl's Nachf.	Wien
28	Eugen Schmidthaussler	Pforzheim
29	Hauptmunzamt	Berlin
30	Hauptmunzamt	Wien
31	Hans Gnad	Wien
32	W. Hobachter	Wien
33	Friedrich Linden FFL	Lüdenscheid
34	Willy Annetsberger WA	München
35	F.W. Assmann & Sohn A	Lüdenscheid
36	Bury & Leonhard	Hanau a M
37	Ad. Baumeister	Lüdenscheid
38		
39	Rudolf Bergs	Gablonz ad N
40	Berg & Nolte B & NL	Ludenscheid
41	Gebr. Bender	Oberstein/Nahe
42	Beidermann & Co	Oberkassel b/Bonn
43	Julius Bauer Söhne	Zella Mehlis i/Thur

44	Jakob Bengel	dar/Oberdonau
45	Franz Jungwirth	Wien
46	Hans Doppler	Wels/ Oberdonau
47	Erhard & Söhn AG	Schwabisch Gmund
48	Richard Feix	Gablonz ad N
49	Josef Feix Söhn JFS	Gablonz ad N
50	Karl Gschiermeister	Wien
51	Eduard Gorlach & Söhn	Gablonz/N
52	Gottleib & Wagner	Idar/Oberstein
53	Glaser & Söhn	Dresden
54		
55	J. E. Hammer & Söhn	Dresden
56	Robert Hauschild	Pforzheim
57	Karl Hensler	Pforzheim
58	Artur Jokel & Co	Gablonz/N
59	Louis Keller	Oberstein
60	Katz & Deyhle	Pfortzheim
61	Rudolf A. Karneth & Söhn RK	Gablonz a N
62	Kerbach & Oesterhelt	Dresden
63	Franz Klamt & Söhne	Gablonz a N
64	Gottl. Fr. Keck & Sohn	Pfortzheim
65	Klein & Quenzer AG	Idar/Oberstein
66	Friedrich Keller	Oberstein
67	R. Kreiseł	Gablonz a N
68	Alfred Knoblock	Gablonz a N
69	Alois Klammer	Innsbruck
70	Lind & Meyrer	Oberstein ad N
71	Rudolf Leukert	Gablonz a N
72	Franz Lipp	Pforzheim
73	Frank Mönert	Gablonz a N
74	Carl Meurer Sohn	Oberstein/Nahe
76	Ernst L. Muller	Pforzheim
77	Bayer. Hauptmunzamt	München
78	Gustav Miksch	Gablonz/N
79		
80	G.H. Osang	Dresden
81	Overhoff & Cie O & C	Lüdenscheid
82	Augustin Prager	Gablonz a N
83	Emil Peukert	Gablonz a N
84	Carl Posllath	Schroben- hausen
85	Julius Pietsch	Gablonz/N
86	Pulmann & Crone	Lüdenscheid
87	Roman Palme	Gablonz a N
88	Werner Redo	Saarlautern
89	Rudolf Richter RRS	Schlag 244 b Gablonz
90	Aug. F. Richter K.G.	Hamburg
91	Josef Rössler & Co.	Gablonz ad N
92	Josef Rücker & Sohn	Gablonz ad N
93	Richard Simm & Sohn RS & S	Gablonz ad N
94		
95	Adolf Scholze	Grunwald ad N
96		
97		
98	Rudolf Souval RS	Wien
99	Schwertner & Cie.	Graz-Eggenberg
100	Rudolf Wächtler & Lange	Mittweida i.Sa.
101	Rudolf Tham	Gablonz ad N
102	Philipp Türks Ww.	Wien
103	Aug. G. Tham	Gablonz ad N
104	Hein Ulbricht's Ww	Kaufing b/Schwanensta dt
105	Heinrich Vogt	Pforzheim
106	Bruder Schneider AG BSW	Wien
107	Carl Wild CW	Hamburg
108	Arno Wallpach	Salzburg
109	Walter & Henlein WH	Gablonz ad N
110	Otto Zappe	Gablonz ad N
111	Ziemer & Söhne	Oberstein
112	Argentor Werke Rust & Hetzel	Wien
113	Hermann Aurich HA	Dresden
114	Ludwig Bertsch	Karlsruhe
115		
116	Funke & Brüninghaus F & BL	Lüdenscheid
117	Hugo Lang	Wiesenthal a N
118	August Menzs & Sohn	Wiesenthal a N
119		
120	Franz Petzl	Wien
121		
122	J. J. Stahl	Strassburg
123	Beck, Hassinger & Co	Strassburg
124	Rudolf Schanes	Wien
125	Eugen Gauss	Pforzheim
126	Eduard Hahn EH	Oberstein/Nahe
127	Moritz Hausch AG	Pforzheim
128	S. Jablonski GmbH	Posen
129	Fritz Kohm	Pforzheim
130	Wilh. Schröder & Co	Lüdenscheid
131	Heinrich Wander	Gablonz
132	Franz Reischauer	Idar-Oberstein
133		
134	Otto Klein	Hanau
135	Julius Moser	Oberstein
	Schwerin & Sohn CS u SC	Berlin
	Sohni, Heubach & Co SH u Co	Oberstein
	Rath	München
	Rudolf Stübiger	Wien

● **Multiple LDO numbers**

The list below comprises manufacturers who had multiple 'L' numbers. These 'L' numbers apparently indicated full licences and part licences to produce certain state awards, such as the Iron Cross and Eagle Order. These two subsequent lists are interesting in that they run from 10 to 26 and 50 to 66. The numerical relationship is identical in both groupings. Whether any intermediate listings are available is uncertain. Both of these lists go some way towards supporting the theory that certain manufacturers produced parts and other manufacturers were engaged in the finishing of those medals. It is possible that these listings are relevant to that process. It is also possible that these numbers followed the first list and that this list is nothing more than an extension of the first list and was introduced in 1943.

LDO NUMBER	FIRM MARK	MAKER'S LOCATION
L/10		Deschler & Sohn München 9, Wirthstrasse 9
L/11		Wilhelm Deumer WD Lüdenscheid, Postfach 161
L/12		C. E. Juncker CEJ Berlin S.W.68, Altejacobstrasse 13
L/13		Paul Meybauer PM Berlin S.W.68, Junkerstrasse 19
L/14		Frederich Orth FO Wien, V1/6 56, Schmalzhofgasse 18
L/15		Otto Schickel Pforzheim
L/16		Steinhauer & Lück S & L Lüdenscheid
L/17		Hermann Wernstein HW Jena Lobstedt
L/18		B. H. Mayer's Hofkunstprageanstalt, Pforzheim
L/19		Ferdinand Hoffstätter Bonn/Rhein, Postfach 161
L/20		No Maker Known
L/21		Foerster & Barth Pforzheim, Tunnelstrasse 71
L/22		Rudolf Souval RS Wien, V11/62, Strasse der Julihamfer 23
L/23		Julius Maurer Oberstein/Nahe
L/24		Fritz Zimmerman FZS Stuttgart-W, Silberburgstrasse 58a
L/25		A. E. Kochert Wien 1, Neuer Markt 15
L/26		Klein & Quenzer Oberstein/Nahe
L/50		Gebr. Godet & Co Berlin W8, Jägerstrasse 19
L/51		E. Fred. Wiedmann Frankfurt-M 5-10, Schifferstrasse 52-54
L/52		C. F. Zimmermann Pforzheim, Dr Fritz Todt Strasse 55
L/53		Hymmen & Co Lüdenscheid, Karl Strasse
L/54		Schauerte & Hohfeld Lüdenscheid
L/55		Wächtler & Lange Rudolf, Mittweida/Sa
L/56		Funcke & Brüninghaus F & BL
L/57		Boerger & Co Berlin SO 16, Adalbertstrasse 42
L/58		Glaser & Sohn Dresden A, Borngasse 5,
L/59		Alois Rettenmaier Schwabisch Gmund, Parlerstrasse 27
L/60		Gustav Brehmer GB Markneukirchen/SR
L/61		Friedrich Linden FLL Lüdenscheid
L/62		Werner Redo Saarlautern
L/63		G. D. Osang Dresden A1, Neue Gasse 30
L/64		F. A. Assmann & Söhn A Lüdenscheid
L/65		Dr Franke & Co, KG Lüdenscheid
L/66		A. D. Schwerdt Stuttgart S, Splittlerstrasse 36

MONKEY METAL

This is the term used to explain the alloy in which the late war badges were produced. It has a high proportion of zinc in its make-up and it deteriorates over the years. This deterioration facilitates the absorption of the gilding that in many cases has been applied to it. It also has a low melting point which makes repairs to badges constructed in this manner particularly difficult. The metal, when of this age, also exudes a very faint acrid smell which is a good indicator of originality.

POT METAL

This is a similar alloy to monkey metal but the quality is better as the use of sub-standard additives to the mixture is less.

WHITE METAL

This is is a blanket term to encompass Cupro-Nickel and German silver and gives the impression of silver. German silver has a Nickel content of 12%. It looks like silver and can be artificially aged. This forms a good patina as found on silver coins and is resistant to wear. It also takes up the design from a die very well but requires great pressure from the minting engine. This metal produces the finest quality of badges, rivalling only the appearance of genuine silver.

ROSE-CUT

This is the name used in conjunction with diamond cutting and produces a hemispherical diamond with curved part in triangular facets. This was particularly popular on the continent from 1900 to 1940, when the diamond industry was decimated in Holland by the escape of the diamond cutters and merchants to England. This industry being mainly a Jewish institution, the SS had the final word with those that remained. The main centre and the style gives rise to the name 'Rotterdam Rose-Cut'. After 1945, the design of cuts changed, in part due to the British influence exerted upon the Dutch cutters from their counterparts in Hatton Garden, London, the British diamond centre.

DOUBLE STRUCK OR REINFORCED STRIKING

This is when the die is reinforced from the reverse, giving the impression of the obverse in not as much detail and in some cases just forming lines in the obverse. It produces a very distinct obverse design.